The Rise of Christianity

✣

The Rise of Christianity

A SOCIOLOGIST

RECONSIDERS HISTORY

✣

RODNEY STARK

PRINCETON UNIVERSITY PRESS

PRINCETON AND OXFORD

Copyright © 1996 by Princeton University Press
Published by Princeton University Press, 41 William Street,
Princeton, New Jersey 08540
In the United Kingdom: 99 Banbury Road, Oxford OX2 6JX
All Rights Reserved

First paperback printing, 2023
Paperback ISBN 9780691248042
Cloth ISBN 9780691027494
E-book ISBN 9780691214290

The Library of Congress has cataloged the cloth edition as follows:

Stark, Rodney.
The rise of Christianity : a sociologist reconsiders
history / Rodney Stark.
p.   cm.
Includes bibliographical references and index.
ISBN 0-691-02749-8 (CL: alk. paper)
1. Church history—Primitive and early church, ca. 30–600.
2. Sociology, Christian—History—Early church, ca. 30–600.
I. Title
BR166.S75   1996
306.6′70 l—dc20   95–44197

This book has been composed in Baskerville

Cover design: Katie Osborne

Cover image: *St Paul Preaching in Athens*, stipple engraving
and color woodcut on paper by George Baxter.
Courtesy of Yale Center for British Art, Paul Mellon Collection.

Printed in the United States of America

FOR FRANCES AND KEITH

✣

✢ *Contents* ✢

✤ *Illustrations* ✤

✢ *Preface* ✢

I HAVE ALWAYS been a history buff, but for most of my career I never really considered working with historical materials myself. I was content to be a sociologist and to spend my time trying to formulate and test more rigorous theories concerning a range of topics—most of them involving the sociology of religion. Then, in 1984, I read Wayne Meeks's *The First Urban Christians*. I bought it on impulse from the History Book Club, and I liked it very much. I was extremely impressed, not only by the many new things I learned about the subject, but also with Meeks's efforts to utilize social science.

Several months later I got lucky again. I came across a religious studies book catalog. In addition to Meeks's book, it listed other new titles in early church history. Here are the three new books I ordered that day: *Christianizing the Roman Empire*, by Ramsay MacMullen; *The Christians as the Romans Saw Them*, by Robert L. Wilken; and *Miracle in the Early Christian World*, by Howard Clark Kee. It would be hard to select three better books on the early Christian era. And, along with Meeks, these authors convinced me that what the field really needed was a more up-to-date and more rigorous brand of social science.

A year later, when I sent off a paper entitled "The Class Basis of Early Christianity: Inferences from a Sociological Model," I informed the journal editor that my primary purpose was to discover whether I was "good enough to play in the Greco-Roman League." Thus I was delighted when several historians of the New Testament era responded so favorably to the essay that they invited me to write a paper that would serve as the focus of the 1986 annual meeting of the Social History of Early Christianity Group of the Society of Biblical Literature. That paper laid out my heretical view that the mission to the Jews had been far more successful and long-lasting than the New Testament and the early church fathers claim. After formal responses to the essay by John Elliott, Ronald Hock, Caroline Osiek, and

L. Michael White, I was engaged in a long question-and-answer session by the discussants and by many members of the large audience. Having long been accustomed to social science meetings where no one bothers to attend the sessions, I was quite unprepared for the intellectual dialogue that took place—it was the most rewarding three hours I have ever spent at an academic meeting. Moreover, at least for me, it answered the question of whether I had anything to contribute to the study of the early church.

I am not a New Testament scholar and shall never be. Nor am I a historian—despite my recent venture into American religious history (Finke and Stark 1992). I am a sociologist who sometimes works with historical materials and who has, in preparation of this volume, done his best to master the pertinent sources, albeit mostly in English. What I am primarily trying to contribute to studies of the early church is better social science—better theories and more formal methods of analysis, including quantification wherever possible and appropriate. Thus in this book I shall try to introduce historians and biblical scholars to real social science, including formal rational choice theory, theories of the firm, the role of social networks and interpersonal attachments in conversion, dynamic population models, social epidemiology, and models of religious economies. Conversely, I shall try to share with social scientists the immense scholarly riches available from modern studies of antiquity.

I am indebted to many scholars for advice and especially for guiding me to sources that I would not have found because of my lack of formal training in the field. I am particularly indebted to my sometime collaborator Laurence Iannaccone of Santa Clara University, not only for his many useful comments, but for many of the fundamental insights that underlie chapters 8 and 9. I am also very grateful to L. Michael White, of Oberlin College, and to my colleague Michael A. Williams, of the University of Washington, for invaluable help in dealing with the sources and for encouraging me to pursue these topics. I must thank William R. Garrett, of St. Michael's College, for valuable suggestions as well as early encouragement. David L. Balch, of Brite Divinity School at Texas Christian University, invited me to participate in an International Conference on the Social History of the Matthean Community and convinced me to write the essay that now is chapter 7. Stanley K. Stowers, of Brown University, graciously invited me there to give several lectures, prompting me to complete my work on the Christianizing of the urban empire. During his tenure as president of the Association for the Sociology of Religion, David Bromley arranged for me to give the Paul Hanly Furfey Lecture, and chapter 5 was the result. Darren Sherkat, of Vanderbilt University, made useful suggestions about several of my forays into the arithmetic of the possible. Finally, Roger S. Bagnall, of Columbia University, steered me away from several unnecessary speculations.

I should also like to thank Benjamin and Linda de Wit, of Chalcedon Books in East Lansing, Michigan, for finding me copies of many classics—often many versions of the same one. Being dependent on translations, much to my surprise I found myself burdened with too many translations. On my shelves are four translations of Eusebius, for example. There are very marked differences among them on many of the passages I have quoted in this study. Which to use? On the basis of prose style, I much preferred the 1965 translation by G. A. Williamson. However, my colleagues with formal training in the area explained that Eusebius actually wrote very dull, awkward prose and thus I ought to rely on the Lawlor and Oulton version. I am not convinced that translators need to capture the dullness of the original if they are true to the meaning of each passage. After making many comparisons I adopted a rule that I have applied in all instances when I have possessed multiple translations: to use the version that most clearly expressed the point that caused me to quote the material, as long as the point is not unique to a particular translation.

Working with the famous ten-volume translations of *The Ante-Nicene Fathers*, edited by Roberts and Donaldson, made me appreciate fully my debt to multiple translations. This was especially true as I wrote about abortion, birth control, and sexual norms in chapter 5; whenever the church fathers wrote candidly on these matters, the Roberts and Donaldson version translated the original Greek into Latin rather than into English. Reading Clement of Alexandria, for example, one encounters frequent blocks of type in Latin. From Jaroslav Pelikan (1987:38) I discovered that this was a very old tradition. Hence Edward Gibbon reported in his *Autobiography* that "my English text is chaste, all licentious passages are left in the obscurity of a learned language" (1961:198). Fortunately for those of us for whom learned languages are obscure, there exist more recent translations, written by scholars having less refined sensibilities than Gibbon or the Victorian gentlemen from Edinburgh. In all, it was a most instructive experience.

This book was a long time coming. From the start I have tested the waters by publishing early versions of many of these chapters in various journals—as is noted at the start of appropriate chapters. Moreover, this project was never my principal undertaking. Since early 1985, when I completed the initial version of what is now chapter 2, I have published a number of books (one of them an introduction to sociology that I have subsequently revised five times). In the midst of these other activities, my effort to reconstruct the rise of Christianity has been a cherished hobby—a justification for reading books and articles that now fill an entire wall of my study. It would be impossible to express adequately how much pleasure I have gained from these authors. I am convinced that students of antiquity are on average the most careful researchers and the most graceful writers in the world of scholarship. Sadly, this concludes my hobby and ends my visit to their domain.

The Rise of Christianity

✠

Rather than cause the triumph of Christianity, the emperor Constantine's "Edict of Milan" was an astute *response* to rapid Christian growth that had already made them a major political force.

Conversion and Christian Growth

FINALLY, all questions concerning the rise of Christianity are one: How was it done? How did a tiny and obscure messianic movement from the edge of the Roman Empire dislodge classical paganism and become the dominant faith of Western civilization? Although this is the only question, it requires many answers—no one thing led to the triumph of Christianity.

The chapters that follow will attempt to reconstruct the rise of Christianity in order to explain why it happened. But in this chapter I will pose the question in a more precise way than has been done. First, I shall explore the arithmetic of growth to see more clearly the task that had to be accomplished. What is the minimum rate of growth that would permit the Christian movement to become as large as it must have been in the time that history allows? Did Christianity grow so rapidly that mass conversions must have taken place—as Acts attests and every historian from Eusebius to Ramsay MacMullen has believed? Having established a plausible growth curve for the rise of Christianity, I will review sociological knowledge of the process by which people convert to new religions in order to infer certain requirements concerning social relations between Christians and the surrounding Greco-Roman world. The chapter concludes with a discussion of the legitimate uses of social scientific theories to reconstruct history in the absence of adequate information on what actually occurred.

Since this book is a work of both history and social science, I have written it for a nonprofessional audience. In this way I can make sure that the social science is fully accessible to historians of the early church, meanwhile preventing social scientists from becoming lost amidst obscure historical and textual references. Before I proceed, however, it seems appropriate to discuss whether an attempt to explain the rise of Christianity is not somewhat sacrilegious. If, for example, I argue that the rise of Christianity benefited from superior fertility or from an excess of females who made possible high rates of exogamous marriage, am I not, thereby, attributing sacred achievements to profane causes? I think not. Whatever one does or does not believe about the divine, obviously God did not cause the world to become Christian, since that remains to be achieved. Rather, the New Testament recounts human efforts to spread the faith. No sacrilege is entailed in the search to understand human actions in human terms. Moreover, I do not reduce the rise of Christianity to purely "material" or social factors. Doctrine receives its due—an essential factor in the religion's success was what Christians believed.

THE ARITHMETIC OF GROWTH

Studies of the rise of Christianity all stress the movement's rapid growth, but rarely are any figures offered. Perhaps this reflects the prevalence among historians of the notion, recently expressed by Pierre Chuvin, that "ancient history remains wholly refractory to quantitative evaluations" (1990:12). Granted, we shall never discover "lost" Roman census data giving authoritative statistics on the religious composition of the empire in various periods. Nevertheless, we *must quantify*—at least in terms of exploring the arithmetic of the possible—if we are to grasp the magnitude of the phenomenon that is to be explained. For example, in order for Christianity to have achieved success in the time allowed, must it have grown at rates that seem incredible in the light of modern experience? If so, then we may need to formulate new social scientific propositions about conversion. If not, then we have some well-tested propositions to draw upon. What we need is at least two plausible numbers to provide the basis for extrapolating the probable rate of early Christian growth. Having achieved such a rate and used it to project the number of Christians in various years, we can then test these projections against a variety of historical conclusions and estimates.

For a *starting* number, Acts 1:14–15 suggests that several months after the Crucifixion there were 120 Christians. Later, in Acts 4:4, a total of 5,000 believers is claimed. And, according to Acts 21:20, by the sixth decade of the first century there were "many thousands of Jews" in Jerusalem who now believed. These are not statistics. Had there been that many converts in Jerusalem, it would have been the first Christian city, since there probably were no more than twenty thousand inhabitants at this time—J. C. Russell (1958) estimated only ten thousand. As Hans Conzelmann noted, these numbers are only "meant to render impressive the marvel that here the Lord himself is at work" (1973:63). Indeed, as Robert M. Grant pointed out, "one must always remember that figures in antiquity . . . were part of rhetorical exercises" (1977:7–8) and were not really meant to be taken literally. Nor is this limited to antiquity. In 1984 a Toronto magazine claimed that there were 10,000 Hare Krishna members in that city. But when Irving Hexham, Raymond F. Currie, and Joan B. Townsend (1985) checked on the matter, they found that the correct total was 80.

Origen remarked, "Let it be granted that Christians were few in the beginning" (*Against Celsus* 3.10, 1989 ed.), but how many would that have been? It seems wise to be conservative here, and thus I shall assume that there were 1,000 Christians in the year 40. I shall qualify this assumption at several later points in the chapter.

Now for an *ending* number. As late as the middle of the third century, Origen admitted that Christians made up "just a few" of the population. Yet only six decades later, Christians were so numerous that Constantine found it expedient to embrace the church. This has caused many scholars to think that something really extraordinary, in terms of growth, happened in the latter half of the third century (cf. Gager 1975). This may explain why, of the few numbers that have been offered in the literature, most are for membership in about the year 300.

Edward Gibbon may have been the first to attempt to estimate the Christian population, placing it at no more than "a twentieth part of the subjects of the empire" at the time of Constantine's conversion ([1776–1788] 1960:187). Later writers have rejected Gibbon's figure as far too low. Goodenough (1931) estimated that 10 percent of the empire's population were Christians by the time of Constantine. If we accept 60 million as the total population at that time—which is the most widely accepted estimate (Boak 1955a; Russell 1958; MacMullen 1984; Wilken 1984)—this would mean that there were 6 million Christians at the start of the fourth century. Von Hertling (1934) estimated the maximum number of Christians in the year 300 as 15 million. Grant (1978) rejected this as far too high and even rejected von Hertling's minimum estimate of 7.5 million as high. MacMullen (1984) placed the number of Christians in 300 at 5 million. Fortunately, we do not need greater precision; if we assume that the actual number of Christians in the year 300 lay within the range of 5–7.5 million, we have an adequate basis for exploring what rate of growth is needed for that range to be reached in 260 years.

Given our starting number, if Christianity grew at the rate of *40 percent per decade*, there would have been 7,530 Christians in the year 100, followed by 217,795 Christians in the year 200 and by 6,299,832 Christians in the year 300. If we cut the rate of growth to 30 percent a decade, by the year 300 there would have been only 917,334 Christians—a figure far below what anyone would accept. On the other hand, if we increase the growth rate to 50 percent a decade, then there would have been 37,876,752 Christians in the year 300—or more than twice von Hertling's maximum estimate. Hence 40 percent per decade (or 3.42 percent per year) seems the most plausible estimate of the rate at which Christianity actually grew during the first several centuries.

TABLE 1.1
Christian Growth Projected at 40 Percent per Decade

Year	Number of Christians	Percent of Population[a]
40	1,000	0.0017
50	1,400	0.0023
100	7,530	0.0126
150	40,496	0.07
200	217,795	0.36
250	1,171,356	1.9
300	6,299,832	10.5
350	33,882,008	56.5

[a] Based on an estimated population of 60 million.

This is a very encouraging finding since it is exceedingly close to the average growth rate of 43 percent per decade that the Mormon church has maintained over the past century (Stark 1984, 1994). Thus we know that the numerical goals Christianity needed to achieve are entirely in keeping with modern experience, and we are not forced to seek exceptional explanations. Rather, history allows time for the normal processes of conversion, as understood by contemporary social science, to take place.

However, before we take up the topic of conversion, it seems worthwhile to pause and consider the widespread impression that Christian growth speeded rapidly during the last half of the third century. In terms of *rate* of growth, it probably did not. But because of the rather extraordinary features of exponential curves, this probably was a period of "miraculous-seeming" growth in terms of *absolute numbers*. All of this is clear in table 1.1.

Progress must have seemed terribly slow during the first century—the projected total is only 7,530 by 100. There was a greater increase in numbers by the middle of the second century, but still the projection amounts to only slightly more than 40,000 Christians. This projection is in extremely close agreement with Robert L. Wilken's estimate of "less than fifty thousand Christians" at this time—"an infinitesimal number in a society comprising sixty million" (1984:31). Indeed, according to L. Michael White (1990:110), Christians in Rome still met in private homes at this time. Then, early in the third century, the projected size of the Christian population picks up a bit and by 250 reaches 1.9 percent. This estimate is also sustained by a prominent historian's "feel" for the times. Discussing the process of conversion to Christianity, Robin Lane Fox advised that we keep "the total number of Christians in perspective: their faith was much the most rapidly growing religion in the Mediterranean, but its total membership was still small in absolute terms, perhaps (at a guess) only 2 percent of the Empire's total population by 250" (1987:317). But even more compelling is how the absolute number (as well as the percent Christian) suddenly shoots upward between 250 and 300, just as historians have reported,[1] and recent archaeological findings from Dura-Europos support this view. Excavations of a Christian building show that during the middle of the third century a house church was extensively remodeled into a building "entirely devoted to religious functions," after which "all domestic activities ceased" (White 1990:120). The renovations mainly involved the removal of partition walls to create an enlarged meeting hall—indicative of the need to accommodate more worshipers. That my reconstruction of Christian growth exhibits the "sudden spurt" long associated with the second half of the third century adds to the plausibility of the figures.

The projections are also extremely consistent with Graydon F. Snyder's (1985) assessment of all known archaeological evidence of Christianity during the first three centuries. Snyder determined that there really isn't any such evidence prior to 180. He interpreted this to indicate that before then it is impossible to distinguish Christian from non-Christian culture in "funerary art, inscriptions, letters, symbols, and perhaps buildings . . . [because] it took over a century for the new community of faith to develop a distinctive mode of self-expression" (Snyder 1985:2). That may be, but it must also be noted that the *survival* of Christian archaeological evidence would have been roughly proportionate to how much there *could have been* to start with. The lack of anything surviving from prior to 180 must be assessed on the basis of the tiny number of Christians who could have left such traces. Surely it is not surprising that the 7,535 Christians at the end of the first century left no trace. By 180, when I project that the total Christian population first passed the 100,000 mark, there would finally have been enough Christians so that it is probable that traces of their existence would survive. Thus Snyder's findings are very compatible with my estimates of a very small Christian population in the first two centuries.

As an additional test of these projections, Robert M. Grant has calculated that there were 7,000 Christians in Rome at the end of the second century (1977:6). If we also accept Grant's estimate of 700,000 as the population of Rome for that year, then 1 percent of the population of Rome had been converted by the year 200. If we set the total population of the empire at 60 million in 200, then, based on the projection for that year, Christians constituted 0.36 percent of the empire's population. This seems to be an entirely plausible matchup, since the proportion Christian should have been higher in Rome than in the empire at large. First of all, historians assume that the church in Rome was exceptionally strong—it was well known for sending funds to Christians elsewhere. In about 170, Dionysius of Corinth wrote to the Roman church: "From the start it has been your custom to treat all Christians with unfailing kindness, and to send contributions to many churches in every city, sometimes alleviating the distress of those in need, sometimes providing for your brothers in the mines" (Eusebius, *Ecclesiastical History* 4.23.6, 1965 ed.). Second, by 200 the Christian proportion of the population of the city of Rome must have been substantially larger than that in the whole of the empire because

Christianity had not yet made much headway in the more westerly provinces. As will be seen in chapter 6, of the twenty-two largest cities in the empire, four probably still lacked a Christian church by the year 200. Although I have estimated the overall number of Christians in the empire, I am fully aware that Christian growth was concentrated in the East—in Asia Minor, Egypt, and North Africa. Moreover, there is general agreement among historians (Harnack 1908; Boak 1955a; Meeks 1983) that the Christian proportion of the population was substantially higher in cities than in the rural areas at this time—hence the term *paganus* or "countryman" came to refer to non-Christians (pagans). In any event, here too the projections closely agree with estimates based on independent sources.

Now, let us peek just a bit further into the future of Christian growth. If growth held at 40 percent per decade for the first half of the fourth century, there would have been 33,882,008 Christians by 350. In an empire having a population of at least 60 million, there might well have been 33 million Christians by 350—for by then some contemporary Christian writers were claiming a majority (Harnack 1908: 2:29). Looking at the rise of a Christian majority as purely a function of a constant rate of growth calls into serious question the emphasis given by Eusebius and others to the conversion of Constantine as the factor that produced the Christian majority (Grant 1977). So long as nothing changed in the conditions that sustained the 40-percent-a-decade growth rate, Constantine's conversion would better be seen as a response to the massive exponential wave in progress, not as its cause.

This interpretation is entirely in keeping with the thesis developed by Shirley Jackson Case in his 1925 presidential address to the American Society of Church History. Case began by noting that attempts by the emperor Diocletian in 303, and continued by his successor Galerius in 305, to use persecution to force Christians to support the state had failed because "by the year 300 Christianity had become too widely accepted in Roman society to make possible a successful persecution on the part of the government" (1928:59). As a result, Case continued, by 311 the emperor Galerius switched tactics and excused the Christians from praying to Roman gods, and asked only that they pray to "their own god for our security and that of the state" (Case 1928:61). Thus Constantine's edict of toleration, issued two years later, was simply a continuation of state policy. Case's assessment of Constantine's edict stressed the impact of Christian growth on this policy:

> In this document one perceives very easily the real basis of Constantine's favor for Christianity. First, there is the characteristic attitude of an emperor who is seeking supernatural support for his government, and secondly, there is a recognition of the fact that the Christian element in the population is now so large, and its support for Constantine and Licinius in their conflict with rivals who still opposed Christianity, is so highly esteemed, that the emperors are ready to credit the Christian God with the exercise of a measure of supernatural power on a par with the other gods of the State. (1928:62)

It is reassuring to have the projections of Christian membership in table 1.1 fit so well with several independent estimates, with major historical perceptions such as the rapid increases during the latter part of the third century, and with the record of Mormon growth achieved over the past century. Keep in mind, however, that the numbers are *estimates*, not recorded fact. They seem very plausible, but I would be entirely comfortable with suggestions that reality may have been a bit lumpier. Perhaps growth was somewhat more rapid in the earliest days and my beginning number of 1,000 Christians in 40 is a bit low. But it also seems likely that there were periodic losses in the early days, some of which may have been very substantial for a group still so small. For example, following the execution of James and the subsequent destruction of Jerusalem, the Christian community in Palestine seems to have died out (Frend

1965, 1984). And while Tacitus's claim that "an immense multitude" (*Annals* 15.44, 1989 ed.) was butchered by Nero in about 65 is much exaggerated (see chapter 8), even the deaths of several hundred Christians would have been a very serious setback.

I have tried to offset such bumps and lumps in the growth curve by starting with a very conservative number. Moreover, my purpose in generating these numbers was not to discover "facts," but to impose needed discipline on the subject. That is, by resorting to simple arithmetic I believe I have demonstrated adequately that the rise of Christianity required no miraculous rates of conversion.

Several years after I had completed this exploration of the arithmetic of early Christian growth, when this book was nearly finished, my colleague Michael Williams made me aware of Roger S. Bagnall's remarkable reconstruction of the growth of Christianity in Egypt (1982, 1987). Bagnall examined Egyptian papyri to identify the proportion of persons with identifiably Christian names in various years, and from these he reconstructed a curve of the Christianization of Egypt. Here are *real* data, albeit from only one area, against which to test my projections. Two of Bagnall's data points are much later than the end of my projections. However, a comparison of the six years within my time frame shows a level of agreement that can only be described as extraordinary—as can be seen in table 1.2.

Bagnall's finding no Christians in 239 can be disregarded. Obviously there were Christians in Egypt then, but because their numbers would still have been very small it is not surprising that none turned up in Bagnall's data. But for later years the matchups are striking, and the correlation of 0.86 between the two curves borders on the miraculous. The remarkable fit between these two estimates, arrived at via such different means and sources, seems to me a powerful confirmation of both.

Although the projections seem very plausible through 350, the rate of Christian growth eventually must have declined rap-

TABLE 1.2
Two Estimates of Christianization Compared

Year	Projected Percent Christian in the Greco-Roman World	Percent Christian in Egypt[a]
239	1.4	0
274	4.2	2.4
278	5.0	10.5
280	5.4	13.5
313	16.2	18.0
315	17.4	18.0
		$r = 0.86$

[a] Bagnall 1982, 1987.

idly at some point during the fourth century. If nothing else, the empire would have begun to run out of potential converts. This is evident when we realize that had the 40 percent growth rate held throughout the fourth century, there would have been 182,225,584 Christians in the year 400. Not only is that total impossible, growth rates must always decline when a movement has converted a substantial proportion of the available population—as the pool of potential converts is progressively "fished out." Or, as Bagnall put it, "the curve of conversion becomes asymptotic, and incremental conversion becomes slight after a time" (1982:123). Clearly, then, the projections from my model are invalid after the year 350. However, since my concerns only involve the *rise* of Christianity, it is not necessary to venture beyond this point.

ON CONVERSION

Eusebius tells us that early Christian missionaries were so empowered by the "divine Spirit" that "at the first hearing whole multitudes in a body eagerly embraced in their souls piety towards the Creator of the universe" (*Ecclesiastical History* 3.37.3,

1927 ed.). Not only do many modern historians of the early church accept Eusebius's claims about mass conversions in response to public preaching and miracle working, but they often regard it as a necessary assumption because of the rapidity of Christianity's rise. Thus in his distinguished study, *Christianizing the Roman Empire*, Ramsay MacMullen urged acceptance of the reports of large-scale conversions as necessary

> to explain better the *rate* of change we are observing. In the whole process, very large numbers are obviously involved . . . [I]t would be hard to picture the necessary scale of conversion if we limited ourselves to . . . evangelizing in private settings . . . [If this mode of conversion], however, is combined with evidence for successes en masse, the two in combination do seem to me adequate to explain what we know happened. (1984:29)

MacMullen's views reflect those of Adolf Harnack (1908: 2:335–336), who characterized the growth of Christianity in terms such as "inconceivable rapidity" and "astonishing expansion," and who expressed his agreement with Augustine's claim that "Christianity must have reproduced itself by means of miracles, for the greatest miracle of all would have been the extraordinary extension of the religion apart from any miracles" (335n.2).

This is precisely why there is no substitute for arithmetic. The projections reveal that Christianity could easily have reached half the population by the middle of the fourth century without miracles or conversions en masse. The Mormons have, thus far, traced the same growth curve, and we have no knowledge of their achieving mass conversions. Moreover, the claim that mass conversions to Christianity took place as crowds spontaneously responded to evangelists assumes that doctrinal appeal lies at the heart of the conversion process—that people hear the message, find it attractive, and embrace the faith. But modern social science relegates doctrinal appeal to a very secondary role, claiming that most people do not really become very attached to the doctrines of their new faith until *after* their conversion.

In the early 1960s John Lofland and I were the first social scientists to actually go out and watch people convert to a new religious movement (Lofland and Stark 1965). Up to that time, the most popular social scientific explanation of conversion involved the pairing of deprivation with ideological (or theological) appeal. That is, one examined the ideology of a group to see what kinds of deprivation it addressed and then concluded (*mirabile dictu!*) that converts suffered from those deprivations (Glock 1964). As an example of this approach, since Christian Science promised to restore health, its converts *must* disproportionately be drawn from among those with chronic health problems, or at least those who suffer from hypochondria (Glock 1964). Of course, one could as plausibly argue the reverse, that only people with excellent health could long hold to the Christian Science doctrine that illness was all in the mind.

In any event, Lofland and I were determined to watch people go through the process of conversion and try to discover what really was involved. Moreover, we wanted to watch conversion, not simply activation. That is, we wanted to look at people who were making a major religious shift, as from Christianity to Hinduism, rather than examine how lifelong Christians got themselves born again. The latter is a matter of considerable interest, but it was not our interest at the time.

We also wanted a group that was small enough so that the two of us could provide adequate surveillance, and new enough so that it was in an early and optimistic phase of growth. After sifting through many deviant religious groups in the San Francisco Bay area we came upon precisely what we were looking for—a group of about a dozen young adults who had just moved to San Francisco from Eugene, Oregon. The group was led by Young Oon Kim, a Korean woman who had once been a professor of religion at Ewha University in Seoul. The movement she served was based in Korea, and in January 1959, she arrived in Oregon

to launch a mission to America. Miss[2] Kim and her young followers were the very first American members of the Unification
Church, widely known today as the Moonies.

As Lofland and I settled back to watch people convert to this
group, the first thing we discovered was that all of the current
members were united by close ties of friendship predating their
contact with Miss Kim. Indeed, the first three converts had been
young housewives, next-door neighbors who became friends of
Miss Kim after she became a lodger with one of them. Subsequently, several of the husbands joined, followed by several of
their friends from work. At the time Lofland and I arrived to
study them, the group had never succeeded in attracting a
stranger.

Lofland and I also found it interesting that although all the
converts were quick to describe how their spiritual lives had
been empty and desolate prior to their conversion, many
claimed they had not been particularly interested in religion
before. One man told me, "If anybody had said I was going to
join up and become a missionary I would have laughed my head
off. I had no use for church at all."

We also found it instructive that during most of her first year
in America, Miss Kim had tried to spread her message directly
by talks to various groups and by sending out many press re-
leases. Later, in San Francisco the group also tried to attract
followers through radio spots and by renting a hall in which to
hold public meetings. But these methods yielded nothing. As
time passed, Lofland and I were able to observe people actually
becoming Moonies. The first several converts were old friends
or relatives of members who came from Oregon for a visit. Subsequent converts were people who formed close friendships
with one or more members of the group.

We soon realized that of all the people the Moonies encountered in their efforts to spread their faith, the only ones who
joined were those *whose interpersonal attachments to members over-
balanced their attachments to nonmembers.* In effect, conversion is

not about seeking or embracing an ideology; it is about bringing one's religious behavior into alignment with that of one's friends and family members.

This is simply an application of the highly respected control theory of deviant behavior (Toby 1957; Hirschi 1969; Stark and Bainbridge 1987; Gottfredson and Hirschi 1990). Rather than asking why people deviate, why they break laws and norms, control theorists ask why anyone ever does conform. Their answer is posed in terms of *stakes in conformity*. People conform when they believe they have more to lose by being detected in deviance than they stand to gain from the deviant act. Some people deviate while others conform because people differ in their stakes in conformity. That is, some people simply have far less to lose than do others. A major stake in conformity lies in our attachments to other people. Most of us conform in order to retain the good opinion of our friends and family. But some people lack attachments. Their rates of deviance are much higher than are those of people with an abundance of attachments.

Becoming a Moonie today is an act of deviance, as was becoming a Christian in the first century. Such conversions violate norms defining legitimate religious affiliations and identities. Lofland and I saw many people who spent some time with the Moonies and expressed considerable interest in their doctrines, but who never joined. In every instance these people had many strong attachments to nonmembers who did not approve of the group. Of persons who did join, many were newcomers to San Francisco whose attachments were all to people far away. As they formed strong friendships with group members, these were not counterbalanced because distant friends and families had no knowledge of the conversion-in-process. In several instances a parent or sibling came to San Francisco intending to intervene after having learned of the conversion. Those who lingered eventually joined up too. Keep in mind that becoming a Moonie may have been regarded as deviant by outsiders, but it was an act of conformity for those whose most significant attachments were to Moonies.

During the quarter century since Lofland and I first published our conclusion—that attachments lie at the heart of conversion and therefore that conversion tends to proceed along social networks formed by interpersonal attachments—many others have found the same to be true in an immense variety of religious groups all around the world. A recent study based on Dutch data (Kox, Meeus, and 't Hart 1991) cited twenty-five additional empirical studies, all of which supported our initial finding. And that list was far from complete.

Although several other factors are also involved in the conversion process, the central sociological proposition about conversion is this: *Conversion to new, deviant religious groups occurs when, other things being equal, people have or develop stronger attachments to members of the group than they have to nonmembers* (Stark 1992).

Data based on records kept by a Mormon mission president give powerful support to this proposition. When missionaries make cold calls, knock on the doors of strangers, this eventually leads to a conversion once out of a thousand calls. However, when missionaries make their first contact with a person in the home of a Mormon friend or relative of that person, this results in conversion 50 percent of the time (Stark and Bainbridge 1985).

A variation on the network proposition about conversion is that successful founders of new faiths typically turn first to those with whom they already have strong attachments. That is, they recruit their first followers from among their family and close friends. Thus Muhammad's first convert was his wife Khadijah; the second was his cousin Ali, followed by his servant Zeyd and then his old friend Abu Bakr. On April 6, 1830, the Mormons were founded by Joseph Smith, his brothers Hyrum and Samuel, and Joseph Smith's friends Oliver Cowdery and David and Peter Whitmer. The rule extends to Jesus too, since it appears that he began with his brothers and mother.

A second aspect of conversion is that people who are deeply committed to any particular faith do not go out and join some other faith. Thus Mormon missionaries who called upon the Moonies were immune, despite forming warm relationships with several members. Indeed, the Moonie who previously had "no use for church at all" was more typical. Converts were not former atheists, but they were essentially unchurched and many had not paid any particular attention to religious questions. Thus the Moonies quickly learned that they were wasting their time at church socials or frequenting denominational student centers. They did far better in places where they came in contact with the uncommitted. This finding has received substantial support from subsequent research. Converts to new religious movements are overwhelmingly from relatively irreligious backgrounds. The majority of converts to modern American cult movements report that their parents had no religious affiliation (Stark and Bainbridge 1985). Let me state this as a theoretical proposition: *New religious movements mainly draw their converts from the ranks of the religiously inactive and discontented, and those affiliated with the most accommodated (worldly) religious communities.*

Had we not gone out and watched people as they converted, we might have missed this point entirely, because when people retrospectively describe their conversions, they tend to put the stress on theology. When asked why they converted, Moonies invariably noted the irresistible appeal of the Divine Principles (the group's scripture), suggesting that only the blind could reject such obvious and powerful truths. In making these claims converts implied (and often stated) that their path to conversion was the end product of a search for faith. But Lofland and I knew better because we had met them well before they had learned to appreciate the doctrines, before they had learned how to testify to their faith, back when they were not seeking faith at all. Indeed, we could remember when most of them regarded the religious beliefs of their new set of friends as quite odd. I recall one who told me that he was puzzled that such nice people could get so worked up about "some guy in Korea" who claimed to be the Lord of the Second Advent. Then, one day, he got worked up about this guy too. I suggest that this is also how people in the first century got themselves worked up about someone who claimed to be the Lord of the First Advent. Robin Lane Fox suggests the same thing: "Above all we should give weight to the presence and influence of friends. It is a force which so often escapes the record, but it gives shape to everyone's personal life. One friend might bring another to the faith. . . . When a person turned to God, he found others, new 'brethren,' who were sharing the same path" (1987:316). Peter Brown has expressed similar views: "Ties of family, marriages, and loyalties to heads of households had been the most effective means of recruiting members of the church, and had maintained the continued adherence of the average Christian to the new cult" (1988:90).

The basis for successful conversionist movements is growth through social networks, through a *structure of direct and intimate interpersonal attachments*. Most new religious movements fail because they quickly become closed, or semiclosed networks. That is, they fail to keep forming and sustaining attachments to outsiders and thereby lose the capacity to grow. Successful movements discover techniques for remaining open networks, able to reach out and into new adjacent social networks. And herein lies the capacity of movements to sustain exponential rates of growth over a long period of time.

Some readers may suspect that the rapid rise in the absolute number of new Christians between 250 and 350 would require mass conversions even though the rate of conversion remained constant at 40 percent per decade. Admittedly, exponential growth curves are counterintuitive and easily seem incredible. Nevertheless, the *dynamics of the conversion process* are not changed even as the absolute numbers reach a rapid growth stage along an exponential curve. The reason is that as movements grow, their social surface expands proportionately. That is, each new member expands the size of the network of attachments between the group and potential converts. As noted above, however, this occurs *only* if the group constitutes an *open network*. Thus if we are to better understand and explain the rise of Christianity, we must discover how the early Christians maintained open networks—for it would seem certain that they did. This last remark sets the stage for a brief discussion of the appropriate scope of social scientific theories and whether it is possible even to apply propositions developed in one time and place to other eras and cultures.

ON SCIENTIFIC GENERALIZATION

Many historians believe that cultures and eras verge on the unique. Thus in his very thoughtful response to my use of the network theory of conversion to discuss the success of the mission to the Jews (see chapter 3), Ronald F. Hock noted that I seem to think that networks, for example, are not "all that different from period to period, society to society" (1986:2–3). He then pointed out that

> the networks utilized by Mormons are those consisting of a member's family, relatives, and friends, but are ancient networks the same? Ancient cities are not modern ones, and ancient networks that were centered in aristocratic households included more than family and friends: domestic slaves, freedmen, and perhaps parasites, teachers, athletic trainers, and travelers. In addition, urban life was lived more in public, so that recruitment could proceed along more extensive and complex networks than we find among Mormons in our more nuclear and anonymous cities and suburbs.

I am certain that Hock is correct, but I am unrepentant. What he is noting are details that might tell us how to discover networks should we be transported to ancient Antioch, but that have no implications for the network proposition per se. *However* people constitute structures of direct interpersonal attachments, those structures will define the lines through which conversion will most readily proceed. The definition of network is not locked to time and space, nor is the conversion proposition.

Many historians seem to have considerable trouble with the idea of general theories because they have not been trained in the distinction between concepts and instances. Proper scientific concepts are abstract and identify a class of "things" to be regarded as alike. As such, concepts must apply to all possible members of the class, all that have been, are, shall be, or could be. The concept of chair, defined as all objects created to seat a lone individual and support his or her back, is an abstraction. We cannot see the concept of chair. It is an intellectual creation existing only in our minds. But we can see many actual chairs, and as we look at some, we discover immense variation in size, shape, materials, color, and the like. Moreover, when we look at chairs used in the ancient world, we perceive some very noticeable differences from the chairs of today. Nevertheless, each is a chair so long as it meets the definition set out above—other somewhat similar objects belong to other object classes such as stools and couches.

These points apply as fully to the concept of social network as to the concept of chair. The concept of social network also exists only in our minds. All that we can see are specific instances of the class—networks involving some set of individuals. As with chairs, the shapes and sizes of social networks may differ greatly across time and space, and the processes by which networks form may vary as greatly as do techniques for making chairs. But these variations in details never result in chairs' becoming pianos, nor do variations in their makeup ever turn social networks into collections of strangers.

It is only through the use of abstract concepts, linked by abstract propositions, that science exists. Consider a physics that must generate a new rule of gravity for each object in the universe. And it is precisely the abstract generality of science that makes it possible for social science to contribute anything to our understanding of history, let alone to justify efforts to reconstruct history from social scientific theories. Let me now turn to that important issue.

SOCIAL THEORY AND
HISTORICAL RECONSTRUCTIONS

During the past several decades historians of the New Testament era have become increasingly familiar with social science and have become increasingly inclined to use social scientific models to infer "what must have happened" in order to fill blanks in the historical and archaeological record. As Robin Scroggs pointed out in an influential essay, "there may be times when a sociological model may actually assist our ignorance. If our data evidence some *parts* of the gestalt of a known model, while being silent about others, we *may* cautiously be able to conclude that the absence of the missing parts is accidental and that the entire model was actually a reality in the early church" (1980:166). Since those lines were published, the practice Scroggs suggested has become common (Barton 1982, 1984; Holmberg 1980; Elliott 1986; Fox 1987; Gager 1975, 1983; Green 1985; Malina 1981, 1986; Meeks 1983, 1993; Kee 1983; Kraemer 1992; Sanders 1993; Theissen 1978, 1982; Wilken 1984; Wire 1991). I have quite mixed reactions to this literature. Some studies I have read with pleasure and admiration. Other examples have made me very uncomfortable because the social science "models" utilized are so inadequate. Some of them are merely metaphors—as Durkheim's "discovery" that religion is society worshiping itself is merely metaphor. How would one falsify that statement, or assertions to the effect that religion is a neurotic illusion or the poetry of the soul? The problem with metaphors is not that they are false, but that they are *empty*. Many of them do seem to ooze profundity, but at best metaphors are merely definitions. Consider the term *charisma*.

Max Weber borrowed this Greek word meaning "divine gift" to identify the ability of some people to convince others that their authority is based on divine sources: "The holder of charisma seizes the task that is adequate for him and demands obedience and a following by virtue of his mission. His success determines whether he finds them. His charismatic claim breaks down if his mission is not recognized by those to whom he feels he has been sent. If they recognize him, he is their master" (1946:246). Charisma is commonly observed in religious leaders, and surely no one would dispute that Jesus and many of the apostles and early evangelists had it. Thus the literature on the early church is saturated with the term. Unfortunately, charisma is too often understood as a nearly magical power possessed by individuals rather than a description of how they are regarded. That is, their power over others is attributed to their charisma, and it is often suggested that particular religious leaders are so potent *because* they had charisma. Roy Wallis, for example, claimed that Moses David (David Berg), founder of the Children of God, maintained control over his followers because of his "charismatic status" (1982:107). But this is entirely circular. It is the same as saying that people believed that Moses David had divine authority because people believed he had divine authority. Because Weber's discussions of charisma did not move beyond definitional and descriptive statements, and said nothing about the causes of charisma, the concept is merely a name attached to a definition. When we see someone whose authority is believed by some people to be of divine origin, we have the option of calling this charisma, but doing so will contribute nothing to our understanding of why this phenomenon occurs. Hence when studies of the early church utilize the term *charisma*, what we usually confront is only a name that too often is thought to explain something, but does not.

Besides metaphors and simple concepts, other "models" used in this literature are nothing but typologies or *sets* of concepts. One of the most popular of these consists of various definitions to distinguish religious groups as *churches* or *sects*. The most useful of these definitions identifies churches and sects as the end points of a continuum based on the degree of tension between the group and its sociocultural environment (Johnson 1963; Stark and Bainbridge 1979, 1987). Sects are religious groups in a relatively high state of tension with their environment; churches are groups in a relatively low state of tension. These are very useful concepts. Unfortunately, they are often used, even by many social scientists, as if they explained something. All such efforts are circular. Thus it is circular to say that a particular religious body rejects the world *because* it is a sect, as Bryan Wilson (1970) often does, since bodies are classified as sects because they reject the world. The concepts of church and sect do nothing more (or less) than allow us to classify various religious bodies. But theories using these concepts do not reside in the concepts themselves. For example, it is well known that religious bodies, especially if they are successful, tend to move from a higher to a lower state of tension—sects often are transformed into churches. But no explanation of this transformation can be found in the definitions of church and sect. Instead, we must use propositions to link the concepts of church and sect to other concepts, such as upward social mobility and regression to the mean, in order to formulate an explanation (Stark and Bainbridge 1985, 1987).

Let me emphasize: concepts are *names*, not *explanations*. The act of naming some objects or phenomena tells us nothing about why they occur or what they influence. Explanation requires theories: abstract statements saying *why* and *how* some set of phenomena are linked, and from which falsifiable statements can be derived (Popper 1959, 1962). Metaphors, typologies, and concepts are passive; they cast no light of their own and cannot illuminate the dark corners of unrecorded history

(Stark and Bainbridge 1979, 1985, 1987). Granted, concepts may permit some useful comparisons among some sets of phenomena—comparisons of the social class composition of two religious movements, for example, can be very revealing. But if a model is to provide more than *classification*, if it proposes to *explain*, then the model must include not simply concepts, but propositions. The difference here is that between a parts catalog and a working diagram of an engine. That is, a model must include a fully specified set of interrelations among the parts. Such a model explains why and how things fit together and function. For this task, only a theory, not a conceptual scheme, suffices.

It is not surprising that scholars trained in history and in textual interpretation might find themselves more comfortable with an older generation of social "scientists" who dealt in metaphors rather than scientific theories, if for no other reason than that their work abounds in literary allusions and is redolent of ancient library dust. But let it be noted that in science, unlike papyrology, older seldom is better. And I regard it as an essential part of my task in this book to familiarize historians of the early church with more powerful and modern social scientific tools, and particularly with real theories rather than with concepts, metaphors, and typologies pretending to have explanatory power.

However, even if we use the best social science theories as our guide for reconstructing history, we are betting that the theories are solid and that the application is appropriate. When those conditions are met, then there is no reason to suppose that we cannot reason from the general rule to deduce the specific in precisely the same way that we can reason from the principles of physics that coins dropped in a well will go to the bottom. Even so, it is better when we can actually see the coins go down. *Need* is the only justification for the application of social science to fill in historical blanks. But we must be very cautious not to fill the blanks with fantasy and science fiction.

In this book I shall attempt to reconstruct the rise of Christianity on the basis of many inferences from modern social scientific theories, making particular use of my own formal theorizing about religion and religious movements (Stark and Bainbridge 1979, 1980, 1985, 1987; Stark and Iannaccone 1991, 1992). I will frequently employ the arithmetic of the possible and the plausible to test various assumptions. To guard against error I shall test my reconstructions against the historical record whenever possible, as I have done in this chapter.[3]

The early church was anything but a refuge for slaves and the impoverished masses, as illustrated by this portrait (ca. 300) of the Christian Galla Placidia and her children, done in gold leaf on glass.

The Class Basis of Early Christianity

FOR MOST of the twentieth century historians and sociologists agreed that, in its formative days, Christianity was a movement of the dispossessed—a haven for Rome's slaves and impoverished masses. Friedrich Engels was an early proponent, claiming that "Christianity was originally a movement of oppressed people: it first appeared as the religion of slaves and emancipated slaves, of poor people deprived of all rights, of peoples subjugated or dispersed by Rome" (Marx and Engels 1967: 316). These views seem to have first gained ascendancy among scholars in Germany. Thus New Testament scholars trace this view to Deissmann ([1908] 1978, 1929), while sociologists look to Troeltsch ([1911] 1931), who claimed that in fact *all* religious movements are the work of the "lower strata." Marxists also look to Germany in this same period for Kautsky's ([1908] 1953) elaborate expansion of Engels's views into an orthodox analysis of Christianity as a proletarian movement, which, he claimed, even achieved true communism briefly. Moreover, many scholars confidently attributed this conception of early Christians' social origins to Paul on the basis of his first letter to the Corinthians, in which he notes that not many of the wise, mighty, or noble are called to the faith. By the 1930s this view of Christian origins was largely unchallenged.[1] Thus the well-known Yale historian Erwin R. Goodenough wrote in a widely adopted college textbook: "Still more obvious an indication of the undesirability of Christianity in Roman eyes was the fact that its converts were drawn in an overwhelming majority from the lowest classes of society. Then as now the governing classes were apprehensive of a movement which brought into a closely

An earlier version of this chapter appeared in *Sociological Analysis* 47 (1986): 216–225.

knit and secret organization the servants and slaves of society" (1931:37).

In recent decades, however, New Testament historians have begun to reject this notion of the social basis of the early Christian movement. E. A. Judge was perhaps the first major scholar of the present generation to raise a vigorous dissent. He began by dismissing the lack of noble Christians as an irrelevancy:

> If the common assertion that Christian groups were constituted from the lower orders of society is meant to imply that they did not draw upon the upper orders of the Roman ranking system, the observation is correct, and pointless. In the eastern Mediterranean it was self-evident that members of the Roman aristocracy would not belong to a local cult association . . . [Moreover they] amounted to an infinitesimally small fraction of the total population. (1960:52)

After a careful analysis of the ranks and occupations of persons mentioned in the sources, Judge concluded:

> Far from being a socially depressed group, then, . . . the Christians were dominated by a socially pretentious section of the population of big cities. Beyond that they seem to have drawn on a broad constituency, probably representing the household dependents of leading members. . . .
>
> But the dependent members of city households were by no means the most debased section of society. If lacking freedom, they still enjoyed security, and a moderate prosperity. The peasantry and persons in slavery on the land were the most underprivileged classes. Christianity left them largely untouched. (60)

Moreover, Judge perceptively noted that the "proof text" in 1 Cor. 1:26–28 had been overinterpreted: Paul did not say his followers included *none* of the wise, mighty, or noble—merely that there were "not many" such persons, which means that there were *some*. Indeed, based on an inscription found in Corinth in 1929 and upon references in Rom. 16:23 and 2 Tim. 4:20, many scholars now agree that among the members of the church at Corinth was Erastus, "the city treasurer" (Furnish 1988:20). And historians now accept that Pomponia Graecina, a woman of the senatorial class, whom Tacitus reported as having been accused of practicing "foreign superstition" in 57 (*Annals* 13.32, 1989 ed.), was a Christian (Sordi 1986). Nor, according to Marta Sordi, was Pomponia an isolated case: "We know from reliable sources that there were Christians among the aristocracy [in Rome] in the second half of the first century (Acilius Glabrio and the Christian Flavians) and that it seems probable that the same can be said for the first half of the same century, before Paul's arrival in Rome" (1986:28).

Since Judge first challenged the proletarian view of the early church, a consensus has developed among New Testament historians that Christianity was based in the middle and upper classes (Scroggs 1980). Thus Jean Danielou and Henri Marrou (1964:240) discussed the prominent role of "rich benefactors" in the affairs of the early church. Robert M. Grant (1977:11) also denied that early Christianity was "a proletarian mass movement," and argued that it was "a relatively small cluster of more or less intense groups, largely middle class in origin." Abraham J. Malherbe (1977:29–59) analyzed the language and style of early church writers and concluded that they were addressing a literate, educated audience. In his detailed study of the church at Corinth in the first century, Gerd Theissen (1982:97) identified wealthy Christians including members of "the upper classes." Robin Lane Fox (1987:311) wrote of the presence "of women of high status." Indeed, soon after Judge's book appeared, the Marxist historian Heinz Kreissig (1967) recanted the proletarian thesis.[2] Kreissig identified the early Christians as drawn from "urban circles of well-situated artisans, merchants, and members of the liberal professions" (quoted in Meeks 1983:214).

Curiously, this new view is a return to an earlier historical tradition. Although Edward Gibbon was often quoted in support of the proletarian thesis—"the new sect of Christians was almost entirely composed of the dregs of the populace, of peasants and mechanics, of boys and women, of beggars and slaves" ([1776–1788] 1960:187)—he had actually preceded this line by identifying it as "a very odious imputation." To the contrary, Gibbon argued, Christianity necessarily would have included many from the lower ranks simply because most people belonged to these classes. But he saw no reason to think that the lower classes were disproportionately represented among Christians.

During the nineteenth century many famous historians went further than Gibbon and argued that the lower classes were disproportionately *under*-represented in the early church. Indeed, W. M. Ramsay wrote in his classic study that Christianity "spread first among the educated more rapidly than among the uneducated; nowhere had it a stronger hold ... than in the household and at the court of the emperors" (1893:57). Ramsay attributed similar views to the famous German classicist Theodor Mommsen. And, just as his many German contemporaries were promulgating the proletarian thesis, Adolf Harnack (1908: 2:35) noted that Ignatius, in his letter to the Christian congregation in Rome, expressed his concern lest they interfere with his martyrdom (see chapter 8). Harnack pointed to the obvious conclusion that Ignatius took it for granted that Christians in Rome had "the power" to gain him a pardon, "a fear which would have been unreasonable had not the church contained members whose riches and repute enabled them to intervene in this way either by bribery or by the exercise of personal influence."

Thus we come full circle. Obviously, if we wish to understand the rise of Christianity, we shall need to know something about its primary recruitment base—who joined? I am satisfied that the new view among historians is essentially correct. Nevertheless, *any* claim about the social basis of early Christianity must remain precarious, at least in terms of direct evidence, and it is unlikely that we shall ever have much more than the fragments of historical data we already possess. But there is another approach to this matter: to reconstruct the probable class basis of Christianity from some very well tested sociological propositions about the social basis of new religious movements. Indeed, this seems the best topic with which to begin my efforts at reconstruction because historians do not regard this as a controversial matter. Thus as I am able to show the close correspondence between my theoretical conclusions and the data assembled by historians, the latter may place greater confidence in the reconstructive enterprise per se. The fundamental thesis is simply put: If the early church was like all the other cult movements for which good data exist, it was not a proletarian movement but was based on the more privileged classes.

CLASS, SECT, AND CULT

William Sims Bainbridge and I have distinguished between *sect* movements and *cult* movements (Stark and Bainbridge 1979, 1985, 1987). The former occur by schism within a conventional religious body when persons desiring a more otherworldly version of the faith break away to "restore" the religion to a higher level of tension with its environment. This is the process of sect formation analyzed by H. Richard Niebuhr (1929). Sociologists can cite both theory and considerable research to show that those who take part in sect movements are, if not the dispossessed, at least of lower social standing than those who stick with the parent body.

Cult movements, on the other hand, are not simply new organizations of an old faith; they are *new faiths*, at least new in the society being examined. Cult movements always start small—someone has new religious ideas and begins to recruit others to the faith, or an alien religion is imported into a society where it then seeks recruits. In either case, as new faiths, cult movements violate prevailing religious norms and are often the target of considerable hostility.

For a long time the thesis that religious movements originate in lower-class deprivation was generalized to all religious movements—not only to sects but to cult movements as well. Thus not only were sects such as the Free Methodists and the Seventh-Day Adventists regarded as lower-class movements, so too were the Mormons, Theosophists, and Moonies. No distinction was made between cults and sects (cf. Wallis 1975); all were seen as protest movements and therefore as essentially proletarian (Niebuhr 1929). Moreover, the proletarian basis of many religious movements often has simply been asserted as if self-evident without the slightest effort's being made to assess who actually joined. Thus Gay confidently informed his readers about English converts to Mormonism, "most of whom were poor" (1971). He gives not the slightest clue as to how he knows this. As we shall see, it very likely was not true *unless*, in the context of nineteenth-century Britain, the Mormons were perceived as a Protestant sect rather than as a new religion.

Recently, however, the manifest absurdity of imputing a proletarian base to many new religious movements has overwhelmed sociological certitude. Indeed, when one examines what is involved in accepting a new faith (as opposed to being recruited by an energetic organization based on a conventional faith), it is easy to see why these movements must draw upon the more privileged for their recruits. As a useful introduction to this discussion, I will assess current sociological theory on the relationship between social class and religious commitment in general.

CLASS AND COMMITMENT

As with the social basis of religious movements, so too sociologists long assumed that the lower classes were more religious than the rich. Since the founders of modern social science, from Marx to Freud, all regarded religion as a compensator for thwarted desires, as false consciousness or neurotic illusion, the prevailing sociological orthodoxy held that religious commitment served primarily to assuage the suffering of the poor and deprived. The results of early survey studies came as a rude surprise: a series of investigators called the roll and found the deprived conspicuously absent from church membership and Sunday services (Stark 1964). This led to a revision of the deprivation thesis when it was discovered that religious commitment consists of a number of somewhat independent dimensions (Glock 1959; Stark and Glock 1968) and that the poor tend to be more religious on some of these dimensions while the rich are more religious on others (Demerath 1965; Glock and Stark 1965; Stark 1971). Thus negative correlations were found between social class and accepting traditional religious beliefs, having religious and mystical experiences, and frequency of personal prayers. In contrast, there are positive correlations between social class and church membership, attendance at worship services, participation in church activities, and saying grace before meals. But there seem to be no correlations between social class and belief in life after death or in the existence of heaven. Recently this array of empirical findings has been encompassed by three propositions linking power or class position to forms of religious commitment.

The starting point is to notice that religion can in fact compensate people for their inability to gain certain things they desire. However, the inability of humans to satisfy desires has *two* quite different aspects. First, some people are unable to gain desired rewards that are only *scarce*—rewards that others are able to obtain, or to obtain in more ample amounts. These include the tangible rewards such as wealth and health, the lack of which underlies all deprivation interpretations of religion. Clearly, religions provide a variety of effective mechanisms by which people can endure such deprivations, including promises that earthly sacrifice will merit heavenly recompense. But we must also recognize a *second* aspect of deprivation: the ability of religion to compensate people for desired rewards that seem to be absolutely *unavailable* to anyone, at least in this life. The most obvious of these, and perhaps the one most intensely sought by humans, is victory over death. No one, rich or poor, can gain eternal life by direct methods in the here and now. The only plausible source of such a reward is through religion, and the fulfillment of this promise is postponed to another world, a world known only through religious means. Finally, we must recognize that as organized social enterprises, religions are a source of *direct rewards* to members. That is, religious organizations reward some people with status, income, self-esteem, social relations, entertainment, and a host of other things they value. These distinctions lead to the following propositions (Stark and Bainbridge 1980).

First: *The power of an individual or group will be* positively *associated with control of religious organizations and with gaining the rewards available from religious organizations.*

Second: *The power of an individual or group will be* negatively *associated with acceptance of religious compensators for rewards that actually exist.*

Third: Regardless *of power, persons and groups will tend to accept religious compensators for rewards that do not exist in this world.*

The second of these propositions captures the long tradition of deprivation theories of religion: that the poor will pray while the rich play. We may call this the *otherworldly* or sectlike form of religious commitment. The first proposition, on the other hand, explains the relative absence of the lower classes from more conventional religious organizations, for it captures the religious expression of privilege. We can call this the *worldly* or churchlike dimension of religious commitment. The third proposition can be called the *universal* aspect of religious commitment, since it notes that in certain respects everyone is potentially deprived and in need of the comforts of faith. It is this proposition that explains why the upper classes are religious at all, why they too are susceptible to faith (something Marxist theories can only dismiss as aberration or as a phoney pose meant to lull the proletariat into false consciousness). Moreover, the third proposition helps explain why the more privileged are drawn to cult movements.

THE APPEAL OF NEW RELIGIONS

It is obvious that people do not embrace a new faith if they are content with an older one. New religions must always make their way in the market openings left them by weaknesses in the conventional religion(s) of a society. In later chapters I shall explore the conditions under which conventional faiths fail to serve substantial population segments. Here it is sufficient to point out that as weaknesses appear in conventional faiths, some people will recognize and respond to these weaknesses sooner than others. For example, as the rise of modern science caused difficulties for some traditional Christian teachings, this was recognized sooner by more educated people. In similar fashion, as the rise of Greek and Roman science and philosophy caused difficulties for pagan teachings, this too was first noticed by the educated (deVries 1967). To state this as a proposition: *Religious skepticism is most prevalent among the more privileged.*

But skepticism does not entail a general immunity to the essential supernaturalism of all religions. For example, although sociologists have long believed that people who give their religious affiliation as "none" are primarily secular humanists, considerable recent research shows this not to be the case. Most such people are merely indicating a lack of conviction in a conventional brand of faith, for they are also the group *most* likely to express interest in belief in unconventional mystical, magical, and religious doctrines. For example, "nones" are the group of Americans most willing to accept astrology, yoga, reincarnation, ghosts, and the like (Bainbridge and Stark 1980, 1981). Moreover, people who report their original religious background as "none" are extremely overrepresented in the ranks of converts to new religious movements (Stark and Bainbridge 1985).

It is surely not surprising that people who lack an anchorage in a conventional faith are most prone to embrace a new one. Nor should it be any surprise that people from privileged backgrounds are more likely to have weakened ties to a conventional faith. But can it really be true that it is the privileged who are most likely to embrace new religious movements? This is precisely what we ought to expect when we realize that conversion to a new religion involves being interested in *new culture*—indeed, in being capable of mastering new culture.

Studies of early adopters of cultural innovations have long found them to be well above average in terms of income and education (Larsen 1962). What is true of new technology, fashions, and attitudes ought also to be true in the realm of faith. For new religions always involve *new ideas.* Consider citizens of the Roman world as they first confronted the Pauline church. This was not simply a call to intensify their commitment to a familiar faith (as sect movements always are). Instead of calling Romans to return to the gods, Paul called them to embrace a new worldview, a new conception of reality, indeed to accept a *new* God. While sects are able to appeal to people of little intellectual capacity by drumming the old, familiar culture, new religions find such people difficult to reach. Thus they must gain their hearings from people of social standing and privilege.

But why would such people join? Most of the time most of them will not, which is why it is so rare for a new religion to succeed despite the thousands of them that are born. But sometimes there is substantial discontent with conventional faith among the more privileged. That the less privileged become discontented when a religious organization becomes too worldly to continue to offer them potent compensators for scarce rewards (proposition 2) is well known—this is the basis of sect movements. But there has been little awareness that sometimes a traditional faith and its organized expression can become so worldly that it cannot serve the *universal* need for religious compensators (proposition 3). That is, religious bodies can become so empty of supernaturalism that they cannot serve the religious needs of the privileged either. At such moments, the privileged will seek new options. Indeed, it is the privileged who will be most aware of erosions of the plausibility structure of conventional faiths.

In short, people must have a degree of privilege to have the sophistication needed to understand new religions and to recognize a need for them. This is not to say that the *most* privileged will be most prone to embrace new religious movements, but only that converts will be from the more, rather than the less, privileged classes. Indeed, Wayne Meeks (1983) proposes *relative deprivation* as a major source of recruits to the early church—that people having substantial privilege, but less than they felt they deserved, were especially likely to convert.

THE CLASS COMPOSITION OF CONTEMPORARY NEW RELIGIONS

Recently a considerable body of data has been amassed on who joins new religious movements (Stark and Bainbridge 1985). Let us begin with the Mormons since they are the most successful new religion to appear in many centuries—indeed, they seem on the threshold of becoming a new world faith (Stark 1984, 1994).

Mormonism was not and is not a proletarian movement. It began in one of the most "prosperous, and relatively sophisticated areas" of western New York, an area with a high proportion of cosmopolitan Yankee residents and one that surpassed other parts of the state in the proportion of children enrolled in school (O'Dea 1957:10). Those who first accepted Joseph Smith's teachings were better educated than their neighbors and displayed considerable intellectualism. Consider too that in their first city, Nauvoo, Illinois, in 1841 the Mormons established a municipal university at a time when higher education was nearly nonexistent in the United States. Moreover, within several years of the church's founding, non-Mormon neighbors in Missouri and Illinois began to complain that the Mormons were buying up the best land and displacing them. These were not collective purchases by the church but private ventures by individual Mormons, which is further evidence of the converts' relative privilege (Arrington and Bitton 1979).[3]

In similar fashion Christian Science sprang to prominence by attracting the relatively affluent, not the downtrodden. Wilson (1961) noted the unusual number of English Christian Scientists with titles and the abundance of well-known and aristocratic family names among members. The U.S. Census data on American denominations, published during the first third of this century, reveal that Christian Science far surpassed all other denominations in terms of per capita expenditures, justifying the impression of the group as disproportionately affluent. Spiritualism, too, found its base in the middle and upper classes both in the United States and in Great Britain (Nelson 1969; Stark, Bainbridge, and Kent 1981). In her studies of members of the Unification Church (more widely known as the Moonies), Eileen Barker (1981, 1984) found English converts to be many times more likely than others their age to be university graduates. The same is true of American converts. Americans who have joined various Hindu faiths also follow the rule: 89 percent of members of Ananda (Nordquist 1978) and 81 percent of members of Satchidanana (Volinn 1982) had attended college.

Survey research studies of general populations confirm these case study results. Table 2.1 is based on a 1973 sample of the San Francisco area (Wuthnow 1976). Here we can see that persons who have attended college were several times as likely to report that they were at least somewhat attracted to three Eastern religions that, in an American setting, qualify as cult movements. Moreover, persons who had gone to college were three times as likely as others to report that they had taken part in

TABLE 2.1
Education and Attraction to Cults

	Attended College	Did Not Attend College
Attracted to:		
Transcendental Meditation	17%	6%
Yoga	27%	12%
Zen	17%	5%
Claimed to have taken part in one of these groups	16%	5%

TABLE 2.2
Education and Involvement in Cults and Sects

	College	High School	Grade School
Sect Involvement			
Has been involved in faith healing	6%	7%	11%
Has been "born again"	27%	36%	42%
Cult Involvement			
Has been involved in:			
Yoga	5%	2%	0%
Transcendental Meditation	7%	3%	2%
Eastern religions	2%	1%	0%
Mysticism	3%	1%	0%

one of these groups. Table 2.2 is based on a 1977 Gallup Poll of the adult U.S. population. The top section of the table shows that the less educated are substantially more likely to report that they have had a "born again" experience, and to have been involved in "faith healing." This is as it should be, for, in an American context, these are *sect* activities—associated with higher-tension Christian denominations. However, the remainder of the table involves *cult* activities. And once again we see

TABLE 2.3
Education of Contemporary American Religious Groups

	Percent Who Attended College
Denominations[a]	
Roman Catholic	48%
Jewish	76%
Episcopal	70%
Congregational (United Church of Christ)	63%
Presbyterian	61%
Methodist	46%
Lutheran	45%
Sects	
Assemblies of God	37%
Nazarene	34%
Jehovah's Witnesses	23%
Worldwide Church of God	10%
Cults	
New Age	67%
Scientology	81%
Wiccan	83%
Eckankar	90%
Deity	100%
Total	81%
Mormons	55%
Irreligious	
None	53%
Agnostic	72%

[a] Baptists have been omitted because they constitute such a mixture of sects and denominations, and because of the confounding effect of race.

that the college educated show the largest proportion of participants, followed by those with only high school educations, with the grade school educated being almost devoid of cult participation.

Finally, table 2.3 reports the findings of the 1989–1990 National Survey of Religious Identification. Conducted by Barry A. Kosmin and his colleagues, it is the largest survey of American religious affiliation ever conducted—113,000 cases. Because the sample was so immense, it is possible to assemble a significant number of persons who named a cult movement when asked their religious affiliation. When we examine the data, it is no surprise that members of the major denominations tend to be college-educated—indeed, three-fourths of American Jews have been to college. Nor is it a surprise that most members of Protestant sects are not well educated—only 10 percent of members of the Worldwide Church of God have attended college.

But notice the cult groups.[4] They are the most educated groups—exceeding even Jews and Episcopalians in terms of the percentage of members who have attended college. Admittedly, the percentages for individual groups are based on small numbers of cases—only twelve people gave their religious affiliation as New Age, and only ten named Eckankar. But the findings are extremely consistent across groups, and when the cases are totaled, we see that, overall, 81 percent of members of American cult movements have been to college. Indeed, cult members are more likely to have attended college than are those who claim no religious preference or who claim to be agnostics.

Technically, the Mormons still constitute a cult movement within the religious definitions operative in the United States. However, they have endured so long and have grown so large that their tension with their social environment has been greatly reduced. And, just as Christianity did not remain a middle- and upper-class movement forever but eventually penetrated all classes, the Mormons are not as singularly based on the educated as are the other cult movements shown in the table. Moreover, these data include all Mormons, not just recent converts—while the data on the other groups would be unlikely to include any second-generation members. Nevertheless, the Mormons display a high proportion of college-attenders (55 percent), thus conforming to the general proposition that new religious movements are based on the privileged.

Clearly, then, not just any unconventional religion is an outlet for proletarian discontent. It is not poor kids who are running off and joining cult movements in contemporary America. Indeed, Volinn (1982) found that more than two-thirds of the members of Satchidanana had college-educated parents! Cult movements, insofar as we have any data on their members, are based on the more, not the less, privileged. But can we apply this rule to early Christianity?

CHRISTIANITY AS A CULT MOVEMENT

During his ministry, Jesus seems to have been the leader of a sect movement within Judaism. Indeed, even in the immediate aftermath of the Crucifixion, there was little to separate the disciples from their fellow Jews. However, on the morning of the third day something happened that turned the Christian sect into a cult movement.

Christians believe that on that day Jesus arose from the dead and during the next forty days appeared repeatedly to various groups of his followers. It is unnecessary to believe in the Resurrection to see that because the apostles believed in it, they were no longer just another Jewish sect. Although it took time for the fact to be recognized fully (in part because of the immense diversity of Judaism in this era), beginning with the Resurrection Christians were participants in a new religion, one that added far too much new culture to Judaism to be any longer an internal sect movement. Of course, the complete break between church and synagogue took centuries, but it seems clear that Jewish authorities in Jerusalem quickly labeled Christians as heretics beyond the boundaries of the community in the same way that Moonies are today excluded from Christian associations.

Moreover, whatever the relationship between Christianity and Judaism, when historians speak of the *early* church, they do not mean the church in Jerusalem but the Pauline church—for this is the church that triumphed and changed history. And there can be no doubt that Christianity was not a sect movement within conventional paganism. The early church was a cult movement in the context of the empire, just as the Mormons were a cult movement in the context of nineteenth-century America (and remain a cult in the eyes of evangelical Christians).

If this is so, and if cult movements are based on a relatively privileged constituency, can we not infer that Paul's missionary efforts had their greatest success among the middle and upper middle classes, just as New Testament historians now believe? In my judgment such an inference is fully justified unless a convincing case can be made that basic social and psychological processes were different in the days of Rome from what they are now—that in antiquity the human mind worked on different principles. Some historians might be tempted to embrace such an assertion, but no competent social scientist would consider it for a moment. Moreover, evidence based on a list of the earliest converts to Islam supports the conclusion that from the start, Muhammad's followers came from among young men of considerable privilege (Watt 1961).

CONCLUSION

I am fully aware that this chapter does not "prove" that the early church had its greatest appeal to the solid citizens of the empire. Had Paul sent out not simply letters but also questionnaires, such proof might be forthcoming. But it is idle to demand certainty where none ever will be forthcoming. Moreover, science does not proceed by testing empirically each and every application of its theories. (When physicists go to a baseball game, they count hits, runs, and errors like everyone else. They do not keep score on whether each fly ball comes back down.) The whole point of theories is to *generalize* and hence to escape the grip of perpetual trial and error. And the point of sociological generalizations such as *Cult movements overrecruit persons of more privileged backgrounds* is to rise above the need to plead ignorance pending adequate evidence on every specific group.

Finally, what difference does it make whether early Christianity was a movement of the relatively privileged or of the downtrodden? In my judgment it matters a great deal. Had Christianity actually been a proletarian movement, it strikes me that the state necessarily would have responded to it as a *political* threat, rather than simply as an illicit religion. With Marta Sordi (1986), I reject claims that the state did perceive early Christianity in political terms. It is far from clear to me that Christianity could have survived a truly comprehensive effort by the state to root it out during its early days. When the Roman state did perceive political threats, its repressive measures were not only brutal but unrelenting and extremely thorough—Masada comes immediately to mind. Yet even the most brutal persecutions of Christians were haphazard and limited, and the state ignored thousands of persons who openly professed the new religion, as we will see in chapter 8. If we postulate a Christianity of the privileged, on the other hand, this behavior by the state seems consistent. If, as is now believed, the Christians were not a mass of degraded outsiders but from early days had members, friends, and relatives in high places—often within the imperial family—this would have greatly mitigated repression and persecution. Hence the many instances when Christians were pardoned. I shall return to these matters in later chapters.

In conclusion, it might be well to confess how I came to write the essay on which this chapter is based. Having begun to read about the early church, I encountered Robin Scroggs's (1980) discussion of the new view that Christianity was not a proletarian movement. My immediate reaction was, "Of course it wasn't; cult movements never are." And that is precisely what this chapter has attempted to spell out.

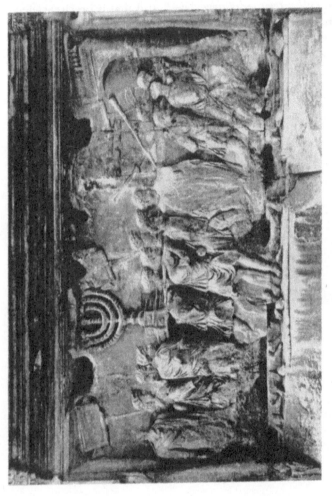

This bas-relief depicts Roman troops carrying the menorah and other sacred loot from the Temple in the year 70. The claim that the mission to the Jews ended at this time is sociologically improbable.

The Mission to the Jews:
Why It Probably Succeeded

Nothing seems more self-evident than the proposition that the rise of Christianity was accomplished despite the failure of the mission to the Jews. The New Testament says so, and so does the uncontested weight of historical and scholarly opinion. Granted, the received wisdom recognizes that Jews made up the bulk of very early converts, as phrases such as "Jewish Christianity" and "the Christian Synagogue" acknowledge. But it is generally assumed that this pattern ended abruptly in the wake of the revolt of 66–74, although some writers will accept a substantial role for Jewish conversion into the second century, regarding the Bar-Kokhba revolt as the "final straw" in Jewish-Christian sympathies.

Perhaps only a sociologist would be foolish enough to suggest that, contrary to the received wisdom, Jewish Christianity played a central role until much later in the rise of Christianity—that not only was it the Jews of the diaspora who provided the initial basis for church growth during the first and early second centuries, but that Jews continued as a significant source of Christian converts until at least as late as the fourth century and that Jewish Christianity was still significant in the fifth century. In any event, that is the argument I shall make in this chapter.

Initially I will base my argument on a number of sociological principles and insights about how movements grow and how people have reacted to religious movements when faced with

A preliminary version of this chapter appeared as "Jewish Conversion and the Rise of Christianity: Rethinking the Received Wisdom," in *Society of Biblical Literature Seminar Papers*, ed. Kent Harold Richards (Atlanta: Scholars Press, 1986), 314–329.

circumstances very like those faced by millions of Hellenized Jews. Indeed, part of my case will rest on how Jews have reacted when faced with similar conditions in recent times. From these materials I reconstruct what *should* have happened. I will then survey various recent archaeological and documentary findings which suggest that my sociological reconstruction represents what *actually* happened.

The reconstructive part of the chapter proceeds in three general steps. First, I sketch the evidential basis for the belief that the Jews did not convert in substantial numbers. Then, I examine a series of sociological propositions and research findings. Finally, I assess the situation of the Hellenized Jews of the diaspora in light of these considerations and try to show why the most plausible conclusion is that large numbers did convert.

How Do We Know That the Jews Rejected Christianity?

Everyone knows that the Jews rejected the Christian message. But how do we know this? The most compelling and solid evidence is that after the triumphant rise of Christianity there still existed a large and obdurate Jewish population. Moreover, the archaeological evidence shows that large synagogues continued to function in various parts of the diaspora during the critical time—the second through fifth centuries. Thus it appears to follow that, while Romans and Greeks flocked to the church, the Jews *must have* stood firm, because they survived to confront the church in later, more fully documented eras.

This leads to the second basis for knowledge that the Jews did not convert: hostile textual references from both sides. Beginning with parts of the New Testament we find the early church fathers depicting the Jews as stubborn and eventually as wicked. It is also known that at some point a curse against Christians (Nazarenes) was inserted into the Jewish Eighteen Benedictions—presumably as a method to prevent Jewish Christians from acting as presenters in the synagogue (Katz 1984; Horbury 1982). The date of this insertion is in doubt. But whenever the curse came into use, the assumption is that reciprocal condemnations reflect bitterness rooted in the failed mission to the Jews.

. And that's all. That is the evidential base I now attempt to reappraise. To do so, I would like to introduce pertinent portions of recent work in the sociology of religion. I begin by examining some historical parallels and go on to introduce some theoretical propositions.

PERTINENT SOCIOLOGY

During the 1960s, sociologists radically revised the conventional wisdom about the assimilation of ethnic groups in American society. Among the leaders were Nathan Glazer and Daniel P. Moynihan (1963), who demonstrated that eastern and southern European ethnics had failed to assimilate into American society—that the melting pot was romantic nonsense. What was their proof? Look around, they said. Look at all the Little Italys and Little Polands. Solidly ethnic communities abound in American cities and hence confound the melting pot thesis.

Nevertheless, the revised view was invalid. When good data became available, it was discovered that the vast majority of these ethnic groups already had assimilated—most had married outside the ethnic group, for example (Alba 1976, 1985). The new myth was a product of the method. As Richard Alba pointed out, if one used Glazer and Moynihan's method, one would always find proof that Italians, for example, do not assimilate so long as *some* have not yet done so—until Little Italy stands empty. The lesson here is that it is possible for Little Italy to seem to thrive while at the same time massive assimilation

51

goes on. The implication is, of course, that active synagogues need not be evidence that large numbers of Jews of the diaspora did not convert. The synagogues of the third and fourth centuries could be the equivalent of Little Italy in the twentieth century. Granted, of course, Little Italy may one day stand empty while some of the synagogues of the diaspora never did. But this does not alter the cautionary lesson.

Let us now examine a second historical parallel. Emancipation of the Jews in most European nations during the nineteenth century resulted in a religious crisis for those Jews who seized the opportunities of full citizenship. As Stephen Steinberg (1965) demonstrated so clearly, emancipated Jews discovered that Judaism was not simply a religion, but an ethnicity—the ghetto was not simply a Gentile imposition but a tribal precinct. To leave the ghetto, one had to abandon a tribal ethnicity. That is, to move freely in the greater society, Jews needed to shed the highly distinctive appearance of ghetto residents—side curls, shawls, and yarmulkes, for example. They also needed to relax dietary restrictions that prevented them from freely associating with Gentiles or entering their social circles. The emancipated Jews discovered, in fact, that one could not keep the Law outside the ghetto. Elsewhere there were no kosher butchers. How could one avoid violating the Sabbath by riding to the synagogue when one lived too far away to walk?

Emancipation caused hundreds of thousands of European Jews to become socially marginal—no longer accepted as Jews (often having been excommunicated from Judaism and shunned by family), and not truly assimilated Gentiles either. The concept of *marginality* has long-standing utility in sociology (Stonequist 1937; Stark and Bainbridge 1987). People are marginalized when their membership in two groups poses a contradiction or cross pressure such that their status in each group is lowered by their membership in the other. The concept takes on power as it is embedded in a proposition: *People will attempt to escape or resolve a marginal position.* Some Jews in the nineteenth century tried to resolve their marginality by assimilation, including conversion to Christianity. Others attempted to resolve their marginality by becoming a new kind of Jew.

Reform Judaism was designed to provide a nontribal, nonethnic religion rooted in the Old Testament (and the Enlightenment), one that focused on theology and ethics rather than on custom and practice (Blau 1964; Steinberg 1965). Samuel Holdheim, the first rabbi of the Reform congregation in Berlin, wrote in 1845 that divine law is given only for a particular time and place:

> A law, even though divine, is potent only so long as the conditions and circumstances of life, to meet which it was enacted, continue; when these change, however, the law also must be abrogated, even though it have God for its author. For God himself has shown indubitably that with the change of the circumstances and conditions of life for which He once gave those laws, the laws themselves cease to be operative, that they *shall* be observed no longer because they *can* be observed no longer. (Quoted in Blau 1964:137)

The Pittsburgh Platform adopted by the Reform movement in its early days in the United States is forthright in its attempt to strip ethnicity from theology. Referring to Orthodox Judaism, the platform proclaimed:

> Today we accept as binding only its moral laws and maintain only such ceremonials as elevate and sanctify our lives, but reject all such as are not adapted to the views and habits of modern civilization.
>
> We hold that all such Mosaic and Rabbinical laws as regulate diet, priestly purity and dress originated in ages and under the influence of ideas altogether foreign to our present mental and spiritual state.
>
> We recognize Judaism as a progressive religion, ever striving to be in accord with the postulates of reason. (Quoted in Steinberg 1965:125)

Indeed, in this same document it was stated frankly, "We consider ourselves no longer a nation but a religious community." Later in this chapter I will attempt to show the great similarity between the circumstances of nineteenth-century emancipated Jews and those of Hellenized Jews in the Greco-Roman world. I shall show the ways in which Christianity offered many of the same things to Hellenized Jews that nineteenth-century Jews found in the Reform movement.

Against this background, let me now introduce several sociological propositions, in addition to the one on marginality. Recall from chapter 1 that *New religious movements mainly draw their converts from the ranks of the religiously inactive and discontented, and those affiliated with the most accommodated (worldly) religious communities.*

One aspect of this proposition is obvious. If people are firmly anchored into one religious institution, they don't up and join another. However, it has also been widely assumed that people who have lost all apparent religious ties and interests (like Americans who answer "None" when asked their religious preference) also don't up and join a new religious movement—that joiners are active seekers after a new faith. But that is not the case. New religious movements do best in places where there is the greatest amount of apparent secularization—for example, in places with low rates of church membership such as the west coasts of the United States and Canada, and northern Europe. Moreover, in these places the converts to new religious movements derive overwhelmingly from unaffiliated and irreligious backgrounds—the same people who would once have given their affiliation as "None" (Stark and Bainbridge 1985).

Indeed, the very great secularity of North American and European Jews in recent times is reflected in the extraordinary rates at which their children have been joining new religious movements (Stark and Bainbridge 1985). For example, more than a third of Americans who joined Hare Krishna are from nonpracticing Jewish families (Shinn 1983). Would people raised in Hellenized Jewish families have been prone to join something too?

The second important proposition is that *People are more willing to adopt a new religion to the extent that it retains cultural continuity with conventional religion(s) with which they already are familiar.* As Nock so aptly put it:

> The receptivity of most people for that which is wholly new (if anything is) is small. . . . The originality of a prophet lies commonly in his ability to fuse into a white heat combustible material which is there, to express and appear to meet the half-formed prayers of some at least of his contemporaries. The teaching of Gotama the Buddha grows out of the eager and baffled asceticism and speculation of his time, and it is not easy even now to define exactly what was new in him except his attitude. The message of John the Baptist and of Jesus gave form and substance to the dreams of a kingdom which had haunted many of their compatriots for generations. (1933:9–10)

The principle of cultural continuity captures the human tendency to maximize—to get the most for the least cost. In the case of adopting a new religious outlook, cost can be measured in terms of how much of what one already knows and more or less accepts one must discard in order to make the shift. To the extent that potential converts can retain much of their original cultural heritage and merely add to it, cost is minimized (Stark and Bainbridge 1987). For example, when persons familiar with the culture of Christianity confront the option of becoming Mormons, they are not asked to discard the Old and New Testaments but to add a third testament to the set. Mormonism does not present itself as an alternative to Christianity, but as its fulfillment. Joseph Smith did not claim to bring revelations from a new source, but to bring more recent tidings from the same source. This principle also applies to Muhammad and to Jesus.

The third proposition is that *Social movements grow much faster when they spread through preexisting social networks.*

This is simply an application of the attachment proposition about conversion developed in chapter 1. For the fact is that typically people do not *seek* a faith; they *encounter* one through their ties to other people who already accept this faith. In the end, accepting a new religion is part of conforming to the expectations and examples of one's family and friends. This limits avenues by which movements can recruit.

Religious movements can grow because their members continue to form new relationships with outsiders. This is a frequent pattern observed in recruitment to religious movements in modern times, especially in large cities. Many new religions have become skilled in making attachments with newcomers and others deficient in interpersonal attachments (Lofland and Stark 1965; Stark and Bainbridge 1985). Movements can also recruit by spreading through preexisting social networks, as converts bring in their families and friends. This pattern has the potential for much faster growth than the one-by-one conversion of social isolates (Stark and Roberts 1982). The best example of this is provided by the Mormons. Although they often get an isolated recruit on the basis of attachments built by missionaries, the primary source of Mormon converts is along network lines. The average convert was preceded into the church by many friends and relatives. It is network growth that so distinguishes the Mormon rate of growth—meanwhile, other contemporary religious movements will count their growth in thousands, not millions, for lack of a network pattern of growth.

The statistics on Christian growth developed in chapter 1 would seem to require that Christianity arose through preexisting networks. For that to have occurred requires converts to have come from communities united by attachments. These networks need not have been rooted in highly stable communities. But the network assumption is not compatible with an image of proselytizers seeking out most converts along the streets and highways, or calling them forth from the crowds in

56

the marketplaces. In addition, network growth requires that missionaries from a new faith *already have, or easily can form,* strong attachments to such networks.

THE SITUATION OF HELLENIZED JEWS IN THE DIASPORA

Now it is time to apply all of the above to the question of how, given their circumstances, Hellenized Jews in the diaspora were likely to have responded to Christianity as it appeared among them. I shall show that because there was extensive similarity between the situation of the Hellenized Jews of New Testament times and that of nineteenth-century emancipated Jews, we can expect something analogous to the Reform movement to have attracted the Hellenized Jews.

It is important to keep in mind how greatly the Hellenized Jews of the diaspora outnumbered the Jews living in Palestine. Johnson (1976) suggests that there were a million in Palestine and four million outside, while Meeks (1983) places the population of the diaspora at five to six million. It is also worth noting that the Hellenized Jews were primarily urban—as were the early Christians outside Palestine (Meeks 1983). Finally, the Hellenized Jews were not an impoverished minority; they had been drawn out from Palestine over the centuries because of economic opportunities. By the first century, the large Jewish sections in major centers such as Alexandria were known for their wealth. As they built up wealthy and populous urban communities within the major centers of the empire, Jews had adjusted to life in the diaspora in ways that made them very marginal vis-à-vis the Judaism of Jerusalem. As early as the third century B.C.E. their Hebrew had decayed to the point that the Torah had to be translated into Greek (Greenspoon 1989). In the process of translation not only Greek words, but Hellenic viewpoints, crept into the Septuagint. Thus Exod. 22:28 was rendered "You shall not revile *the gods,*" which Roetzel (1985) interprets as a gesture toward accommodation with pagans. In any event, the Jews outside Palestine read, wrote, spoke, thought, and worshiped in Greek. Of the inscriptions found in the Jewish catacombs in Rome, fewer than 2 percent were in Hebrew or Aramaic, while 74 percent were in Greek and the remainder in Latin (Finegan 1992:325–326). Many Jews in the diaspora had taken Greek names, and they had incorporated much of the Greek enlightenment into their cultural views, just as emancipated Jews responded to the eighteenth-century Enlightenment. Moreover, many Hellenized Jews had embraced some elements of pagan religious thought. In short, large numbers were no longer Jews in the ethnic sense and remained only partly so in the religious sense (Goldstein 1981; Frend 1984: Green 1985).

But neither were they Greeks, for Judaism could not easily be separated from an ethnicity intrinsic to the Law. The Law set Jews apart as fully in the first century as in the nineteenth and prevented them from full participation in civic life (Hengel 1975). In both eras the Jews were in the unstable and uncomfortable condition of social marginality. As Tcherikover put it, Hellenized Jews found it degrading to live among Greeks and embrace Greek culture and yet to remain "enclosed in a spiritual Ghetto and be reckoned among the 'barbarians.'" He pointed to the urgent need for "a compromise, a synthesis, which would permit a Jew to remain a Jew" and still be able to claim full entry into "the elect society of the Greeks" (1958:81).

Perhaps the "God-Fearers" can help reveal the difficulty that the Hellenized Jews had with the ethnic impositions of Judaism. Judaism had long attracted Gentile "fellow travelers," who found much intellectual satisfaction in the moral teachings and monotheism of the Jews, but who would not take the final step of fulfilling the Law. These people are referred to as God-Fearers. For Hellenized Jews who had social and intellectual problems with the Law, the God-Fearers could easily have been a very tempting model of an alternative, fully Greek Judaism—a Judaism that Rabbi Holdheim might have judged appropriate to the changed circumstances and conditions of life. But the God-Fearers were not a movement. The Christians were.

When the Apostolic Council decided not to require converts to observe the Law, they created a religion free of ethnicity. Tradition has it that the first fruit of this break with the Law was the rapid success of the mission to the Gentiles. But who would have been the first to hear of the break? Who would have had the greatest initial benefits from it? What group, in fact, best fulfills the sociological propositions outlined above?

CULTURAL CONTINUITY

Christianity offered twice as much cultural continuity to the Hellenized Jews as to Gentiles. If we examine the marginality of the Hellenized Jews, torn between two cultures, we may note how Christianity offered to retain much of the religious content of *both* cultures and to resolve the contradictions between them. Indeed, Theissen described Pauline Christianity as "accommodated Judaism" (1982:124).

Little need be said of the extent to which Christianity maintained cultural continuity with Judaism. Indeed, much of the New Testament is devoted to displaying how Christianity extends and fulfills the Old. And for much of this century scholars have stressed the ways in which Christianity presented a remarkably familiar face to the non-Jewish, Greco-Roman culture as well (Harnack 1908; Nock 1933; Kee 1983; Wilken 1984; MacMullen 1981, 1984; Frend 1984). But if we look at these "two cultural faces" of early Christianity, it seems clear that its greatest appeal would have been for those to whom *each* face mattered: the Jews of the diaspora.

ACCOMMODATED JUDAISM

Not only were the Hellenized Jews socially marginal, they were also relatively worldly, accommodated, and secular. The example of Philo is compelling. Much has been made of Philo's "anticipations" of many Christian doctrines, and it has been suggested that he may have influenced as well as foreshadowed many of Paul's teachings. This could have had the effect of preparing sophisticated opinion for the Christian message. But these matters are secondary to my argument. Whatever else Philo may represent, he offers dramatic proof of the extensive accommodation of Judaism in the diaspora (Collins 1983).

Early in the first century we find an esteemed leader of the Alexandrian Jewish community whose interpretations of the Torah amazingly resemble those of the early Reform rabbis: divine authority is subordinated to reason and to symbolic and allegorical interpretation; faith is accommodated to time and place. Like the Reform rabbis, Philo was stuck between two worlds. How could he be fully Hellenized but remain in some sense Jewish? To this end, he tried to offer "reasonable" explanations of the laws—God forbids eating of the flesh of birds of prey and of carnivorous mammals in order to elevate the virtue of peace. What he could not explain in this way, he recast as allegory. As Collins pointed out, "The allegorical interpretation of scripture by Philo and others is an evident method for reducing the dissonance between the Jewish scriptures and philosophical religion" (1983:9). Frend has made the same point, arguing that Philo attempted to interpret the Law "exclusively through the mirror of Greek philosophy" (1984:35). As a result, the self-evident religious and historical meaning of much of the Torah was "lost among the spiritual and moral sentiments whereby Philo sought to demonstrate the harmony and rationality of the universe" (Frend 1984:35).

A major aspect of accommodation is a turn toward worldliness and away from otherworldliness, with the result that the supernatural becomes ever more remote and inactive. Here too Philo's writings are a model of the accommodation process. Granted, he had a real penchant for mysticism and could write of his soul's being "on fire." But his commitment was to Platonic philosophy, and this was a lens through which the supernatural could be barely glimpsed through layers of abstraction, Reason, and Perfection. In Philo, the thundering and jealous Yahweh of the Old Testament is replaced by a remote, abstract Absolute Being. It has been said of many modern Christian theologians that their primary aim is to find ways to express disbelief as belief. It seems to me that the same could be said of Philo, *and of his peers.*

I suggest there are two primary reasons to believe that Philo expressed fashionable opinion and thus revealed the extensive accommodation of Hellenized Judaism. First, he made his views well known while retaining public esteem. Second, later in the century when the question of Christians and the Law arose, it was not Gentile converts to Christianity "who first detached themselves from the law, but Jewish Christians" (Conzelmann 1973:83). These Jewish Christians were not part of the church in Palestine but were Hellenized converts. One must suppose that their nonobservance predated their conversion, or, at the very least, that they had observed the Law only superficially. Again, the parallels with Reform Jews, and with the present-day affinity of Jews from nonpracticing homes for novel religious movements, seem compelling.

NETWORKS

I now examine the implications of network growth for the mission to the Jews. Let us put ourselves in the position of the evangelists: here we are in Jerusalem in the year 50. The Apostolic

Council has just met and decided that we should leave Palestine and go out and spread the glad tidings. Where should we go? Whom should we seek out when we get there? Put another way, who will welcome us? Who will listen? I suggest that the answer would have been obvious: we should go to the major communities of Hellenized Jews (Roberts 1979).

In all the major centers of the empire were substantial settlements of diasporan Jews *who were accustomed to receiving teachers from Jerusalem.* Moreover, the missionaries were likely to have family and friendship connections within at least some of the diasporan communities. Indeed, if Paul is a typical example, the missionaries were themselves Hellenized Jews.

In addition, the Hellenized Jews were the group best prepared to receive Christianity. We have already seen how Christianity appealed to both their Jewish and their Hellenic sides. It built a distinctly Hellenized component on Jewish foundations. But, unlike the Platonic conceptions of Philo, Christianity presented an exceedingly vigorous otherworldly faith, capable of generating strong commitment.

We also ought to note that diasporan Jews would be less dubious about a messiah come to Palestine—a part of the empire that many Gentiles would regard as a backwater. Nor would the Jews have been so easily put off by the facts of the Crucifixion. Indeed, the cross was a symbol used to signify the Messiah in Hebrew manuscripts prior to the Crucifixion (Finegan 1992:348). In contrast, many Gentiles apparently had trouble with the notion of deity executed as a common criminal. The socially marginal Jews of the diaspora knew that Roman justice was often opportunistic, and they could also understand the machinations of the high priests in Jerusalem.

Finally, it seems reasonable to suppose that the escalating conflict between Rome and various Jewish nationalist movements added to the burden of marginality experienced by Hellenized Jews. In the wake of the destruction of the Temple, with Jewish nationalists plotting new revolts, multitudes of

Hellenized Jews who no longer felt strong ethnic ties to Palestine must have been very tempted to step aside (Grant 1972; Downey 1962).

These are the reasons that ought to have caused the first missionaries to concentrate on the Hellenized Jews. And virtually all New Testament historians agree that they *did so*, and *were successful*, but *only* in the beginning. These facts are agreed upon: (1) many of the converts mentioned in the New Testament can be identified as Hellenized Jews; (2) much of the New Testament assumes an audience familiar with the Septuagint (Frend 1984); (3) Christian missionaries frequently did their public teaching in the synagogues of the diaspora—and may have continued to do so far into the second century (Grant 1972); (4) archaeological evidence shows that the early Christian churches outside Palestine were concentrated in the Jewish sections of cities—as Eric Meyers put it, "on opposite sides of the street, so to speak" (1988:76; see also Pearson 1986; White 1985, 1986).

The critical issue thus comes into view. What justifies the assumption that the powerful social forces that initially achieved such a favorable response in diasporan communities suddenly became inoperative? Frend asserts that between 145 and 170 there was a major shift in which Christianity abandoned its Jewish connections (1984:257). But he does not say how he knows, nor does he explain why such a shift should have occurred or did occur. There is nothing in the sociological propositions examined above to justify a sudden shift in recruitment patterns, nor is there an empirical example to cite. Granted, sociological "models" are fallible, but we ought not to dismiss them without due cause. Here, an adequate cause to prefer the received over the sociological wisdom would be persuasive historical evidence that Jewish conversion did peter out by the second century and that Jewish Christianity was absorbed in a sea of Gentile converts.

I find no compelling case in the sources that the mission to the Jews ended in this way. To the contrary, the pertinent texts seem surprisingly (to me) supportive of my revisionist views (which are compatible with Georg Strecker's [1971] interpretations as well). First of all, historians acknowledge that neither the "Jewish War" nor the Bar-Kokhba revolt had really serious direct impact on most Jewish communities in the diaspora. That is, these conflicts brought destruction and depopulation in Palestine, but their "significance for the diaspora communities was minimal" (Meeks and Wilken 1978:5). If this is so, then why must we assume that one or the other of these conflicts severed connections between the Christian and Jewish communities? Indeed, would the destruction of the Temple and of the center of "ethnic" Judaism not have added to the growing weakness of traditional Orthodoxy in the diaspora and thus have increased the potential appeal of Christianity? We must not mistake what could well have been a "remnant" Orthodox Judaism of the fifth and sixth centuries for the dominant Judaism of the Hellenized communities of the second through fourth centuries.

Moreover, I think examination of the Marcion affair reveals that a very Jewish Christianity still was overwhelmingly dominant in the mid–second century. The Marcion movement was very much what one would have expected Christianity to become *if*, from very early on, the church in the West had been the Gentile-dominated movement, increasingly in conflict with the Jews of the diaspora, that it is alleged to have been.

Even today, after nearly two millennia of rationalization, the fit between the Old and the New Testaments often seems awkward. In the second century, with the canon still in flux, many must have perceived very serious "difficulties and internal contradictions," as Gerhard May has put it (1987–1988:148). Paul Johnson described the situation rather more bluntly, asserting that compared with the New, the Old Testament seems to be talking of "a quite different God," and that the clarity and integrity of post-Pauline Christian writings suffered from trying to reconcile the two traditions (1976:46).

In the face of these problems, what would be the most parsimonious and obvious solution for a religious movement consisting overwhelmingly of "Gentile" Christians? I think it would be the precise solution Marcion adopted: to strip the New Testament of all those parts concerned with justifying Christianity to the Jews, and then to drop the Old Testament from the canon entirely. If we are Christians, why should we worry about non-Christians or about pre-Christian doctrines? If Jewish texts do not jibe with the Pauline tradition, why not simply complete the break with Judaism? Whether Marcion himself came from a Jewish background, as is sometimes claimed, is irrelevant to the theological elegance of his solution. Indeed, the speed with which Marcion built a substantial movement suggests that his solution pleased many. But the crucial point is this: the traditional Christian faction seems to have easily ousted Marcion and successfully condemned *Antitheses* as heresy.

I do not believe that the traditionalists won out because of superior theology. Rather, the whole affair suggests to me that in the middle of the second century the church still was dominated by people with Jewish roots and strong current ties to the Jewish world. Notice that this was *after* the Bar-Kokhba revolt and at the very time Frend (1984) suggests that Jewish influences in the church rapidly waned. To me, the Marcion affair suggests that the mission to the Jews remained a very high priority far later than has been recognized.

Since "everyone" has known that Christian-Jewish connections were insignificant by the mid–second century, it is understandable that no one has drawn the obvious (to me) conclusions about the persistence well into the fifth century of "Judaizing" tendencies within Christianity. The facts are clear. In this period large numbers of Christians showed such an affinity for Jewish culture that it could be characterized as "a widespread Christian infatuation with Judaism" (Meeks and Wilken 1978:31). This is usually explained on the basis of lingering attractions of Judaism and renewed conversion to Judaism (Simon 1964; Wilken 1971, 1983). Perhaps so. But this is also exactly what one would expect to find in Christian communities containing many members of relatively recent Jewish ancestry, who retained ties of family and association with non-Christian Jews, and who therefore *still retained* a distinctly Jewish aspect to their Christianity. Indeed, it is quite uncertain just *when* it became unacceptable for Christians to observe the Law.

Put another way, what was at issue may not have been the Juda*izing* of Christianity, but that in many places a substantial Jewish Christianity *persisted*. And if this was the case, there is no reason to suppose that Jewish Christians had lost the ability to attract new converts from their networks of Hellenized families and friends. Hence, rather than seeing these affinities as signs of renewed conversion to Judaism, I suggest that a more plausible reading is to see them as signs that Jewish conversion to Christianity *continued*.

For the moment, assume that Jewish conversion to Christianity was still a major factor in the fourth and early fifth centuries—major in the sense that a substantial rate of defection from Judaism to Christianity continued, even though this would by then have become a minor source of converts to the now-huge Christian population. Such an assumption allows us to make better sense of the anti-Jewish polemics of Christian figures such as John Chrysostom. I think we can safely accept Chrysostom's claims about widespread Christian involvement in Jewish circles, since his audience would have known the true state of affairs. But rather than dismiss Chrysostom as merely a raving bigot or as an unscrupulous manipulator of Jewish scapegoats, why not see him as an early leader in the movement to *separate* a church and synagogue that were still greatly intertwined?

Postulate a world in which there are a great many Christians with Jewish friends and relatives and who, therefore, turn up at Jewish festivals and even in the synagogues from time to time. Moreover, this has gone on for centuries. Now suppose you are a newly appointed bishop who has been told that it is time to get serious about making a Christian world. How can you convince people that they ought to avoid even the appearance of dabbling in Judaism? By confronting them with the need to choose, not between Gentile and Jewish Christianity, but between Christianity and traditional, Orthodox Judaism—a Judaism whose adherents could be attacked as "Christ-killers" who consorted with demons (as Jewish Christianity could not). In this fashion Chrysostom could stress that it was time for Jewish-Christians to become assimilated, unhyphenated Christians. Seen this way, the increasingly emphatic attacks on Judaism in this later period reflect efforts to consolidate a diverse and splintered faith into a clearly defined catholic structure. I find this a more plausible interpretation than the thesis that the attacks were reactions against a new wave of conversion to Judaism. Why should the "ethnic" burden of Orthodoxy suddenly have ceased to matter to potential converts? And that takes us back to the "God-Fearers."

It seems to me that MacLennan and Kraabel (1986) are correct to dismiss the role of the "God-Fearers" as go-betweens taking Christianity to the Jews of the diaspora. There were plenty of Jewish Christians, including Paul, filling that role. I think they are also correct that the extent of Jewish conversion to Christianity during the first two centuries was "higher than is usually assumed." But I find difficulties with their conclusion that the God-Fearers may have been primarily mythical. Their evidence is, in my judgment, *too late*. A lack of mention of Gentile donors in synagogue inscriptions from the third and fourth centuries can be material *only if* we assume that the God-Fearers did not take the Christian option when it appeared, but continued to be marginal hangers-on of the synagogue. That is not consistent with good sociology. And it is inconsistent with the New Testament. Acts does not suggest that one would find the God-Fearers still lingering in the back of the synagogues, but that by early in the second century, at the latest, they would have long since moved into the churches.

What we ought to look for in the synagogues are signs of lingering connections with Christianity. MacLennan and Kraabel tell us that the archaeological evidence fails to show much Gentile presence around the synagogues in the Jewish settlements in the diaspora. But they also tells us that this is where the churches were! If they are correct that the people in these churches were not Gentiles, who could they have been other than Jewish Christians? And in fact, the weight of pertinent recent evidence seems to support this conclusion.

RECENT PHYSICAL EVIDENCE

There is recent physical evidence (or what insiders sometimes call *realia*) suggesting that the Christian and Jewish communities remained closely linked—intertwined, even—until far later than is consistent with claims about the early and absolute break between church and synagogue. The *realia* are both archaeological and documentary.

Eric Meyers (1983, 1988) reported that a wealth of archaeological findings in Italy (especially in Rome and Venosa) show that "Jewish and Christian burials reflect an interdependent and closely related community of Jews and Christians in which clear marks of demarcation were blurred until the third and fourth centuries C.E." (1988:73–74). Shifting to data from Palestine, Meyers noted excavations in Capernaum (on the shores of the Sea of Galilee) that reveal "a Jewish synagogue and a Jewish-Christian house church on opposite sides of the street. . . . Following the strata and the structures, both communities apparently lived in harmony until the seventh century C.E." (1988:76). Finally, Meyers suggested that only when a triumphant Christianity began, late in the fourth century, to pour money into Palestine for church building and shrines was there any serious rupture with Jews.

Roger Bagnall reported a surviving papyrus (*P.Oxy.* 44) from the year 400 wherein a man "explicitly described as a Jew" leased a ground-floor room and a basement storage room in a house from two Christian sisters described as apotactic monastics:

> The rent is in line with other lease payments for parts of the city known from the period, and the whole transaction is distinguished by its routineness. All the same, the sight of two Christian nuns letting out two rooms in their house to a Jewish man has much to say about not only the flexibility of the monastic life but also the ordinariness of [Christian-Jewish] relationships. (1993:277–278)

These data may strike social scientists as thin, but they seem far less ambiguous and far more reliable than the evidence with which students of antiquity must usually work.

Conclusion

In the nineteenth century, many newly emancipated Jews in western Europe responded to their marginal situation by turning to Reform Judaism—preserving some semblance of their religious heritage while jettisoning its heavy burdens of ethnicity. Had it not been for the preceding centuries of Christian hostility, they might very well have taken up Christianity instead, for it too would have been more compatible with the modern enlightenment and would have released them from the confines of the Law, the two concerns most urgently expressed in Reform writings. In the early centuries of the Christian era such a barrier had not yet been erected between Jews and Christians. In those days too, Jews were caught on the cleft of marginality, to which Christianity offered an appropriate resolution.

Keep in mind, too, that there were far more than enough Jews in the diaspora to have provided the numbers needed to fulfill plausible growth curves well into the Christian era. In chapter 1, I calculated a total of slightly more than a million Christians by the year 250. Only approximately *one* out of every *five* Jews in the diaspora need have converted to meet that total in the absence of any Gentile conversions—and I hardly mean to suggest that there were none of these before 250. Moreover, the diasporan Jews were in the right places to provide the needed supply of converts—in the cities, and especially in the cities of Asia Minor and North Africa. For it is here that we find not only the first churches, but, during the first four centuries, the most vigorous Christian communities.

I have tried to show what *should have happened*, why the mission to the Jews of the diaspora should have been a considerable *long-run* success. Although I reconfirm my respect for the gap between "should" and "did," I cautiously suggest that a very substantial conversion of the Jews actually did take place. Indeed, Ephraim Isaac recently reported that according to Ethiopian tradition, when Christianity first appeared there, "half of the population was Jewish and . . . most of them converted to Christianity" (1993:60).

AFTERWORD

Long after the initial version of this chapter had been published and as this book neared completion, I finally read the classic two-volume work by Johannes Weiss ([1914] 1959). Midway in the second volume I discovered that Weiss also rejected the traditional view positing the failure of the mission to the Jews. Noting that portions of the New Testament suggest that "the mission to the Jews has been abandoned as completely hopeless," Weiss then devoted many pages of textual analysis to rejecting this claim (2:666–703). He asserted that the church "did not abandon its mission to the Jews," and suggested that serious dialogue and interaction continued well into the third century and probably later. He noted, for example, that Origen mentioned having taken part in a theological debate with Jews before "umpires" sometime during the first half of the third century (2:670).

This discovery encouraged me to feel that I was on the right track, and discouraged me from imagining that I could ever finally master this enormous literature.

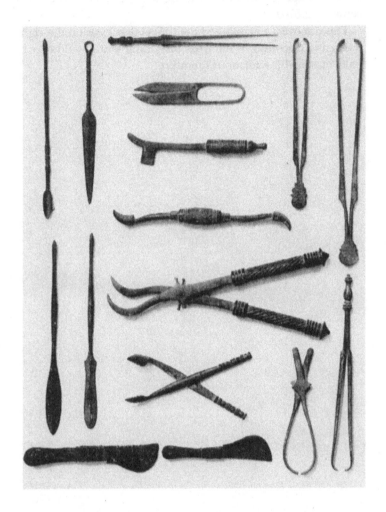

As these surgical instruments found in Pompeii reveal, the Romans understood human anatomy. But because they did not know germs even existed, they could not treat communicable diseases.

Epidemics, Networks,
and Conversion

IN 165, during the reign of Marcus Aurelius, a devastating epidemic swept through the Roman Empire. Some medical historians suspect that it was the first appearance of smallpox in the West (Zinsser [1934] 1960). But whatever the actual disease, it was lethal. During the fifteen-year duration of the epidemic, from a quarter to a third of the empire's population died from it, including Marcus Aurelius himself, in 180 in Vienna (Boak 1947; Russell 1958; Gilliam 1961; McNeill 1976). Then in 251 a new and equally devastating epidemic again swept the empire, hitting the rural areas as hard as the cities (Boak 1955a, 1955b; Russell 1958; McNeill 1976). This time it may have been measles. Both smallpox and measles can produce massive mortality rates when they strike a previously unexposed population (Neel et al. 1970).

Although, as we shall see, these demographic disasters were reported by contemporary writers, the role they likely played in the decline of Rome was ignored by historians until modern times (Zinsser [1934] 1960; Boak 1947). Now, however, historians recognize that acute depopulation was responsible for policies once attributed to moral degeneration. For example, massive resettlement of "barbarians" as landholders within the empire and their induction into the legions did not reflect Roman decadence but were rational policies implemented by a state with an abundance of vacant estates and lacking manpower (Boak 1955a). In his now-classic and pioneering work

An earlier version of this chapter appeared as "Epidemics, Networks, and the Rise of Christianity," in *Semeia* 56 (1992): 159–175 (L. Michael White, guest editor).

on the impact of epidemics on history, Hans Zinsser pointed out that

> again and again, the forward march of Roman power and world organization was interrupted by the only force against which political genius and military valor were utterly helpless—epidemic disease . . . and when it came, as though carried by storm clouds, all other things gave way, and men crouched in terror, abandoning all their quarrels, undertakings, and ambitions, until the tempest had blown over. ([1934] 1960:99)

But while historians of Rome have been busy making good the oversights of earlier generations, the same cannot be said of historians of the early Christian era. The words "epidemic," "plague," and "disease" do not even appear in the index of the most respected recent works on the rise of Christianity (Frend 1984; MacMullen 1984). This is no small omission. Indeed, Cyprian, Dionysius, Eusebius, and other church fathers thought the epidemics made major contributions to the Christian cause. I think so too. In this chapter I suggest that had classical society not been disrupted and demoralized by these catastrophes, Christianity might never have become so dominant a faith. To this end, I shall develop three theses.

The first of these can be found in the writings of Cyprian, bishop of Carthage. The epidemics swamped the explanatory and comforting capacities of paganism and of Hellenic philosophies. In contrast, Christianity offered a much more satisfactory account of why these terrible times had fallen upon humanity, and it projected a hopeful, even enthusiastic, portrait of the future.

The second is to be found in an Easter letter by Dionysius, bishop of Alexandria. Christian values of love and charity had, from the beginning, been translated into norms of social service and community solidarity. When disasters struck, the Christians were better able to cope, and this resulted in *substantially higher rates of survival.* This meant that in the aftermath of each epidemic, Christians made up a larger percentage of the population even without new converts. Moreover, their noticeably better survival rate would have seemed a "miracle" to Christians and pagans alike, and this ought to have influenced conversion.

Let me acknowledge that, as I consulted sources on the historical impact of epidemics, I discovered these two points discussed briefly in William H. McNeill's superb *Plagues and Peoples* (1976:108–109). I could not recall having read them before. I must have done so, but at a time when I was more interested in the fall of Rome than in the rise of Christianity. In any event, both points have a substantial social scientific pedigree as elements in the analysis of "revitalization movements"—the rise of new religions as a response to social crises (Wallace 1956, 1966; Thornton 1981; Champagne 1983; Stark and Bainbridge 1985, 1987).

My third thesis is an application of control theories of conformity (Hirschi 1969; Stark and Bainbridge 1985, 1987). When an epidemic destroys a substantial proportion of a population, it leaves large numbers of people without the interpersonal attachments that had previously bound them to the conventional moral order. As mortality mounted during each of these epidemics, large numbers of people, especially pagans, would have *lost the bonds* that once might have restrained them from becoming Christians. Meanwhile, the superior rates of survival of Christian social networks would have provided pagans with a much greater probability of replacing their lost attachments with new ones to Christians. In this way, very substantial numbers of pagans would have been shifted from mainly pagan to mainly Christian social networks. In any era, such a shifting of social networks will result in religious conversions, as was outlined in chapter 1.

In what follows I will expand each of these arguments and offer evidence that it applies. But first, I must sketch the extent of these two epidemics and their demographic impact.

THE EPIDEMICS

The great epidemic of the second century, which is sometimes referred to as the "Plague of Galen," first struck the army of Verus during its campaigns in the East in 165 and from there spread across the empire. The mortality was so high in many cities that Marcus Aurelius spoke of caravans of carts and wagons hauling the dead from cities. Hans Zinsser noted that

> so many people died that cities and villages in Italy and in the provinces were abandoned and fell into ruin. Distress and disorganization was so severe that a campaign against the Marcomani was postponed. When, in 169, the war was finally resumed, Haeser records that many of the Germanic warriors—men and women—were found dead on the field without wounds, having died from the epidemic. ([1934] 1960:100)

We cannot know the actual mortality rate with any certainty, although there is no doubt that it was high. Seeck's 1910 estimate that over half the empire's population perished now seems too high (see Littman and Littman 1973). Conversely, Gilliam's conclusion that only 1 percent died is incompatible even with his own assertion that "a great and destructive epidemic took place under Marcus Aurelius" (1961:249).

The Littmans (1973) propose a rate of 7 to 10 percent, but they arrive at it by selecting smallpox epidemics in Minneapolis during 1924–1925 and in western Prussia in 1874 as the relevant comparisons, and ignoring the far higher fatalities for smallpox epidemics in less modern societies with populations lacking substantial prior exposure. I am most persuaded by McNeill's (1976) estimate that from a quarter to a third of the population perished during this epidemic. Such high mortality is consistent with modern knowledge of epidemiology. It is also consistent with analyses of subsequent manpower shortages (Boak 1955a).

Almost a century later a second terrible epidemic struck the

Roman world. At its height, five thousand people a day were reported to have died in the city of Rome alone (McNeill 1976). And for this epidemic we have many contemporary reports, especially from Christian sources. Thus Cyprian, bishop of Carthage, wrote in 251 that "many of us are dying" from "this plague and pestilence" (*Mortality*, 1958 ed.). Several years later Dionysius, bishop of Alexandria, wrote in an Easter message that "out of the blue came this disease, a thing . . . more frightful than any disaster whatever" (Eusebius, *The History of the Church*, 1965 ed.).

These disasters were not limited to the cities. McNeill (1976) suggests that the death toll may have been even higher in rural areas. Boak (1955b) has calculated that the small town of Karanis, in Egypt, may have lost more than a third of its population during the first epidemic. Calculations based on Dionysius's account suggest that two-thirds of Alexandria's population may have perished (Boak 1947). Such death rates have been documented in many other times and places when a serious infectious disease has struck a population not recently exposed to it. For example, in 1707 smallpox killed more than 30 percent of the population of Iceland (Hopkins 1983). In any event, my concern here is not epidemiological. It is, rather, with the human experience of such crisis and calamity.

CRISIS AND FAITH

Frequently in human history, crises produced by natural or social disasters have been translated into crises of faith. Typically this occurs because the disaster places demands upon the prevailing religion that it appears unable to meet. This inability can occur at two levels. First, the religion may fail to provide a satisfactory explanation of *why* the disaster occurred. Second, the religion may seem to be *unavailing* against the disaster, which becomes truly critical when all nonreligious means also prove inadequate—when the supernatural remains the only

77

plausible source of help. In response to these "failures" of their traditional faiths, societies frequently have evolved or adopted new faiths. The classic instance is the series of messianic movements that periodically swept through the Indians of North America in response to their failures to withstand encroachments by European settlers (Mooney 1896). The prevalence of new religious movements in societies undergoing rapid modernization also illustrates the point. Bryan Wilson (1975) has surveyed many such episodes from around the world.

In a now-famous essay, Anthony F. C. Wallace (1956) argued that *all* religions arise in response to crises. That seems a needlessly extreme view, but there is abundant evidence that faith seldom is "blind," in the sense that religions frequently *are discarded* and new ones accepted in troubled times, and surely periods of raging epidemics meet the requirements outlined by Wallace.

In this chapter I will contrast Christianity's ability to explain the epidemics with that of its competitors in the Greco-Roman world. I also will examine the many ways in which Christianity not only seemed to be, but actually was, *efficacious.* This too is typical. Indeed, this is why the term "revitalization movement" is applied to new religions that arise during times of crisis—the name indicates the positive contributions such movements often make by "revitalizing" the capacity of a culture to deal with its problems.

How do religions "revitalize?" Primarily by effectively mobilizing people to attempt collective actions. Thus the new religious movements among the North American Indians during the eighteenth and nineteenth centuries initially revitalized these societies by greatly reducing drunkenness and despair, and then provided an effective framework for joining fragmented bands into an organized political unit capable of concerted action. That these proved unable to withstand white encroachments in the long run must not obscure the obvious early benefits and how these "proved" the new faith's validity. In this way new ideas or theologies often generate new social arrangements that are better suited to the new circumstances.

Social scientists typically are trained to be suspicious of "theological" or "ideological" explanations and often suppose that these are epiphenomena easily reduced to the "real" causes, which are material in nature. This is true even of some social scientists who specialize in studies of early Christianity. However, I shall demonstrate in this chapter, and many times throughout the book, that ideas often are critical factors in determining not only individual behavior but, indeed, the path of history. To be more specific, for people in the Greco-Roman world, to be a Christian or a pagan was not simply a matter of "denominational preference." Rather, the *contents* of Christian and pagan beliefs were *different* in ways that greatly determined not only their explanatory capacities but also their relative capacities to mobilize human resources.

To assess these differences between pagans and Christians, let us imagine ourselves in their places, faced with one of these terrible epidemics.

Here we are in a city stinking of death. All around us, our family and friends are dropping. We can never be sure if or when we will fall sick too. In the midst of such appalling circumstances, humans are driven to ask *Why*? Why is this happening? Why them and not me? Will we all die? Why does the world exist, anyway? What is going to happen next? What can we do?

If we are pagans, we probably already know that our priests profess ignorance. They do not know why the gods have sent such misery—or if, in fact, the gods are involved or even care (Harnack 1908, vol. 2). Worse yet, many of our priests have fled the city, as have the highest civil authorities and the wealthiest families, which adds to the disorder and suffering.

Suppose that instead of being pagans we are philosophers. Even if we reject the gods and profess one or another school of Greek philosophy, we still have no answers. Natural law is no help in saying why suffering abounds, at least not if we seek to find *meaning* in the reasons. To say that survival is a matter of luck makes the life of the individual seem trivial. Cicero expressed the incapacity of classical as well as modern humanism to provide meaning (or perhaps I should say "meaningfulness"), when he explained that "it depends on fortune or (as we should say) 'conditions' whether we are to experience prosperity or adversity. Certain events are, indeed, due to natural causes beyond human control" (quoted in Cochrane [1940] 1957:100).

Moreover, for a science that knows nothing of bacteria (let alone viruses) the phrase "natural causes" in connection with these great epidemics is simply how philosophers say, "Who knows?" I am not here disputing that survival was in fact substantially random or that the epidemics had natural causes. But I do claim that people will prefer explanations which assert that such events reflect underlying historical intentions, that the larger contours of life are coherent and explicable. Not only were the philosophers of the time unable to provide such meanings, but from the point of view of classical science and philosophy these events were indeed beyond human control, for no useful medical courses of action could be suggested. Indeed, the philosophers of the period could think of nothing more insightful than to anthropomorphize society and blame senility. As Cochrane put it, "while a deadly plague was ravaging the empire . . . the sophists prattled vaguely about the exhaustion of virtue in a world growing old" ([1940] 1957:155).

But if we are Christians, our faith does claim to have answers. McNeill summed them up this way:

> Another advantage Christians enjoyed over pagans was that the teaching of their faith made life meaningful even amid sudden and surprising death. . . . [E]ven a shattered remnant of survivors who had somehow made it through war or pestilence or both could find warm, immediate and healing consolation in the vision of a heavenly existence for those missing relatives and

friends. . . . Christianity was, therefore, a system of thought and feeling thoroughly adapted to a time of troubles in which hardship, disease, and violent death commonly prevailed. (1976:108)

Cyprian, bishop of Carthage, seems almost to have welcomed the great epidemic of his time. Writing in 251 he claimed that only non-Christians had anything to fear from the plague. Moreover, he noted that although

the just are dying with the unjust, it is not for you to think that the destruction is a common one for both the evil and the good. The just are called to refreshment, the unjust are carried off to torture; protection is more quickly given to the faithful; punishment to the faithless. . . . How suitable, how necessary it is that this plague and pestilence, which seems horrible and deadly, searches out the justice of each and every one and examines the minds of the human race; whether the well care for the sick, whether relatives dutifully love their kinsmen as they should, whether masters show compassion for their ailing slaves, whether physicians do not desert the afflicted. . . . Although this mortality has contributed nothing else, it has especially accomplished this for Christians and servants of God, that we have begun gladly to seek martyrdom while we are learning not to fear death. These are trying exercises for us, not deaths; they give to the mind the glory of fortitude; by contempt of death they prepare for the crown. . . . [O]ur brethren who have been freed from the world by the summons of the Lord should not be mourned, since we know that they are not lost but sent before; that in departing they lead the way; that as travellers, as voyagers are wont to be, they should be longed for, not lamented . . . and that no occasion should be given to pagans to censure us deservedly and justly, on the ground that we grieve for those who we say are living. (*Mortality* 15–20, 1958 ed.)

His fellow bishop Dionysius addressed his Alexandrian members in similar tones. "Other people would not think this a time for festival," he wrote, but "far from being a time of distress, it is a time of unimaginable joy" (*Festival Letters*, quoted by Eusebius, *Ecclesiastical History* 7.22, 1965 ed.). Acknowledging the huge death rate, Dionysius noted that though this terrified the pagans, Christians greeted the epidemic as merely "schooling and testing." Thus, at a time when all other faiths were called to question, Christianity offered explanation and comfort. Even more important, Christian doctrine provided a *prescription for action*. That is, the Christian way appeared to work.

SURVIVAL RATES AND THE GOLDEN RULE

At the height of the second great epidemic, around 260, in the Easter letter already quoted above, Dionysius wrote a lengthy tribute to the heroic nursing efforts of local Christians, many of whom lost their lives while caring for others.

> Most of our brother Christians showed unbounded love and loyalty, never sparing themselves and thinking only of one another. Heedless of danger, they took charge of the sick, attending to their every need and ministering to them in Christ, and with them departed this life serenely happy; for they were infected by others with the disease, drawing on themselves the sickness of their neighbors and cheerfully accepting their pains. Many, in nursing and curing others, transferred their death to themselves and died in their stead. . . . The best of our brothers lost their lives in this manner, a number of presbyters, deacons, and laymen winning high commendation so that death in this form, the result of great piety and strong faith, seems in every way the equal of martyrdom.

Dionysius emphasized the heavy mortality of the epidemic by asserting how much happier survivers would be had they merely, like the Egyptians in the time of Moses, lost the firstborn from each house. For "there is not a house in which there is not one dead—how I wish it had been only one." But while the epidemic had not passed over the Christians, he suggests that pagans fared much worse: "Its full impact fell on the heathen."

Dionysius also offered an explanation of this mortality differential. Having noted at length how the Christian community nursed the sick and dying and even spared nothing in preparing the dead for proper burial, he wrote:

> The heathen behaved in the very opposite way. At the first onset of the disease, they pushed the sufferers away and fled from their dearest, throwing them into the roads before they were dead and treated unburied corpses as dirt, hoping thereby to avert the spread and contagion of the fatal disease; but do what they might, they found it difficult to escape.

But should we believe him? If we are to assess Dionysius's claims, it must be demonstrated that the Christians actually did minister to the sick while the pagans mostly did not. It also must be shown that these different patterns of responses would result in substantial differences in mortality.

CHRISTIAN AND PAGAN RESPONSES

It seems highly unlikely that a bishop would write a pastoral letter full of false claims about things that his parishioners would know from direct observation. So if he claims that many leading members of the diocese have perished while nursing the sick, it is reasonable to believe that this happened. Moreover, there is compelling evidence from pagan sources that this was characteristic Christian behavior. Thus, a century later, the emperor Julian launched a campaign to institute pagan charities in an effort to match the Christians. Julian complained in a letter to the high priest of Galatia in 362 that the pagans needed to equal the virtues of Christians, for recent Christian growth was caused by their "moral character, even if pretended," and by their "benevolence toward strangers and care for the graves of the dead." In a letter to another priest, Julian wrote, "I think that when the poor happened to be neglected and overlooked by the priests, the impious Galileans observed this and devoted themselves to benevolence." And he also wrote, "The impious Galileans support not only their poor, but ours as well, everyone can see that our people lack aid from us" (quoted in Johnson 1976:75; Ayerst and Fisher 1971:179–181).

Clearly, Julian loathed "the Galileans." He even suspected that their benevolence had ulterior motives. But he recognized that his charities and that of organized paganism paled in comparison with Christian efforts that had created "a miniature welfare state in an empire which for the most part lacked social services" (Johnson 1976:75). By Julian's day in the fourth century it was too late to overtake this colossal result, the seeds for which had been planted in such teachings as "I am my brother's keeper," "Do unto others as you would have them do onto you," and "It is more blessed to give than to receive" (Grant 1977).

Julian's testimony also supported the claim that pagan communities did not match Christian levels of benevolence during the epidemics, since they did not do so even in normal times when the risks entailed by benevolence were much lower. But there is other evidence.

Some of the most detailed reporting on epidemics in the classical world is to be found in Thucydides' *History of the Peloponnesian War* (2.47–55). Thucydides was himself a survivor of a deadly plague that struck Athens in 431 B.C.E, having contracted the disease in the first days of the epidemic. Modern medical writers praise Thucydides' careful and detailed account of symptoms (Marks and Beatty 1976). At least as much can be said for his account of public responses.

Thucydides began by noting the ineffectiveness of both science and religion:

> The doctors were quite incapable of treating the disease because
> of their ignorance of the right methods. . . . Equally useless were
> prayers made in the temples, consultation of the oracles, and so

forth; indeed, in the end people were so overcome by their sufferings that they paid no further attention to such things. (49,
1954 ed.)

Then he reported that once the contagious nature of the disease was recognized, people "were afraid to visit one another."
As a result,

> they died with no one to look after them; indeed there were
> many houses in which all the inhabitants perished through lack
> of any attention. . . . The bodies of the dying were heaped one
> on top of the other, and half-dead creatures could be seen stag-
> gering about in the streets or flocking around the fountains in
> their desire for water. The temples in which they took up their
> quarters were full of the dead bodies of people who had died
> inside them. For the catastrophe was so overwhelming that men,
> not knowing what would happen next to them, became indiffer-
> ent to every rule of religion or of law. . . . No fear of god or law
> of man had a restraining influence. As for the gods, it seemed to
> be the same thing whether one worshipped them or not, when
> one saw the good and the bad dying indiscriminately. (51–53,
> 1954 ed.)

Although separated from it by nearly seven centuries, this description of how pagan Athens reacted to a killing epidemic is
strikingly similar to Dionysius's account of pagan responses to
the epidemic in Alexandria. Thucydides acknowledged that
some, who like himself had recovered from the disease and
thus were immune, did try to nurse the sick, but their numbers
seem to have been few. Moreover, Thucydides accepted that it
was only sensible to flee epidemics and to shun contact with the
sick.

It is also worth noting that the famous classical physician
Galen lived through the first epidemic during the reign of
Marcus Aurelius. What did he do? He got out of Rome quickly,
retiring to a country estate in Asia Minor until the danger re-
ceded. In fact, modern medical historians have noted that
Galen's description of the disease "is uncharacteristically in-

complete," and suggest that this may have been due to his hasty departure (Hopkins 1983). Granted, this is but one man's response, albeit that of a man much admired by later generations as the greatest physician of the age. But although at least one modern medical historian has felt the need to write an exculpatory essay on Galen's flight (Walsh 1931), it was not seen as unusual or discreditable at the time. It was what any prudent person would have done, had they the means—unless, of course, they were "Galileans."

Here issues of doctrine must be addressed. For something distinctive did come into the world with the development of Judeo-Christian thought: the linking of a highly *social* ethical code with religion. There was nothing new in the idea that the supernatural makes behavioral demands upon humans—the gods have always wanted sacrifices and worship. Nor was there anything new in the notion that the supernatural will respond to offerings—that the gods can be induced to exchange services for sacrifices. What was new was the notion that more than self-interested exchange relations were possible between humans and the supernatural. The Christian teaching that God loves those who love him was alien to pagan beliefs. MacMullen has noted that from the pagan perspective "what mattered was . . . the service that the deity could provide, since a god (as Aristotle had long taught) could feel no love in response to that offered" (1981:53). Equally alien to paganism was the notion that because God loves humanity, Christians cannot please God unless they *love one another*. Indeed, as God demonstrates his love through sacrifice, humans must demonstrate their love through sacrifice on behalf of *one another*. Moreover, such responsibilities were to be extended beyond the bonds of family and tribe, indeed to "all those who in every place call on the name of our Lord Jesus Christ" (1 Cor. 1:2). These were revolutionary ideas.

Pagan and Christian writers are unanimous not only that Christian Scripture stressed love and charity as the central duties of faith, but that these were sustained in everyday behavior.

I suggest reading the following passage from Matthew (25:35–40) as if for the very first time, in order to gain insight into the power of this new morality when it was *new*, not centuries later in more cynical and worldly times:

> For I was hungry and you gave me food, I was thirsty and you gave me drink, I was a stranger and you welcomed me, I was naked and you clothed me, I was sick and you visited me, I was in prison and you came to me. . . . Truly, I say to you, as you did it to one of the least of these my brethren, you did it to me.

When the New Testament was *new*, these were the norms of the Christian communities. Tertullian claimed: "It is our care of the helpless, our practice of loving kindness that brands us in the eyes of many of our opponents. 'Only look,' they say, 'look how they love one another!' " (*Apology* 39, 1989 ed.).

Harnack quoted the duties of deacons as outlined in the *Apostolic Constitutions* to show that they were set apart for the support of the sick, infirm, poor, and disabled: "They are to be doers of good works, exercising a general supervision day and night, neither scorning the poor nor respecting the person of the rich; they must ascertain who are in distress and not exclude them from a share in church funds, compelling also the well-to-do to put money aside for good works" (1908: 1:161).

Or let us read what Pontianus reports in his biography of Cyprian about how the bishop instructed his Carthaginian flock:

> The people being assembled together, he first of all urges on them the benefits of mercy. . . . Then he proceeds to add that there is nothing remarkable in cherishing merely our own people with the due attentions of love, but that one might become perfect who should *do something more than heathen men or publicans*, one who, overcoming evil with good, and practicing a merciful kindness like that of God, should love his enemies as well. . . . Thus the good was done to all men, not merely to the household of faith. (Quoted in Harnack 1908: 1:172–173)

And, as we have seen, that is precisely what most concerned Julian as he worked to reverse the rise of Christianity and restore paganism. But for all that he urged pagan priests to match these Christian practices, there was little or no response because *there were no doctrinal bases or traditional practices* for them to build upon. It was not that Romans knew nothing of charity, but that it was not based on service to the gods. Pagan gods did not punish ethical violations because they imposed no ethical demands—humans offended the gods only through neglect or by violation of ritual standards (MacMullen 1981:58). Since pagan gods required only propitiation and beyond that left human affairs in human hands, a pagan priest could not preach that those lacking in the spirit of charity risked their salvation. Indeed, the pagan gods offered no salvation. They might be bribed to perform various services, but the gods did not provide an escape from mortality. We must keep that in sight as we compare the reactions of Christians and pagans to the shadow of sudden death. Galen lacked belief in life beyond death. The Christians were certain that this life was but prelude. For Galen to have remained in Rome to treat the afflicted would have required bravery far beyond that needed by Christians to do likewise.

DIFFERENTIAL MORTALITY

But how much could it have mattered? Not even the best of Greco-Roman science knew anything to do to *treat* these epidemics other than to avoid all contact with those who had the disease. So even if the Christians did obey the injunction to minister to the sick, what could they do to help? At the risk of their own lives they could, in fact, save an immense number of lives. McNeill pointed out: "When all normal services break down, quite elementary nursing will greatly reduce mortality. Simple provision of food and water, for instance, will allow persons who are temporarily too weak to cope for themselves to recover instead of perishing miserably" (1976:108).

Some hypothetical numbers may help us grasp just how much impact Christian nursing could have had on mortality rates in these epidemics. Let us begin with a city having 10,000 inhabitants in 160, just before the first epidemic. In chapter 1, I calculated that Christians made up about 0.4 percent of the empire's population at this time, so let us suppose that 40 of this city's inhabitants are Christians, while 9,960 are pagans—a ratio of 1 Christian to 249 pagans. Now, let us assume an epidemic generating mortality rates of 30 percent over its course in a population left without nursing. Modern medical experts believe that conscientious nursing *without any medications* could cut the mortality rate by two-thirds or even more. So let us assume a Christian mortality rate of 10 percent. Imposing these mortality rates results in 36 Christian and 6,972 pagan survivors in 170, after the epidemic. Now the ratio of Christians to pagans is 1 to 197, a substantial shift.

However, there is no reason to suppose that the conversion of pagans to Christianity would have slowed during the epidemic—indeed, as we shall see, the rate might well have risen at this time. In keeping with the projected Christian conversion rate of 40 percent a decade, we must add 16 converts to the Christian total and subtract these 16 from the pagan total. This yields a ratio of 1 Christian per 134 pagans.

To keep things simple, let us suppose that the population of this city was static over the next 90 years, until hit by the second epidemic, and that the conversion rate of 40 percent a decade remained in effect. Let us also assume that the mortality rates of 10 and 30 percent apply again. After this epidemic was over, in 260, there would be 997 Christians and 4,062 pagans in this city. And this is a ratio of 1 Christian to 4 pagans. Had the two epidemics not occurred, and had conversion been the only factor determining the relative sizes of the Christian and pagan populations, then in 260 there would have been 1,157 Christians and 8,843 pagans, or a ratio of 1 Christian to 8 pagans. In fact, of course, the population would not have been static for this period. In the days before modern medicine, epidemics were always especially hard on the young and on pregnant women and those suffering from childbirth-related infections (Russell 1958). Hence in the aftermath of serious epidemics the birthrate declined. With a much lower mortality rate, the Christian birthrate would have been much less influenced, and this too would have increased the ratio of Christians to pagans.

Thus an immense Christian gain would have occurred without their having made a single convert during the period. But, as noted, these same trends ought to have resulted in many converts. For one thing, if, during the crisis, Christians fulfilled their ideal of ministering to *everyone*, there would be many pagan survivors who owed their lives to their Christian neighbors. For another, no one could help but notice that Christians not only found the capacity to risk death but were much less likely to die.

As Kee (1983) has so powerfully reminded us, miracle was intrinsic to religious credibility in the Greco-Roman world. Modern scholars have too long been content to dismiss reports of miracles in the New Testament and in other similar sources as purely literary, not as things that happened. Yet we remain aware that in tabernacles all over modern America, healings are taking place. One need not propose that God is the active agent in these "cures" to recognize their reality both as events and as perceptions. Why then should we not accept that "miracles" were being done in New Testament times too, and that people expected them as proof of religious authenticity? Indeed, MacMullen regards it as self-evident that a great deal of conversion was based on a "visible show of divinity at work" (1981:126). He suggests that martyrdom would have been perceived as a miracle, for example.

Against this background, consider that a much superior Christian survival rate hardly could seem other than miraculous. Moreover, superior survival rates would have produced a much larger proportion of Christians who were *immune*, and who could, therefore, pass among the afflicted with seeming invulnerability. In fact, those Christians most active in nursing the sick were likely to have contracted the disease very early and to have survived it as they, in turn, were cared for. In this way was created a whole force of miracle workers to heal the "dying." And who was to say that it was the soup they so patiently spooned to the helpless that healed them, rather than the prayers the Christians offered on their behalf?

MORALITY, FLIGHT, AND ATTACHMENTS

I have stressed the importance of social networks in the conversion process. It is useful therefore to engage in some comparative analysis of epidemics' impact on the social networks of Christians and pagans, and how this would have changed their relative patterns of attachments. In general, I will demonstrate that an epidemic would have caused chaos in pagan social relations, leaving large numbers with but few attachments to other pagans meanwhile greatly increasing the relative probabilities of strong bonds between pagans and Christians.

Let us return to our hypothetical city and focus our attention on three varieties of interpersonal attachments: (1) Christian-Christian; (2) Christian-pagan; and (3) pagan-pagan. If we apply the differential mortality rates used above (10 percent for Christians, 30 percent for pagans), we can calculate the *survival odds* for each variety of *attachment*. That is, our interest here is not in the survival of individuals but in that of an attachment; hence our measure is the odds that both persons survive the epidemic. The survival rate for Christian-Christian bonds is 0.81 (or 81 percent). The survival rate for Christian-pagan bonds is 0.63. The survival rate for pagan-pagan bonds is 0.49. Thus not only are attachments among pagans almost twice as likely to perish as attachments among Christians, pagan bonds to Christians are also much more likely to survive than those uniting pagans to one another.

These attachment survival rates take only differential mortality into account. But attachments are also severed if one person leaves. Since we know that substantial numbers of pagans fled epidemics (while Christians stayed), this too must be considered. Let us suppose that 20 percent of the pagan population fled. Now the survival rate of pagan-pagan attachments is 0.25 and that of Christian-pagan attachments is 0.45, while the Christian-Christian rate remains 0.81.

These rates assume, of course, that Christian victims of an epidemic received nursing care, while pagans did not. In fact, however, our sources testify that *some pagans* were nursed by Christians. Given the relative sizes of the Christian and pagan populations at the onset of the epidemic, Christians would not have had the resources to nurse all or even most sick pagans. Presumably, proximity and attachments would have determined which pagans would be cared for by Christians. That is, pagans who lived near Christians and/or who had close Christian friends (even relatives) would have been most likely to be nursed. Let us assume that Christian nursing was as conducive to survival for pagans as it was for Christians. That means that pagans nursed by Christians had noticeably higher survival rates than other pagans. But it also means that we should recalculate the Christian-pagan attachment survival rate. If we assume that pagans in these relationships had as good a chance of living as did the Christians, then the survival rate for these attachments is 0.81—more than three times the survival rate of pagan-pagan attachments.

Another way to look at this is to put oneself in the place of a pagan who, before the epidemic, had five very close attachments, four with pagans and one with a Christian. We could express this as a Christian-to-pagan attachment ratio of 1 to 4. Let us assume that this pagan remains in the city and survives. Subtracting mortality and flight results in a Christian-pagan attachment ratio of 0.8 to 1. What has happened is that where once there were four pagans to one Christian in this pagan's intimate circle, now there is, in effect, one of each—a dramatic equalization.

Not only would a much higher proportion of pagan survivors' attachments be to Christians simply because of the greater survival rate of those relationships; further, during and after the epidemic the formation of new relationships would be increasingly biased in favor of Christians. One reason is that the nursing function is itself a major opportunity to form new bonds. Another is that it is easier to attach to a social network that is more rather than less intact. To see this, let us once again focus on the pagan who, after the epidemic, has one close Christian and one close pagan attachment. Suppose that he or she wishes to replace lost attachments—perhaps to remarry. The Christian friend still has many other attachments to extend to this pagan. The pagan friend, however, is very deficient in attachments. For the Christian, there is an 80 percent probability that any one of his or her Christian friends and relatives survived the epidemic and remained in the city. For the pagan, these odds are only 50 percent.

The consequence of all this is that pagan survivors faced greatly increased odds of conversion because of their increased attachments to Christians.

CONCLUSION

Several modern writers have warned against analyzing the rise of Christianity as though it were inevitable, as earlier generations of Christian historians tended to do. That is, since we know that indeed the tiny and obscure Jesus Movement managed, over the course of several centuries, to dominate Western civilization, our historical perceptions suffer from overconfidence. As a result, scholars more often recount, rather than try to account for, the Christianization of the West, and in doing so seem to take "the end of paganism for granted," as Peter Brown (1964:109) has noted.

In fact, of course, the rise of Christianity was long and perilous. There were many crisis points when different outcomes could easily have followed. Moreover, in this chapter I have argued that had some crises *not occurred*, the Christians would have been deprived of major, possibly crucial opportunities.

MacMullen has warned us that this "enormous thing called

paganism, then, did not one day just topple over dead" (1981:134). Paganism, after all, was an active, vital part of the rise of Hellenic and Roman empires and therefore *must* have had the capacity to fulfill basic religious impulses—at least for centuries. But the fact remains that paganism did pass into history. And if some truly devastating blows were required to bring down this "enormous thing," the terrifying crises produced by two disastrous epidemics may have been among the more damaging. If I am right, then in a sense paganism did indeed "topple over dead" or at least acquire its fatal illness during these epidemics, falling victim to its relative inability to confront these crises socially or spiritually—an inability suddenly revealed by the example of its upstart challenger. I shall return to these themes in the final two chapters.

The Role of Women in
Christian Growth

AMIDST contemporary denunciations of Christianity as patriarchal and sexist, it is easily forgotten that the early church was so especially attractive to women that in 370 the emperor Valentinian issued a written order to Pope Damasus I requiring that Christian missionaries cease calling at the homes of pagan women. Although some classical writers claimed that women were easy prey for *any* "foreign superstition," most recognized that Christianity was unusually appealing because within the Christian subculture women enjoyed far higher status than did women in the Greco-Roman world at large (Fox 1987; Chadwick 1967; Harnack 1908, vol. 2).

But if historians have long noted this fact, they have made no serious efforts to explain it. Why were women accorded higher status in Christian circles than elsewhere in the classical world? In what follows I shall attempt to link the increased power and privilege of Christian women to a very major shift in sex ratios. I demonstrate that an initial shift in sex ratios resulted from Christian doctrines prohibiting infanticide and abortion; I then show how the initial shift would have been amplified by a subsequent tendency to overrecruit women. Along the way I shall summarize evidence from ancient sources as well as from modern archaeology and historical demography concerning the status of women in the early church. I will also build a case for accepting that relatively high rates of intermarriage existed between Christian women and pagan men, and will suggest how these would have generated many "secondary" conversions to Christianity. Finally, I will demonstrate why Christian and

An earlier version of this chapter was given as the Paul Hanly Furfey Lecture, 1994.

Because infanticide was outlawed, and because women were more likely than men to convert, among Christians there soon were far more women than men, while among pagans men far outnumbered women.

pagan subcultures must have differed greatly in their fertility rates and how a superior birthrate also contributed to the success of the early church.

CHRISTIAN AND PAGAN SEX RATIOS

Men greatly outnumbered women in the Greco-Roman world. Dio Cassius, writing in about 200, attributed the declining population of the empire to the extreme shortage of females (*The Roman History*, 1987 ed.). In his classic work on ancient and medieval populations, J. C. Russell (1958) estimated that there were 131 males per 100 females in the city of Rome, and 140 males per 100 females in Italy, Asia Minor, and North Africa. Russell noted in passing that sex ratios this extreme can occur only when there is "some tampering with human life" (1958:14). And tampering there was. Exposure of unwanted female infants and deformed male infants was legal, morally accepted, and widely practiced by all social classes in the Greco-Roman world (Fox 1987; Gorman 1982; Pomeroy 1975; Russell 1958). Lindsay reported that even in large families "more than one daughter was practically never reared" (1968:168). A study of inscriptions at Delphi made it possible to reconstruct six hundred families. Of these, only six had raised more than one daughter (Lindsay 1968).

The subject of female infanticide will be pursued at length later in the chapter. For now, consider a letter written by one Hilarion to his pregnant wife Alis, which has been reported by many authors because of the quite extraordinary contrast between his deep concern for his wife and his hoped-for son, and his utter callousness toward a possible daughter:

> Know that I am still in Alexandria. And do not worry if they all come back and I remain in Alexandria. I ask and beg you to take good care of our baby son, and as soon as I receive payment I shall send it up to you. If you are delivered of a child [before I

97

come home], if it is a boy keep it, if a girl discard it. You have sent me word, "Don't forget me." How can I forget you. I beg you not to worry. (Quoted in Lewis 1985:54)

This letter dates from the year 1 B.C.E., but these patterns persisted among pagans far into the Christian era. Given these practices, even in childhood, before the onset of the high female mortality associated with fertility in premodern times, females were substantially outnumbered among pagans in the Greco-Roman world. Moreover, it was not just the high mortality from childbirth that continued to increase the sex ratios among adults. As we shall see in detail later in the chapter, abortion was a major cause of death among women in this era.

However, things were different among Christians as their distinctive subculture began to emerge. There are few hard data on the sex composition of Christian communities. Harnack calculated that in his Epistle to the Romans Paul sent personal greetings to fifteen women and eighteen men (1908: 2:67). If, as Harnack implies, it seems likely that there were proportionately more men than women among those Christians of sufficient prominence to merit Paul's special attention, then this 15/18 sex ratio would indicate that the congregation in Rome must already have been predominately female. A second basis for inference is an inventory of property removed from a Christian house-church in the North African town of Cirta during a persecution in 303. Among the clothes the Christians had collected for distribution to the needy were sixteen men's tunics and eighty-two women's tunics, as well as forty-seven pairs of female slippers (Frend 1984; Fox 1987). Presumably this partly reflects the ratio of men to women among the donors. But even though better statistics are lacking, the predominance of women in the churches' membership was, as Fox reported, "recognized to be so by Christians and pagans" (1987:308). Indeed, Harnack noted that the ancient sources

simply swarm with tales of how women of all ranks were converted in Rome and in the provinces; although the details of these stories are untrustworthy, they express correctly enough the general truth that Christianity was laid hold of by women in particular, and also that the percentage of Christian women, especially among the upper classes, was larger than that of men. (1908: 2:73)

These conclusions about Christian sex ratios merit our confidence when we examine *why* sex ratios should have been so different among the Christians. First, by prohibiting all forms of infanticide and abortion, Christians removed major causes of the gender imbalance that existed among pagans. Even so, changes in mortality alone probably could not have resulted in Christian women's coming to outnumber Christian men. However, there was a second factor influencing Christian sex ratios: women were more likely than men to become Christians. This, combined with the reduction in female mortality, *would* have caused a surplus of women in the Christian subcultures.

SEX BIAS IN CONVERSION

In his widely admired monograph on the early church, the British historian Henry Chadwick noted that "Christianity seems to have been especially successful among women. It was often through the wives that it penetrated the upper classes of society in the first instance" (1967:56). Peter Brown noted that "women were prominent" among upper-class Christians and that "such women could influence their husbands to protect the church" (1988:151). Marcia, concubine of the emperor Commodus, managed to convince him to free Callistus, a future pope, from a sentence of hard labor in the mines of Sardinia (Brown 1988). Although Marcia failed to secure the conversion of Commodus, other upper-class women often did bring husbands and admirers to faith.

It will be helpful here to distinguish between primary and secondary conversions. In *primary conversion*, the convert takes an active role in his or her own conversion, becoming a committed adherent based on positive evaluations of the particular faith, albeit that attachments to members play a major role in the formation of a positive evaluation. *Secondary conversion* is more passive and involves somewhat reluctant acceptance of a faith on the basis of attachments to a primary convert. For example, after person A converted to a new faith, that person's spouse agreed to "go along" with the choice, but was not eager to do so and very likely would not have done so otherwise. The latter is a secondary convert. In the example offered by Chadwick, upper-class wives were often primary converts and some of their husbands (often grudgingly) became secondary converts. Indeed, it frequently occurred that when the master of a large household became a Christian, all members of the household including the servants and slaves were expected to do so too.

The ancient sources and modern historians agree that primary conversion to Christianity was far more prevalent among females than among males. Moreover, this appears to be typical of new religious movements in recent times. By examining manuscript census returns for the latter half of the nineteenth century, Bainbridge (1982) found that approximately two-thirds of the Shakers were female. Data on religious movements included in the 1926 census of religious bodies show that 75 percent of Christian Scientists were women, as were more than 60 percent of Theosophists, Swedenborgians, and Spiritualists (Stark and Bainbridge 1985). The same is true of the immense wave of Protestant conversions taking place in Latin America. In fact, David Martin (1990) suggests that a substantial proportion of male Protestants in Latin America are secondary converts.[1]

There have been several interesting efforts to explain why women in many different times and places seem to be far more responsive than men to religion (Thompson 1991; Miller and Hoffman 1995). However, this is not an appropriate place to pursue the matter. Here it is sufficient to explore the impact of differential conversion rates on the sex ratios of the Christian subcultures in the Greco-Roman world. Given several reasonable assumptions, simple arithmetic suffices to assess the magnitude of the changes differential conversion rates could have produced.

Let us begin with a Christian population with equal numbers of men and women. Let us assume a growth rate from *conversion alone* of 30 percent per decade. That is, for the moment we will ignore any natural increase and assume that births equal deaths. Let us also suppose that the sex ratio among converts is two women for every man. As noted above, this is entirely in line with recent experience. Given these reasonable assumptions, we can easily calculate that it will take only fifty years for this Christian population to be 62 percent female. Or if we assume a growth rate of 40 percent per decade, the Christian population will be 64 percent female in fifty years.

If we were to factor in reasonable assumptions about natural increase and differential mortality, we would decrease this sex ratio to some extent. But even so, the Christian subcultures would have had a substantial surplus of women in a world accustomed to a vast surplus of men. Later in this chapter I shall consider how a surplus of women should have resulted in substantial secondary conversions via marriages to pagans. But for now I wish to focus on the simple conclusion that there are abundant reasons to accept that Christian women enjoyed a favorable sex ratio, and to show how that resulted in Christian women's enjoying superior status in comparison with their pagan counterparts.

Sex Ratios and the Status of Women

One of the more significant and original contributions to social thought in recent years is the Guttentag and Secord (1983) theory linking cross-cultural variations in the status of women to cross-cultural variations in sex ratios. The theory involves a remarkably subtle linking of dyadic and social structural power and dependency. For the purposes of this chapter it is sufficient merely to note Guttentag and Secord's conclusion that to the extent that males outnumber females, women will be enclosed in repressive sex roles as men treat them as "scarce goods." Conversely, to the extent that females outnumber males, the Guttentag and Secord theory predicts that women will enjoy relatively greater power and freedom.

As they applied their theory to various societies in different eras, Guttentag and Secord noted that it illuminated the marked differences in the relative status and power of Athenian and Spartan women. That is, *within* the classical world, the status of women varied substantially in response to variations in sex ratios.

In Athens, women were in relatively short supply owing to female infanticide, practiced by all classes, and to additional deaths caused by abortion. The status of Athenian women was very low. Girls received little or no education. Typically, Athenian females were married at puberty and often before. Under Athenian law a woman was classified as a child, regardless of age, and therefore was the legal property of some man at all stages in her life. Males could divorce by simply ordering a wife out of the household. Moreover, if a woman was seduced or raped, her husband was legally compelled to divorce her. If a woman wanted a divorce, she had to have her father or some other man bring her case before a judge. Finally, Athenian women could own property, but control of the property was always vested in the male to whom she "belonged" (Guttentag and Secord 1983; Finley 1982; Pomeroy 1975).

Spartans also practiced infanticide, but without gender bias—only healthy, well-formed babies were allowed to live. Since males are more subject to birth defects and are more apt to be sickly infants, the result was a slight excess of females from infancy, a trend that accelerated with age because of male mortality from military life and warfare. Keep in mind that mortality rates in military encampments far surpassed civilian rates until well into the twentieth century. At age seven all Spartan boys left home for military boarding schools, and all were required to serve in the army until age thirty; they then passed into the active reserve, where they remained until age sixty. A subjugated peasantry known as helots supplied all of the males in the domestic labor force. Although men could marry at age twenty, they could not live with their wives until they left the active army at age thirty.

Spartan women enjoyed status and power unknown in the rest of the classical world. They not only controlled their own property, they controlled that of their male relatives when the latter were away with the army. It is estimated that women were the sole owners of at least 40 percent of all land and property in Sparta (Pomeroy 1975). The laws concerning divorce were the same for men and women. Women received as much education as men, and Spartan women received a substantial amount of physical education and gymnastic training. Spartan women seldom married before age twenty, and, unlike their Athenian sisters who wore heavy, concealing gowns and were seldom seen by males outside their household, Spartan women wore short dresses and went where they pleased (Guttentag and Secord 1983; Finley 1982; Pomeroy 1975).

RELATIVE STATUS OF CHRISTIAN WOMEN

If Guttentag and Secord's theory is correct, then we would have to predict that the status of Christian women in the Greco-Roman world would more closely approximate that of Spartan women than that of women in Athens.

Although I began this chapter with the assertion that Christian women did indeed enjoy considerably greater status and power than did pagan women, this needs to be demonstrated at greater length. The discussion will focus on two primary aspects of female status: within the family and within the religious community.

Wives, Widows, and Brides

First of all, a major aspect of women's improved status in the Christian subculture is that Christians did not condone female infanticide. Granted, this was the result of the prohibition of *all* infanticide. But the more favorable Christian view of women is also demonstrated in their condemnation of divorce, incest, marital infidelity, and polygamy. As Fox put it, "fidelity, without divorce, was expected of every Christian" (1987:354). Moreover, although rules prohibiting divorce and remarriage evolved slowly, the earliest church councils ruled that "twice-married Christians" could not hold church office (Fox 1987). Like pagans, early Christians prized female chastity, but unlike pagans they rejected the double standard that gave pagan men so much sexual license (Sandison 1967). Christian men were urged to remain virgins until marriage (Fox 1987), and extramarital sex was condemned as adultery. Chadwick noted that Christianity "regarded unchastity in a husband as no less serious a breach of loyalty and trust than unfaithfulness in a wife" (1967:59). Even the great Greek physician Galen was prompted to remark on Christian "restraint in cohabitation" (quoted in Benko 1984:142).

Should they be widowed, Christian women also enjoyed very substantial advantages. Pagan widows faced great social pressure to remarry; Augustus even had widows fined if they failed to remarry within two years (Fox 1987). Of course, when a pagan widow did remarry, she lost all of her inheritance—it became the property of her new husband. In contrast, among Christians, widowhood was highly respected and remarriage was, if anything, mildly discouraged. Thus not only were well-to-do Christian widows enabled to keep their husband's estate, the church stood ready to sustain poor widows, allowing them a choice as to whether or not to remarry. Eusebius provides a letter from Cornelius, bishop of Rome, written in 251 to Bishop Fabius of Antioch, in which he reported that "more than fifteen hundred widows and distressed persons" were in the care of the local congregation, which may have included about 30,000 members at this time (*The History of the Church*, 1965 ed., and see editor's note to p. 282).

In all these ways the Christian woman enjoyed far greater marital security and equality than did her pagan neighbor. But there was another major marital aspect to the benefits women gained from being Christians. They were married at a substantially older age and had more choice about whom they married. Since, as we shall see, pagan women frequently were forced into prepubertal, consummated marriages, this was no small matter.

In a now-classic article, the historical demographer Keith Hopkins (1965a) surveyed a century of research on the age of marriage of Roman women—girls, actually, most of them. The evidence is both literary and quantitative. In addition to the standard classical histories, the literary evidence consists of writings by lawyers and physicians. The quantitative data are based on inscriptions, most of them funerary, from which the age at marriage can be calculated (cf. Harkness 1896).

As to the histories, silence offers strong testimony that Roman girls married young, very often before puberty. It is possible to calculate that many famous Roman women married at a tender age: Octavia and Agrippina married at 11 and 12, Quintilian's wife bore him a son when she was 13, Tacitus wed a girl of 13, and so on. But in reviewing the writing about all of these aristocratic Romans, Hopkins (1965a) found only one case in which the ancient writer mentioned the bride's age— and this biographer was himself a Christian ascetic! Clearly, having been a child bride was not thought by ancient biographers to be worth mentioning. Beyond silence, however, the Greek historian Plutarch reported that Romans "gave their girls in marriage when they were twelve years old, or even younger" (quoted in Hopkins 1965a:314). Dio Cassius, also a Greek writing Roman history, agreed: "Girls are considered . . . to have reached marriageable age on completion of their twelfth year" (*The Roman History*, 1987 ed.).

Roman law set 12 as the minimum age at which girls could

marry. But the law carried no penalties, and legal commentaries from the time include such advice as: "A girl who has married before 12 will be a legitimate wife, when she becomes 12." Another held that when girls under age 12 married, for legal purposes they should be considered engaged until they reached 12. Hopkins concluded: "We have no means of knowing whether lawyers represented advanced, typical or conservative opinions in these matters. What we do know is that in the fragments of their opinions that survive there is no sneer or censure against marriages before 12, and there are no teeth in the laws [against it]" (1965a:314).

The quantitative data are based on several studies of Roman inscriptions, combined by Hopkins (1965a), from which age at marriage could be calculated. Hopkins was also able to separate these Roman women on the basis of religion. The results are presented in table 5.1. Pagans were three times as likely as Christians to have married before age 13 (10 percent were wed by age 11). Nearly half (44 percent) of the pagans had married by age 14, compared with 20 percent of the Christians. In contrast, nearly half (48 percent) of the Christian females had not wed before age 18, compared with a third (37 percent) of the pagans.

These differences are highly significant statistically. But they seem of even greater social significance when we discover that not only were a substantial proportion of pagan Roman girls married before the onset of puberty, to a man far older than themselves, but these marriages typically were consummated at once.

When the French historian Durry (1955) first reported his findings that Roman marriages involving child brides normally were consummated even if the bride had not yet achieved puberty, he acknowledged that this ran counter to deeply held ideas about the classical world. But there is ample literary evidence that consummation of these marriages was taken for granted. Hopkins (1965a) noted that one Roman law did deal

TABLE 5.1
Religion and Age at Marriage of Roman Females

	Pagans	Christians
Under 13	20%	7%
13–14	24%	13%
15–17	19%	32%
18 or over	37%	48%
n =	145	180

Significance < .0001

Note: Calculated from Hopkins 1965a.

with the marriage of girls under age 12 and intercourse, but it was concerned only with the question of her adultery. Several Roman physicians suggested that it might be wise to defer intercourse until menarche, but did not stress the matter (Hopkins 1965a).

Unfortunately, the literary sources offer little information about how prepubertal girls felt about these practices. Plutarch regarded it as a cruel custom and reported "the hatred and fear of girls forced contrary to nature." I suggest that, even in the absence of better evidence and even allowing for substantial cultural differences, it seems likely that many Roman girls responded as Plutarch claimed. Thus here too Christian girls enjoyed a substantial advantage.

Gender and Religious Roles

It is well known that the early church attracted an unusual number of high-status women (Fox 1987; Grant 1977; 1970; Harnack 1908, vol. 2). But the matter of interest here concerns the roles occupied by women *within* early Christian congregations. Let me emphasize that by "early Christianity" I mean the period covering approximately the first five centuries. After that, as

Christianity became the dominant faith of the empire and as sex ratios responded to the decline in the differential conversion of women, the roles open to women became far more limited.

As to the status of women in the early church, there has been far too much reliance on 1 Cor. 14:34–36, where Paul *appears* to prohibit women even from speaking in church. Laurence Iannaccone (1982) has made a compelling case that these verses were the opposite of Paul's position and were in fact a quotation of claims being made at Corinth that Paul then refuted. Certainly the statement is at variance with everything else Paul wrote about the proper role for women in the church. Moreover, Paul several times acknowledged women in leadership positions in various congregations.

In Rom. 16:1–2 Paul introduces and commends to the Roman congregation "our sister Phoebe" who is a "deaconess of the church at Cenchrea" who had been of great help to him. Deacons were of considerable importance in the early church. They assisted at liturgical functions and administered the benevolent and charitable activities of the church. Clearly, Paul regarded it as entirely proper for a woman to hold that position. Nor was this an isolated case. Clement of Alexandria wrote of "women deacons," and in 451 the Council of Chalcedon specified that henceforth a deaconess must be at least forty and unmarried (Ferguson 1990). From the pagan side, in his famous letter to the emperor Trajan, Pliny the Younger reported that he had tortured two young Christian women "who were called deaconesses" (1943 ed.).

Not only did Paul commend Phoebe the deaconess to the Romans, he also sent his greetings to prominent women in the Roman congregation, including Prisca, whom he acknowledges for having "risked her neck" on his behalf. He asks that the recipients of his letter "greet Mary, who has worked so hard among you," and sends his greetings to several other women (Rom. 16:1–15). Moreover, in 1 Tim. 3:11 Paul again mentions women in the role of deacons, noting that to qualify for such an appointment women must be "serious, no slanderers, but temperate and faithful in all things."

That women often served as deacons in the early church was long obscured because the translators of the King James Version chose to refer to Phoebe as merely a "servant" of the church, not as a deacon, and to transform Paul's words in 1 Timothy into a comment directed toward the *wives* of deacons.[2] But this reflects the sexist norms of the seventeenth century, not the realities of early Christian communities. Indeed, early in the third century the great Christian intellectual Origen wrote the following comment on Paul's letter to the Romans:

> This text teaches with the authority of the Apostle that . . . there are, as we have already said, women deacons in the Church, and that women, who have given assistance to so many people and who by their good works deserve to be praised by the Apostle, ought to be accepted in the diaconate. (Quoted in Gryson 1976:134)

All important modern translations of the Bible now restore the original language used by Paul in these two letters, but somehow the illusions fostered by the King James falsifications remain the common wisdom. Nevertheless, there is virtual consensus among historians of the early church as well as biblical scholars that women held positions of honor and authority within early Christianity (Frend 1984; Gryson 1976; Cadoux 1925). Peter Brown noted that Christians differed not only from pagans in this respect, but from Jews: "The Christian clergy . . . took a step that separated them from the rabbis of Palestine . . . [T]hey welcomed women as patrons and even offered women roles in which they could act as collaborators" (1988:144–145). And none of his colleagues would have regarded the following claim by the distinguished Wayne Meeks as controversial: "Women . . . are Paul's fellow workers as evangelists and teachers. Both in terms of their position in the larger society and in terms of their participation in the Christian communities, then, a number of women broke through the normal expectations of female roles" (1983:71).

Close examination of Roman persecutions also suggests that women held positions of power and status within the Christian churches. The actual number of Christians martyred by the Romans was quite small, and the majority of men who were executed were officials, including bishops (see chapter 8). That a very significant proportion of martyrs were women led Bonnie Bowman Thurston (1989) to suggest that they must also have been regarded by the Romans as holding some sort of official standing. This is consistent with the fact that the women tortured and then probably executed by Pliny were deaconesses.

Thus, just as the Guttentag and Secord theory predicts, the very favorable sex ratio enjoyed by Christian women was soon translated into substantially more status and power, both within the family and within the religious subculture, than was enjoyed by pagan women. Let me note that women in Rome and in Roman cities enjoyed greater freedom and power than women in the empire's Greek cities (MacMullen 1984). However, it was in the Greek cities of Asia Minor and North Africa that Christianity made its greatest early headway, and it is these communities that are the focus of this analysis. Granted, even in this part of the empire, pagan women sometimes held important positions within various mystery cults and shrines. However, these religious groups and centers were themselves relatively peripheral to power within pagan society, for authority was vested primarily in secular roles. In contrast, the church was the primary social structure of the Christian subculture. Daily life revolved around the church, and power resided in church offices. To the extent that women held significant roles within the church, they enjoyed greater power and status than did pagan women. Indeed, participation in Mithraism, which has often been regarded as early Christianity's major competitor, was limited to males (Ferguson 1990).

Now I would like to pursue an additional and equally remarkable consequence of the very different sex ratios prevailing among pagans and Christians. In the pagan world that surrounded the early Christians, an excess number of men caused wives to be in short supply. But within the Christian subculture it was husbands who were in short supply. Herein lay an excellent opportunity for gaining secondary converts.

Exogamous Marriage and Secondary Conversion

Both Peter and Paul sanctioned marriage between Christians and pagans. Peter advised women with unconverted husbands to be submissive so that the men might be won to faith "when they see your reverent and chaste behavior" (1 Pet. 3:1-2). Paul gives similar advice, noting that "an unbelieving husband is consecrated through his wife" (1 Cor. 7:13-14). Both passages are commonly interpreted as directed toward persons whose conversion postdated their marriage. In such circumstances, as Wayne Meeks explained, the Christian "divorce rule takes precedence over the preference for group endogamy" (1983:101). But I suggest that these passages may reflect a far greater tolerance for exogamous marriage than has been recognized. My reasons are several.

We know that there was a very substantial oversupply of marriageable Christian women and that this was acknowledged to be a problem. Fox reported the concern among church leaders "to match an excess of Christian women to a deficiency of Christian men" (1987:309). Indeed, in about the year 200 Callistus, bishop of Rome, upset many of his fellow clerics when he ruled that Christian women could live in "just concubinage" without entering into marriage (Brown 1988; Fox 1987; Latourette 1937). Although Hippolytus and other contemporaries denounced the pope's action as giving license to adultery, Harnack defended Callistus on the basis of the circumstances he faced: "These circumstances arose from the fact of Christian girls in the church outnumbering youths, the indulgence of Callistus itself proving unmistakably the female element in the church, so far as the better classes were concerned, was in the majority" (1908: 2:83–84). In particular, Callistus was trying to deal with the problem facing upper-class women whose only marital options *within* the Christian community were to men of far inferior rank. Should they have entered into legal marriages with such men, highborn women would have lost many legal privileges and control of their wealth. If highborn Christian women found it so difficult to find grooms that the bishop of Rome permitted "just concubinage," how was he to condemn middle- and lower-class Christian women who wed pagans, especially if they did so within the church guidelines concerning the religious training of the children? The case of Pomponia Graecina, the aristocratic early convert mentioned in chapter 2, is pertinent here. It is uncertain whether her husband Plautius ever became a Christian, although he carefully shielded her from gossip, but there seems to be no doubt that her children were raised as Christians. According to Marta Sordi, "in the second century [her family] were practicing Christians (a member of the family is buried in the catacomb of St. Callistus)" (1986:27). As we see later in the chapter, superior fertility played a significant role in the rise of Christianity. But had the oversupply of Christian women resulted in an oversupply of unwed, childless women, their potential fertility would have been denied to Christian growth. Summing up his long study of the sources, Harnack noted that many mixed marriages were reported and that in virtually all cases "the husband was a pagan, while the wife was a Christian" (1908: 2:79).

Finally, the frequency with which early church fathers condemned marriage to pagans *could* demonstrate that Christians "refused their sons and daughters in marriage to nonmembers" (MacMullen 1984:103). But it could also reflect the reverse, since people tend not to keep harping on matters that are not significant. Tertullian offers an interesting example. Writing in about the year 200 he violently condemned Christian women who married pagans, describing the latter as "slaves of the Devil" (quoted in Fox 1987:308). He also wrote two angry treatises condemning Christian women's use of makeup, hair dye, fancy clothes, and jewelry (1959 ed.). I certainly would not conclude from the latter that most Christian women in Tertullian's time dressed plainly and rejected cosmetics. Were that the case, Tertullian would have been an irrelevant fool—which he so obviously was not. I incline to a similar interpretation of his attack on Christian women for marrying pagans—Tertullian's anger reflects the frequency of such marriages. In fact, Tertullian felt it necessary to acknowledge that one of his colleagues claimed that "while marriage to a pagan was certainly an offence, it was an extremely trivial offence" (quoted in Harnack 1908: 2:82). Michael Walsh seems to agree that intermarriage was common. Commenting upon a proposal by Ignatius of Antioch that Christians should marry only with the permission of their local bishop, Walsh wrote:

> Ignatius' proposal may have been an attempt to encourage marriage between Christians, for inevitably marriages between Christians and pagans were common, especially in the early years. The Church did not at first discourage this practice, which had its advantages: it might bring others into the fold. (1986:216)

This view is further supported by the lack of concern in early Christian sources about losing members via marriage to pagans. Peter and Paul hoped that Christians would bring their spouses into the church, but neither seemed to have the slightest worry that Christians would revert to, or convert to, paganism. Moreover, pagan sources agree. The composure of the Christian martyrs amazed and unsettled many pagans. Pliny noted the "stubbornness and unbending obstinacy" ("Letter," 1943 ed.) of the Christians brought before him—under threat of death they would not recant. The emperor Marcus Aurelius also remarked on the obstinacy of Christian martyrs (*The Communings*, 1916 ed.). And Galen wrote of Christians that "their contempt of death (and of its sequel) is patent to us every day" (quoted in Benko 1984:141). Galen's reference was to the willingness of Christians to nurse the sick during the great plague that struck the empire at this time, killing millions, including Marcus Aurelius (see chapter 4). The high levels of commitment that the early church generated among its members should have made it safe for them to enter exogamous marriages.

That Christians seldom lost out via exogamous marriages is also in keeping with modern observations of high-tension religious movements. Female Jehovah's Witnesses frequently marry outside the group (Heaton 1990). Seldom does this result in their defection, and it often results in the conversion of the spouse. Indeed, this phenomenon is so general that Andrew Greeley (1970) has proposed the rule that whenever a mixed marriage occurs, the less religious person will usually join the religion of the more religious member.

But how much intermarriage was there and how much did it matter in terms of producing secondary converts? What we do know is that secondary conversion was quite frequent among the Roman upper classes (Fox 1987; Chadwick 1967). This was partly because many married upper-class women became Christians and then managed to convert their spouses—this was especially common by the fourth century. But it also occurred because many upper-class Christian women did marry pagans, some of whom they subsequently were able to convert (Harnack 1908, vol. 2). Indeed, Peter Brown wrote of Christian women as a "gateway" into pagan families where "they were the wives, servants, and nurses of unbelievers" (1988:154).

In truth, there is no abundance of direct evidence that intermarriages between Christian women and pagan men were widespread. But, in my judgment, a compelling case can be made by resort to reason. It is reasonable to assume that—given the great surplus of marriageable Christian women, existing in the midst of a world in which women were in short supply, and given that Christians seem not to have feared that intermarriage would result in their daughters' abandoning their faith—such marriages ought to have been common. And from what we know about conversion mechanisms, these intermarriages ought to have resulted in a lot of secondary conversions.

As discussed in detail in chapter 1, conversion is a network phenomenon based on interpersonal attachments. People join movements to align their religious status with that of their friends and relatives who already belong. Hence, in order to offer plausible accounts of Christianity's rise, we need to discover mechanisms by which Christians formed attachments with pagans. Put another way, we need to discover how Christians managed to remain an *open network*, able to keep building bonds with outsiders, rather than becoming a closed community of believers. A high rate of exogamous marriage is one such mechanism. And I think it was crucial to the rise of Christianity.

Indeed, exogamous marriage had another major consequence. It prevented the surplus of Christian women from resulting in an abundance of childless, single women. To the contrary, it seems likely that Christian fertility substantially exceeded that of pagans and that this too helped Christianize the Greco-Roman world.

THE FERTILITY FACTOR

In 59 B.C.E. Julius Caesar secured legislation that awarded land to fathers of three or more children, though he failed to act on Cicero's suggestion that celibacy be outlawed. Thirty years later, and again in the year 9, the emperor Augustus promulgated laws giving political preference to men who fathered three or more children and imposing political and financial sanctions upon childless couples, upon unmarried women over the age of twenty, and upon unmarried men over the age of twenty-five. These policies were continued by most emperors who followed Augustus, and many additional programs were instituted to promote fertility. Trajan, for example, provided substantial child subsidies (Rawson 1986).

But nothing worked. As Tacitus tells us, "childlessness prevailed" (*Annals* 3.25, 1989 ed.). As the distinguished Arthur E. R. Boak remarked, "[policies with] the aim of encouraging families to rear at least three children were pathetically impotent" (1955a:18). As a result, the population of the Roman Empire began to decline noticeably during the last years of the Republic, and serious population shortages had developed by the second century, *before* the onset of the first great plague (Boak 1955a).

Thus although plagues played a substantial role in the decline of the Roman population, of far greater importance was the low fertility rate of the free population in the Greco-Roman world (both rural and urban) and the extremely low fertility of the large slave population (Boak 1955a). By the start of the Christian era, Greco-Roman fertility had fallen below replacement levels, leading to centuries of natural *decrease* (Parkin 1992; Devine 1985; Boak 1955a). As a result, the devastating effects of the major plagues were never remedied, for even in good times the population was not replacing itself. By the third century, there is solid evidence of a decline in both the number and the size of Roman towns in the West, even in Britain (Collingwood and Myres 1937).

That the empire could continue as long as it did depended on a constant influx of "barbarian" settlers. As early as the second century, Marcus Aurelius had to draft slaves and gladiators and hire Germans and Scythians in order to fill the ranks of the army (Boak 1955a). After defeating the Marcomanni, Aurelius settled large numbers of them within the empire in return for their accepting obligations to supply soldiers. Boak commented that Aurelius "had no trouble finding vacant land on which to place them" (1955a:18).

Meanwhile, in keeping with the biblical injunction to "be fruitful and multiply," Christians maintained a substantial rate of natural *increase*. Their fertility rates were considerably higher than those of pagans, and their mortality rates were considerably lower.

To conclude this chapter I shall first establish the basis for the very low fertility rates of the Greco-Roman world. Next, I will examine factors that sustained high fertility among Jews and subsequently among Christians. Although it is impossible to know actual fertility rates in this period, these cultural contrasts are sufficient to strongly suggest that superior Christian fertility played a significant role in the rise of Christianity.

SOURCES OF LOW FERTILITY

A primary cause of low fertility in the Greco-Roman world was a male culture that held marriage in low esteem. In 131 B.C.E. the Roman censor Quintus Caecilius Metellus Macedonicus proposed that the senate make marriage compulsory because so many men, especially in the upper classes, preferred to stay single. Acknowledging that "we cannot have a really harmonious life with our wives," the censor pointed out that since "we cannot have any sort of life without them," the long term welfare of the state must be served. More than a century later Augustus quoted this passage to the senate to justify his own legislation on behalf of marriage, and it was not greeted with any greater enthusiasm the second time around (Rawson 1986:11). For the fact was that men in the Greco-Roman world found it difficult to relate to women. As Beryl Rawson has reported, "one theme that recurs in Latin literature is that wives are difficult and therefore men do not care much for marriage" (1986:11).

Although virginity was demanded of brides, and chastity of wives, men tended to be quite promiscuous and female prostitutes abounded in Greco-Roman cities—from the twopenny *diobolariae* who worked the streets to high-priced, well-bred courtesans (Pomeroy 1975). Greco-Roman cities also sustained substantial numbers of male prostitutes, as bisexuality and homosexuality were common (Sandison 1967).

Infanticide

However, even when Greco-Roman men did marry, they usually produced very small families—not even legal sanctions and inducements could achieve the goal of an average of three children per family. One reason for this was infanticide—far more babies were born than were allowed to live. Seneca regarded the drowning of children at birth as both reasonable and commonplace. Tacitus charged that the Jewish teaching that it is "a deadly sin to kill an unwanted child" was but another of their "sinister and revolting" practices (*The Histories* 5.5, 1984 ed.). It was common to expose an unwanted infant out-of-doors where it could, in principle, be taken up by someone who wished to rear it, but where it typically fell victim to the elements or to animals and birds. Not only was the exposure of infants a very common practice, it was justified by law and advocated by philosophers.

Both Plato and Aristotle recommended infanticide as legitimate state policy.[3] The Twelve Tables—the earliest known Roman legal code, written about 450 B.C.E.—permitted a father to expose any female infant and any deformed or weak male infant (Gorman 1982:25). During recent excavations of a villa in the port city of Ashkelon, Lawrence E. Stager and his colleagues made

> a gruesome discovery in the sewer that ran under the bathhouse. . . . The sewer had been clogged with refuse sometime in the sixth century A.D. When we excavated and dry-sieved the desiccated sewage, we found [the] bones . . . of nearly 100 little babies apparently murdered and thrown into the sewer. (1991:47)

Examination of the bones revealed them to be newborns, probably day-olds (Smith and Kahila 1991). As yet, physical anthropologists have not been able to determine the gender of these infants who apparently had just been dropped down the drain shortly after birth. But the assumption is that they were all, or nearly all, girls (Stager 1991). Girls or boys, these bones reveal a major cause of population decline.

Abortion

In addition to infanticide, fertility was greatly reduced in the Greco-Roman world by the very frequent recourse to abortion. The literature details an amazingly large number of abortion techniques—the more effective of which were exceedingly dangerous. Thus abortion not only prevented many births, it killed many women before they could make their contribution to fertility, and it resulted in a substantial incidence of infertility in women who survived abortions. A consideration of the primary methods used will enable us to more fully grasp the impact of abortion on Greco-Roman fertility and mortality.

A frequent approach involved ingesting slightly less than fatal doses of poison in an effort to cause a miscarriage. But, of course, poisons are somewhat unpredictable and tolerance levels vary greatly; hence in many cases both the mother and the fetus were killed. Another method introduced poisons of various sorts into the uterus to kill the fetus. Unfortunately, in many cases the woman failed to expel the dead fetus and died unless she was treated almost immediately by mechanical methods of removal. But these methods, which were often used as the initial mode of abortion as well, were also extremely dangerous, requiring great surgical skill as well as good luck in an age that was ignorant of bacteria.

The commonly used mechanical methods all involved long needles, hooks, and knives. Tertullian, writing in about 203, described an abortion kit used by Hippocrates:

> a flexible frame for opening the uterus first of all, and keeping it open; it is further furnished with an annular blade, by means of which the limbs within the womb are dissected with anxious but unfaltering care; its last appendage being a blunted or covered hook, wherewith the entire fetus is extracted by a violent delivery. There is also a copper needle or spike by which the actual death is managed. (*A Treatise on the Soul* 25, 1989 ed.)

The famous Roman medical writer Aulas Cornelius Celsus offered extensive instructions on using similar equipment in his

De medicina, written in the first century. Celsus warned surgeons that an abortion "requires extreme caution and neatness, and entails very great risk." He advised that "after the death of the foetus" the surgeon should slowly force his "greased hand" up the vagina and into the uterus (keep in mind that soap had yet to be invented). If the fetus was in a headfirst position, the surgeon should then insert a smooth hook and fix it "into an eye or ear or the mouth, even at times into the forehead, then this is pulled upon and extracts the foetus." If the fetus was positioned crosswise or backwards, then Celsus advised that a blade be used to cut up the fetus so it could be taken out in pieces. Afterwards, Celsus instructed surgeons to tie the woman's thighs together and to cover her pubic area with "greasy wool, dipped in vinegar and rose oil" (*De medicina* 7.29, 1935–1938 ed.).

Given the methods involved, it is not surprising that abortion was a major cause of death among women in the Greco-Roman world (Gorman 1982). Since abortion was so dangerous to women in this era, it might be asked why it was so widely practiced. The sources mention a variety of reasons, but concealment of illicit sexual activity receives the greatest emphasis—unmarried women and women who became pregnant while their husbands were absent often sought abortions (Gorman 1982). Economic reasons are also cited frequently. Poor women sought abortions to avoid a child they could ill afford, and rich women sought them in order to avoid splitting up the family estate among many heirs.

However, the very high rates of abortion in the Greco-Roman world can only be fully understood if we recognize that in perhaps the majority of instances it was men, rather than women, who made the decision to abort. Roman law accorded the male head of family the literal power of life and death over his household, including the right to order a female in the household to abort. The Roman Twelve Tables mentioned earlier did suggest censure for husbands who ordered their wives to abort without good reason, but no fines or penalties were specified. Moreover, the weight of Greek philosophy fully supported these Roman views. In his *Republic* Plato made abortions mandatory for all women who conceived after age forty, on the grounds of limiting the population (5.9, 1941 ed.), and Aristotle followed suit in his *Politics*: "There must be a limit fixed to the procreation of offspring, and if any people have a child as a result of intercourse in contravention of these regulations, abortion must be practiced" (7.14.10, 1986 ed.). It is hardly surprising that a world which gave husbands the right to order the exposure of their infant daughters would give them the right to order their wives and mistresses to abort. Thus the emperor Domitian, having impregnated his niece Julia, ordered her to have an abortion—from which she died (Gorman 1982).

Birth Control

The Romans had an adequate understanding of the biology of reproduction and developed a substantial inventory of preventive measures. Medical historians now are convinced that various plants such as Queen Anne's lace, chewed by women in antiquity, were somewhat effective in reducing fertility (Riddle, Estes, and Russell 1994). In addition, a number of contraceptive devices and medicines were inserted into the vagina to kill sperm or block the path of semen to the uterus. Various ointments, honey, and pads of soft wool were used for the latter purpose (Noonan 1965; Clark 1993). Unborn lamb stomachs and goat bladders served as condoms; these, however, were too expensive for anyone but the very rich (Pomeroy 1975). Even more popular (and effective) were sexual variations that keep sperm out of the vagina. One frequently used method was withdrawal. Another substituted mutual masturbation for intercourse. Surviving Roman and Greek art frequently depicts anal intercourse, and a number of classical writers mention women "playing the boy," a reference to anal sex (Sandison 1967:744). Pomeroy attributes the preference of Greco-Roman males for women with large buttocks "to the practice of anal intercourse"

(1975:49). Having reported a wealth of literary references, Lindsay claims that heterosexual anal intercourse was "very common" and "was used as the simplest, most convenient, and most effective form of contraception" (1968:250–251). Oral sex seems to have been much less common than anal sex (understandably so, given the lack of cleanliness), but it is depicted in a number of erotic Greek paintings, especially on vases (Sandison 1967). Finally, given their attitudes about marriage and their distant relationships with their wives, many Greco-Roman men seem to have depended on the most reliable of all means of birth control, avoiding sex with their wives.

Too Few Women

In the final analysis, a population's capacity to reproduce is a function of the proportion of that population consisting of women in their childbearing years, and the Greco-Roman world had an acute shortage of women. Moreover, many pagan women still in their childbearing years had been rendered infertile by damage to their reproductive systems from abortions or from contraceptive devices and medicines. In this manner was the decline of the Roman Empire's population ensured.

CHRISTIAN FERTILITY

The differential fertility of Christians and pagans is not something I have deduced from the known natural decrease of the Greco-Roman population and from Christian rejection of the attitudes and practices that caused pagans to have low fertility. This differential fertility was taken as fact by the ancients. Thus, at the end of the second century, Minucius Felix wrote a debate between a pagan and a Christian in which Octavius, the Christian spokesman, noted "that day by day the number of us is increased," which he attributed to "[our] fair mode of life" (*Octavius* 31, 1989 ed.). It could hardly have been otherwise, because Christians pursued a lifestyle that could only result in comparatively higher fertility—a point fully appreciated by Tertullian, who noted: "To the servant of God, forsooth, offspring is necessary! For our own salvation we are secure enough, so that we have leisure for children! Burdens must be sought by us for ourselves which are avoided by the majority of the Gentiles, who are compelled by laws [to have children], who are decimated by abortions" (*To His Wife* 1.5, 1989 ed.).

If a major factor in lower fertility among pagans was a male-oriented culture that held marriage in low esteem, a major factor in higher fertility of Christians was a culture that sanctified the marital bond. As noted, Christians condemned promiscuity in men as well as in women and stressed the obligations of husbands toward wives as well as those of wives toward husbands. Writing to the church in Corinth, after having allowed that celibacy was probably to be preferred, Paul quickly went on to define proper marital relations among Christians:

> But because of the temptation to immorality, each man should have his own wife and each woman her own husband. The husband should give to his wife her conjugal rights, and likewise the wife to her husband. For the wife does not rule over her own body, but the husband does; likewise the husband does not rule over his own body, but the wife does. Do not refuse one another except perhaps by agreement for a season, that you may devote yourselves to prayer; but then come together again, lest Satan tempt you through lack of self-control. I say this by way of concession, not of command. I wish that all were as I myself am. But each has his own special gift from God, one of one kind and one of another. (1 Cor. 7:2–7)

The symmetry of the relationship Paul described was at total variance, not only with pagan culture, but with Jewish culture as well—just as allowing women to hold positions of religious importance was at variance with Jewish practice. And if Paul expressed a more conventionally patriarchal view of the marriage relationship in Eph. 5:22—"Wives, be subject to your husbands

123

as to the Lord. For the husband is the head of the wife as Christ is head of the church"—he devoted the next ten verses to admonishing men to love their wives.

Apart from the question of female roles, in most other respects the views of family and fertility sustained by Christians revealed the Jewish origins of the movement. These views can best be described as very family-oriented and pro-natal. Indeed, as time passed, Christians began to stress that the primary purpose of sex was procreation and therefore that it was a marital duty to have children. In addition to these pronounced differences in attitudes, there were dramatic behavioral differences that distinguished Christians from pagans in their treatment of pregnant women and infants.

Abortion and Infanticide

From the start, Christian doctrine absolutely prohibited abortion and infanticide, classifying both as murder. These Christian prohibitions reflected the Jewish origins of the movement. Among Jews, according to Josephus: "The law, moreover, enjoins us to bring up our offspring, and forbids women to cause abortion of what is begotten, or to destroy it afterward; and if any woman appears to have done so, she will be a murderer of her child" (1960 ed.). In similar fashion, the Alexandrian Jewish writing known as the *Sentences of Pseudo-Phocylides* advised: "A woman should not destroy the unborn babe in her belly, nor after its birth throw it before dogs and vultures as prey" (quoted in Gorman 1982:37).

These views are repeated in the earliest Christian writing on the subject. Thus, in the second chapter of the *Didache*, a manual of church teachings probably written in the first century (Robinson 1976), we find the injunction "Thou shalt not murder a child by abortion nor kill them when born." Justin Martyr, in his *First Apology*, written toward the middle of the second century, noted, "We have been taught that it is wicked to expose even newly-born children ... [for] we would then be murderers" (27–29, 1948 ed.). In the second century, Athenagoras wrote in chapter 35 of his *Plea* to the emperor Marcus Aurelius,

> We say that women who use drugs to bring on an abortion commit murder, and will have to give an account to God for the abortion ... [for we] regard the very foetus in the womb as a created being, and therefore an object of God's care ... and [we do not] expose an infant, because those who expose them are chargeable with child-murder. (1989 ed.)

By the end of the second century, Christians not only were proclaiming their rejection of abortion and infanticide, but had begun direct attacks on pagans, and especially pagan religions, for sustaining such "crimes." In his *Octavius*, Minucius Felix charged:

> And I see that you at one time expose your begotten children to wild beasts and to birds; at another, that you crush when strangled with a miserable kind of death. There are some women [among you] who, by drinking medical preparations, extinguish the source of the future man in their very bowels, and thus commit a parricide before they bring forth. And these things assuredly come down from your gods. For Saturn did not expose his children, but devoured them. With reason were infants sacrificed to him in some parts of Africa. (33, 1989 ed.)

Birth Control

Initially, Christian teaching about the use of contraceptive devices and substances may have been somewhat ambiguous (Noonan 1965). However, since it is not clear the extent to which the contraceptive methods used by the ancients actually worked (and many, such as amulets worn around the ankle, clearly did not), it may not have mattered whether they were permitted or condemned. Of far greater importance to Christian fertility were religious objections to the most effective means of birth control—objections mostly taken over from Judaism. That is, Jews and Christians were opposed to sexual practices that diverted sperm from the vagina. As the biblical story of Onan makes clear, withdrawal and mutual masturbation were sins in that the seed was spilled upon the ground. Thus Clement of Alexandria wrote, "Because of its divine institution for the propagation of man, the seed is not to be vainly ejaculated, nor is it to be damaged, nor is it to be wasted" (quoted in Noonan 1965:93). Both Jews and Christians condemned anal intercourse. In Rom. 1:26 Paul wrote: "For this cause God gave them up unto vile affections: for even their women did change the natural use into that which is against nature." As for oral sex, Barnabas wrote: "Thou shalt not . . . become such as those men of whom we hear as working iniquity with their mouth for uncleanness, neither shalt thou cleave unto impure women who work iniquity with their mouths" (*The Epistle* 10, 1988 ed.). In all these ways did Christians reject the cultural patterns that were causing the Greco-Roman pagan population to decline.

An Abundance of Fertile Women

A final factor in favor of high Christian fertility was an abundance of women who were far less likely to be infertile. Since only women can have babies, the sex composition of a population is (other things being equal) a crucial factor in its level of fertility. That the Christian community may well have been 60 percent female offered the Christian subculture a tremendous potential level of fertility. Of course, given the moral restrictions of the group, Christian women also needed to be married in order to have children. But, as I tried to establish earlier, there is no reason to suppose that they did not have high marriage rates, given the abundance of eligible males in the surrounding populace. Moreover, there is every reason to suppose that the overwhelming majority of children from these "mixed marriages" were raised within the church.

Christian Fertility

A number of sophisticated scholars have tried to estimate the fertility rate of the Roman Empire (Parkin 1992; Durand 1960; Russell 1958), but the fact remains that we will never have firm knowledge. What can be established is that mortality was high; thus a high fertility rate was necessary to prevent a population decline. It also seems very likely that fertility was substantially lower than needed for replacement, and, as noted above, there is substantial evidence that the Greco-Roman population did become smaller during the Christian era. Beyond these generalities, it is doubtful that we shall obtain more precise information.

As for the fertility of the Christian population, the literature is empty. It was for this reason that I devoted much attention to establishing that the primary causes of a population decline in the Greco-Roman world did not apply to the Christian subculture. It thus seems entirely proper to assume that Christian population patterns would have resembled the patterns that normally apply in societies having an equivalent level of economic and cultural development. So long as they do not come up against limits imposed by available subsistence, such populations are normally quite expansive. Lack of subsistence was not a factor in this time and place, as the frequent settlement of barbarians to make up population shortages makes clear. We can therefore assume that during the rise of Christianity the Christian population grew not only via conversion, but via fertility. The question is, how much of their growth was due to fertility alone?

Unfortunately, we simply do not have good enough data to attempt a quantitative answer to this question—not even a sufficient basis for hypothetical figures. All that can be claimed is that a nontrivial portion of Christian growth probably was due to superior fertility.

Conclusion

In this chapter I have attempted to establish four things. First, Christian subcultures in the ancient world rapidly developed a very substantial surplus of females, while in the pagan world around them males greatly outnumbered females. This shift was the result of Christian prohibitions against infanticide and abortion and of substantial sex bias in conversion. Second, fully in accord with Guttentag and Secord's theory linking the status of women to sex ratios, Christian women enjoyed substantially higher status within the Christian subcultures than pagan women did in the world at large. This was especially marked vis-à-vis gender relations within the family, but women also filled leadership positions within the church. Third, given a surplus of Christian women and a surplus of pagan men, a substantial amount of exogamous marriage took place, thus providing the early church with a steady flow of secondary converts. Finally, I have argued that the abundance of Christian women resulted in higher birthrates—that superior fertility contributed to the rise of Christianity.

Christianizing the Urban Empire: A Quantitative Approach

I<small>N HIS</small> brilliant study of the early church, Wayne Meeks (1983) uses the title of his book to emphasize that Christianity was first and foremost an *urban* movement. Or, as he put it early in the first chapter, "within a decade of the crucifixion of Jesus, the village culture of Palestine had been left far behind, and the Greco-Roman city became the dominant environment of the Christian movement" (1983:11). In the remainder of the book Meeks offers many insights about the spread of Christianity; his primary emphasis, however, is not on cities, but on urbanites. His aim is to help us recognize *who* embraced the new movement and why.

My concern in this chapter is not so much with who or why as with *where*. What characteristics of cities were conducive to Christianization? To this end I will apply some standard tools used by urban sociologists and conduct a quantitative analysis using a data set consisting of the twenty-two largest cities of the Greco-Roman world circa 100. I will develop and test some hypotheses about why Christianity arose more rapidly in some places than in others. However, rather than present the hypotheses first and then move to the statistical analysis, I shall develop and test each seriatim. The reason for this format is that each variable must be discussed at some length as it enters the analysis, and each variable reflects a hypothesis.

A preliminary version of this chapter appeared as "Christianizing the Urban Empire," in *Sociological Analysis* 52 (1991): 77–88.

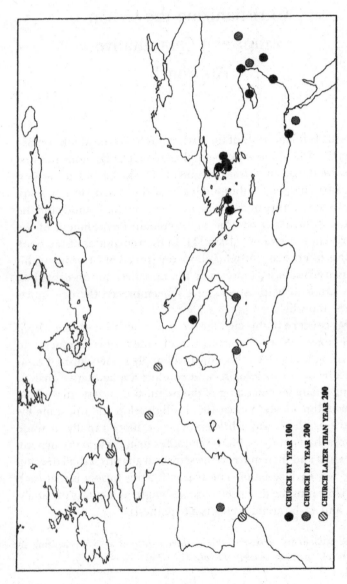

Christianity was an urban movement and, like many new faiths before it, it arose in the east and spread westward, as can be seen in this map showing the twenty-two largest cities of the Roman Empire (ca. 100).

SELECTING CITIES BY SIZE

Despite libraries stuffed with books on many Greco-Roman cities, the sad fact is that, as Lewis Mumford has pointed out, "the city itself remains a shadow" (1974:vii). Indeed, it has required Herculean efforts even to estimate such an elementary and essential fact as the population of these cities. Fortunately, Tertius Chandler made it his life's work to try to discover the populations of ancient cities. Assisted by Gerald Fox (with Kingsley Davis performing the vital role of midwife), he was finally able to publish his extraordinary work (Chandler and Fox 1974). In *Three Thousand Years of Urban Growth*, Chandler and Fox offer a plausible and well-documented basis for estimating the populations of the world's largest cities in 100. Among these are twenty Greco-Roman cities. However, because Chandler and Fox chose to list only those cities having a population of 40,000 or more, they provided no population estimates for Athens or Salamis, although these are usually included in lists of important Greco-Roman cities. I added these two cities, bringing the total to twenty-two. I was unable to muster any Chandler-like scholarship to determine their populations at this time. But, after a good deal of poking around, I settled on 35,000 for Salamis and 30,000 for Athens.[1] If these prove faulty, be assured that removing them from the analysis has no effect on the results I report below.

Here are the twenty-two cities and their estimated populations:

Rome	650,000
Alexandria	400,000
Ephesus	200,000
Antioch	150,000
Apamea	125,000
Pergamum	120,000
Sardis	100,000
Corinth	100,000

Gadir (Cadiz)	100,000
Memphis	90,000
Carthage	90,000
Edessa	80,000
Syracuse	80,000
Smyrna	75,000
Caesarea Maritima	45,000
Damascus	45,000
Cordova	45,000
Mediolanum (Milan)	40,000
Augustodunum (Autun)	40,000
London	40,000
Salamis	35,000
Athens	30,000

CHRISTIANIZATION

How can we measure the receptivity of cities to Christianity, that is, their relative degree of Christianization at various times? My method is neither original nor (I would hope) particularly controversial. I have simply followed Adolf Harnack (1908, vol. 2) in using the notion of the *expansion* of Christianity—for in order to rise, a movement must spread. In his masterwork, Harnack identified those communities in the empire that possessed local Christian churches by the year 180. Later scholars have added much to Harnack's original reconstruction, drawing on the many important archaeological finds of recent decades. However, owing to the lack of quantitative inclination among scholars in this area, it is only in the numerous historical atlases that this literature has been pulled together. Through study of many an atlas, I found four that seemed to reflect solid scholarship on this particular topic, and these are shown in table 6.1, along with Harnack's original findings (Blaiklock 1972; Aharoni and Avi-Yonah 1977; Frank 1988; Chadwick and Evans 1987; Harnack 1908).

Table 6.1
Coding Christianization

	Source 1[a]	Source 2[b]	Source 3[c]	Source 4[d]	Source 5[e]	Code[f]
Caesarea Maritima	2	2	2	2/1	2	2
Damascus	2	2	2	2/1	0	2
Antioch	2	2	2	2/1	2	2
Alexandria	2	2	2	2/1	2	2
Pergamum	2	2	2	2/1	2	2
Salamis	2	2	2	2/1	2	2
Sardis	2	2	2	2/1	2	2
Smyrna	2	2	2	2/1	0	2
Athens	2	2	2	2/1	2	2
Corinth	2	2	2	2/1	0	2
Ephesus	2	2	2	2/1	2	2
Rome	2	2	2	2/1	2	2
Apamea	1	1/0	1	0	2	1
Cordova	1	1/0	1	0	1	1
Edessa	1	1/0	1	2/1	1	1
Syracuse	1	1/0	1	2/1	1	1
Carthage	1	1/0	1	2/1	1	1
Memphis	2	1/0	1	2/1	1	1
Mediolanum (Milan)	0	1/0	0	0	0	0
Augustodunum (Autun)	0	1/0	0	0	0	0
Gadir (Cadiz)	0	1/0	0	0	0	0
London	0	1/0	0	0	0	0

[a] Aharoni and Avi-Yonah 1977 (map of cities with churches by end of first century and map of cities with churches by end of the second century).

[b] Chadwick and Evans 1987 (map of cities known to have had churches by the end of the first century).

[c] Frank 1988 (map of cities known to have had a church by the end of the first century and by 180 C.E.).

[d] Harnack 1908 (map of cities known to have had a church by 180 C.E.).

[e] Blaiklock 1972 (map shaded to show cities known to have had a church by end of first century and by end of second century).

[f] In the codes used when the chapter appeared as an essay in *Sociological Analysis*, Memphis was scored 2 rather than 1 and Cordova was scored 0 rather than 1. Upon further research I decided to make these corrections. However, they did not alter the statistical results in any important way.

I have quantified the expansion of Christianity in terms of three thresholds. The cities most receptive to Christianity are those known to have had a church by 100. They receive a score of two. The next most receptive are those cities known to have had a church by 200. They receive a score of one. The least receptive cities are those still lacking a church by 200. Their score is zero. The result is a three-value, ordinal measure of Christianization.

Cities scored two are: Caesarea Maritima, Damascus, Antioch, Alexandria, Pergamum, Salamis, Sardis, Smyrna, Athens, Corinth, Ephesus, and Rome.

Cities scored one are: Apamea, Carthage, Cordova, Edessa, Memphis, and Syracuse.

Cities scored zero are: Augustodunum (Autun), Gadir (Cadiz), London, and Mediolanum (Milan).

Let us pause here for our first hypothesis. Is there any reason to suppose that *city size* would have influenced Christianization? Harnack thought so: "The larger the town or city, the larger (even relatively, it is probable) was the number of Christians" (1908: 2:327). Moreover, there is a solid theoretical basis for such a hypothesis in the sociological literature. In his well-known subcultural theory of urbanism, Claude S. Fischer offered this proposition: "The more urban the place, the higher the rates of unconventionality" (1975:1328). Fischer's thesis is that the larger the population, in absolute numbers, the easier it is to assemble a "critical mass" needed to form a deviant subculture. Here he specifically includes deviant religious movements. During the period in question Christianity obviously qualifies as a deviant religious movement in that it clearly was at variance with prevailing religious norms. Therefore, Fischer's theory of urbanism predicts that Christians would have assembled the critical mass needed to form a church sooner, the larger the city.

As can be seen in table 6.2 below, there is a positive correlation in support of Fischer's thesis. Although this correlation falls slightly short of significance at the .05 level, it is not at all clear that significance is an appropriate standard here, since the data are not based on a random sample. Indeed, it was with great reservations that I included significance levels in the table.

LOCATION

One thing we know with certainty about these cities is *where* they were. And that means we can measure travel distances from one to another. Therefore, I have determined the distance of each of these twenty-two cities from Jerusalem.

We know where Christianity began. If we want to discover how it spread, we ought to take into account how far it had to go to get to various cities. The issue here is not simply that missionaries had to go farther to get from Jerusalem to Mediolanum than to Sardis. Indeed, anyone could cross the empire from one end to the other in a summer, and travel was common. Meeks (1983:17) reports a merchant's grave inscription found in Phrygia that attests to his having traveled to Rome seventy-two times, a distance of well over a thousand miles, and Ronald Hock (1980) estimates that Paul covered nearly ten thousand miles on his missions. As Meeks put it, "the people of the Roman Empire traveled more extensively and more easily than anyone before them did or would again until the nineteenth century" (1983:17).

My interest is in the primary consequences of all this travel and trade: communication, cultural contact, and networks of interpersonal relationships based on kinship, friendship, or commerce. As I will discuss below, these were vital factors in preparing the way for the Christian missionaries—in determining what kind of reception awaited them. I propose to use distance from Jerusalem as a gradient of these factors.

Given this interest, simple distance as the crow flies is inadequate. Instead, in making the actual measurements I have attempted to trace known travel routes. Moreover, the bulk of trade and of long-distance travel was by boat—Paul traveled as much or more by sea as by land. Therefore, I have assumed sea travel whenever it was feasible and measured distances along the commonly used routes. First, I sketched the route from Jerusalem to a given city on a map. Then, I used a map meter to measure the distance—this makes it easy to follow curves and turn corners. Each measurement was made several times. And the final measurement was then converted to miles on the basis of the map's legend. The routes themselves may be subject to modest errors, but I would not expect errors in excess of plus or minus 10 percent. In order to see the potential impact of errors of that magnitude, I created an additional mileage measure by flipping a coin and adding or subtracting 10 percent depending on whether the coin came up heads or tails. The distorted measure in fact correlated .99 with the original, and each yields identical results with other variables.

In addition to seeking to use travel distances to estimate the degree to which the way was prepared for Christians by the prior ties to Jerusalem and to Jewish culture, we can also use distance as a way to measure the degree of Romanization and the tightness of Roman control. Using the same tactics described above, I therefore measured the travel distance to each city from Rome. Finally, I created a ratio of the two sets of distances to summarize the relative weights of Roman and Jewish influence. The actual distances in miles follow. (The distance given between Athens and Rome is calculated on the assumption that the traveler's boat did not take the portage at Corinth.)

	From Jerusalem	From Rome
Alexandria	350	1,400
Antioch	250	1,650
Apamea	280	1,600
Athens	780	1,000

CHRISTIANIZING THE URBAN EMPIRE

Augustodunum (Autun)	1,920	525
Caesarea Maritima	60	1,575
Carthage	1,575	425
Cordova	2,440	1,225
Corinth	830	800
Damascus	130	1,600
Edessa	550	1,775
Ephesus	640	1,185
Gadir (Cadiz)	2,520	1,200
London	2,565	1,190
Mediolanum (Milan)	1,900	260
Memphis	360	1,500
Pergamum	840	1,200
Rome	1,480	0
Salamis	270	1,450
Sardis	700	1,300
Smyrna	820	1,150
Syracuse	1,100	375

In chapter 3, I stressed the importance of cultural continuity in the success of new religious movements. Specifically, *people are more willing to adopt a new religion to the extent that it retains cultural continuity with conventional religion(s) with which they are already familiar.* In the instance at hand, the way was paved for Christianity to the extent that people were already familiar with Jewish culture—the "God-Fearers" being an apt example. Here were people familiar with Jewish theology, who accepted the idea of monotheism, but who were unwilling to become ethnic Jews in order to fully participate in the Jewish religion. Presumably, the principle of cultural continuity as a facilitating factor in the spread of Christianity can, to some extent, be estimated by distance from Jerusalem. And table 6.2 shows an immense negative correlation between distance from Jerusalem and Christianization (−.74), which is highly statistically significant.

THE DIASPORA

In chapter 3, I argued that, in fact, the mission to the Jews was quite successful and that a steady and significant flow of Hellenized Jewish converts to Christianity probably continued into the late fourth or early fifth century. To recapitulate, my case rests on several sociological propositions. The first is cultural continuity. Not only was Christianity highly continuous with the Jewish heritage of diasporan Jews, it was also highly congruent with their Hellenic cultural elements. The second proposition is that *social movements recruit primarily on the basis of interpersonal attachments that exist, or form, between the convert and members of the group.* And who were the friends and relatives of the early Christian missionaries setting out from Jerusalem to spread their faith? The Jews of the diaspora, of course. In fact, many of the missionaries were, like Paul himself, diasporan Jews.

Even if I am wrong about how late Jewish conversion continued, everyone is agreed that Jews were the primary sources of converts until well into the second century. As Harnack put it:

> The synagogues of the Diaspora . . . formed the most important presupposition for the rise and growth of Christian communities throughout the empire. The network of the synagogues furnished the Christian propaganda with centres and courses for its development, and in this way the mission of the new religion, which was undertaken in the name of the God of Abraham and Moses, found a sphere already prepared for itself. (1908: 1:1)

So, in addition to using distance to measure Jewish cultural influences, we ought to seek a measure of Jewish presence in cities. There simply is no good way to calculate the probable size of the Jewish population in these cities. The best substitute I could obtain is information on which of these cities are known to have had a synagogue in about 100. The data come from

TABLE 6.2
Pearson Product Moment Correlations

	Pop. 100 C.E.	From Jerusalem	Synagogues	From Rome	Romanized	Gnostics
Christianization	.32	−.74[a]	.69[a]	.42[b]	−.71[a]	.59[a]
Population 100 C.E.		−.06	.41[b]	.21	−.29	.48[a]
Miles from Jerusalem			−.46[b]	−.54[a]	.68[a]	−.49[b]
Synagogues				.28	−.44[b]	.41[b]
Miles from Rome					−.84[a]	.37
Romanized						−.43[b]

[a] Significance level: <.01.
[b] Significance level: <.05.

many of the atlases noted above and others, and from MacLennan and Kraabel (1986). The result is a dichotomous variable scoring cities with a synagogue as one, and the others as zero. The following cities received a score of one: Caesarea Maritima, Damascus, Antioch, Alexandria, Sardis, Athens, Rome, Corinth, and Ephesus. Table 6.2 shows that there is a powerful, positive correlation between synagogues and Christianization (.69). Clearly, then, Christianity took root sooner where there were Jewish communities.

Now what about Roman culture and power? In the beginning Christianity did best in Greek cities and soon incurred considerable official Roman antagonism. It seems realistic to treat Roman power as a function of distance—the farther from Rome, the less the local impact of Roman policy. Once again we may simply trace the trade routes to each city from Rome and measure the distances. However, since our interest really centers on the interaction of Roman and Eastern culture and influence, we can divide the distance to Jerusalem by the distance to Rome. The higher the ratio, the greater the relative weight of

TABLE 6.3
Regression: Dependent Variable Is Christianization

Independent Variables	Unstandardized Betas	Standardized Betas	Standard Error	T
Synagogues	0.731	0.466	0.236	3.099[a]
Romanized	−0.220	−0.499	0.077	−3.317[a]

Multiple R-Square = 0.672   Y-Intercept = 1.374

[a] Significant beyond .001.

Roman influence; hence this variable is identified as Romanization (Rome, of course, is excluded from this analysis). Table 6.2 shows that distance from Rome is negatively correlated (−.42) with Christianization, but the really potent effect is from Romanization (−.71). The more Roman and the less Eastern (Greek and Jewish) influence on a city's culture, the later its first church—Rome itself being the obvious exception.

Table 6.3 shows the result of entering Christianization, synagogues, and Romanization into a regression equation. Each of the independent variables displays a robust effect, and together they explain an amazing 67 percent of the variance in Christianization.

GNOSTICS

Not only were there many new religious movements active in the urban empire in this era, there were many Christianities. Almost from the start, factions espousing rather different views of Christ and of Scripture arose, each seeking to be *the* Christianity. Since the discovery of the Nag Hammadi manuscripts, there has been immense interest in the groups known as the Gnostics or the Christian Gnostics (Layton 1987; Williams 1985). A map published by Layton (1987:6–7) makes it possible to create a measure of Gnostic presence similar to the measure of Christianization. Cities known to have had active Gnostic groups prior to the year 200 were scored two. Those having Gnostic groups prior to the year 400 were scored one. Cities not known to have had Gnostic groups by 400 were scored zero. Those scored two were Alexandria, Antioch, Caesarea Maritima, Carthage, Ephesus, Pergamum, Rome, Sardis, and Smyrna. Those scored one were Apamea, Damascus, Edessa, and Memphis. The others were scored zero.

Table 6.2 shows a substantial positive correlation between Gnostics and Christianization (.59). Moreover, Gnostic presence is significantly correlated with population size, in agreement with Fischer's theory. The table also shows a significant correlation between Gnostic presence and synagogues. These findings are worth pursuing at greater length.

For the past century there has been a serious debate about the connections between Gnosticism, on the one hand, and Christianity and Judaism, on the other. Late in the nineteenth century, Harnack (1894) was content to classify the Gnostics as a Christian heresy, as an acutely Hellenized brand of Christianity. Soon thereafter, however, many scholars (e.g., Friedlander 1898) began to trace the origins of the Gnostics to Jewish roots, and to regard Christianity and Gnosticism as *parallel offshoots* of first-century Judaism. Despite the Christian content of most of the manuscripts discovered at Nag Hammadi, the debate continues, and the view that the two movements were parallel probably has more support these days than does the view that the Gnostics were primarily a competing stream within Christianity. Birger Pearson, echoing Friedlander, puts this position most forcefully: "Gnosticism is not, in its origins, a 'Christian' heresy, but . . . it is, in fact, a 'Jewish' heresy" (1973:35).

If we bear that in mind, table 6.4 is of more than passing interest. Here regression analysis is used to assess the net effects of Christianization and Jewish presence on the rise of Gnosticism. The results are very conclusive—at least from the statisti-

141

TABLE 6.4
Regression: Dependent Variable Is Gnosticism

Independent Variables	Unstandardized Betas	Standardized Betas	Standard Error	T
Christianization	0.678	0.578	0.299	2.262[a]
Synagogues	−0.022	−0.012	0.470	−0.047

Multiple R-Square = 0.344   Y-Intercept = 0.067

[a] Significant beyond .05.

cal point of view. When the effects of Christianization are held constant, no direct Jewish effects remain. Whereas Jewish presence has a very substantial impact on the spread of Christianity (see table 6.3), only Christianity seems to have any impact on the rise of Gnosticism. This suggests a causal order fully in keeping with Harnack's original position: that Christianity began as a Jewish heresy and its initial appeal was to Jews, but that Gnosticism began subsequently as a Christian heresy, appealing mainly to Christians (from whom it adopted its very stridently anti-Jewish content).

Such statistical evidence is not, of course, conclusive proof that Gnosticism was a Christian heresy. But it seems worth noting here that participants in this debate may well be talking past one another. As I understand the proponents of the Jewish origins of Gnosticism, their concern has been to trace the origins of some of the central mystical notions of the Gnostics to prior Jewish writers. But as sociologists understand these matters, heresy per se has little to do with the pedigree of ideas and consists primarily of the embodiment of "deviant" ideas in a *social movement*. Put another way, writings can be heretical, but only human beings can be heretics. Moreover, the origins of ideas and of movements need not, and often are not, the same. Consider the many modern groups with spurious claims to unbroken descent from ancient pagan cults. Judged by their doctrines, their claims to be of ancient origin are true. But an examination of their "human history" reveals them to be of contemporary origins. Thus Gnostic writers could have been profoundly influenced by the writings of earlier Jewish mystics without representing a social movement coexisting with Christianity and deriving from pre-Christian origins among Jews. Although the data in table 6.4 have no implications for the origins of Gnostic ideas, they do encourage the conclusion that Gnosticism, as a social movement, was a Christian heresy.

CONCLUSION

Whatever the impact of table 6.4 on historical interpretations of Gnosticism, it is obvious that the other findings reported in this chapter are not going to greatly revise social histories of the rise of Christianity. Even without quantification, every competent historian has known that the Christian movement arose most rapidly in the Greco-Roman cities of Asia Minor, sustained by the very large communities of the Jewish diaspora. Indeed, the findings of greatest substantive interest are probably those lending support to Fischer's propositions about city size and subcultural deviance.

In my judgment, the real surprises are statistical, not substantive. The magnitudes and stability of the statistical outcomes are amazing and strongly testify that a data set based on these twenty-two cities can be of great scholarly value—to the extent that we are able to identify and secure interesting variables.

It strikes me that many additional variables could be created by scholars with the proper training. It would be very interesting to build rates for these cities (and perhaps other aggregate units) based on the immense collections of inscriptions. For example, since historians are agreed that Christianity was one of many new religions to come out of the East, can we use inscriptions to estimate when and where these "Oriental cults" gained followings? In chapter 9 we will examine a variable based on when and whether the Isis cult had a temple in these cities, but many more could be coded.

Initially, I had hoped to create measures of social disorganization of these cities, especially factors that disrupt integration by reducing the strength of interpersonal attachments. It is axiomatic that conformity to the norms is the result of attachments—to the extent that we value our relationships with others, we will conform in order to retain their esteem. When people lack attachments, they have much greater freedom to deviate from the norms. In modern studies, unconventional behavior is strongly correlated with various measures of population turnover and instability. For example, where larger proportions of the U.S. and Canadian populations are newcomers or have recently moved from one residence to another, rates of participation in unconventional religious activities are high (Stark and Bainbridge 1985).

I began by examining data on when and how a city was founded, or refounded, and the ethnic heterogeneity of its population. I was fascinated that both Corinth and Carthage had stood empty when Caesar decided to refound them in order to transport large numbers of Rome's "undesirable" population. To this he added a bunch of retired legionnaires who, in turn, drew numbers of women to the city from nearby villages. Talk about Dodge City, or some other wild and wooly place. As I proceeded, however, I began to realize that *all* the cities of the empire were incredibly disorganized, even compared with rapidly growing and industrializing cities of the nineteenth century, the ones that caused early sociologists to express endless gloom and doom. What Rome had achieved was political unity at the expense of cultural chaos. No one has captured this fact more lucidly that Ramsay MacMullen in the opening sentences of his remarkable work on paganism:

> It was a proper melting pot. If we imagined the British Empire of a hundred years ago all in one piece, all of its parts touching each other, so one could travel . . . from Rangoon to Belfast with-

out the interposition of any ocean, and if we could thus sense as one whole an almost limitless diversity of tongues, cults, traditions, and levels of education, then the true nature of the Mediterranean world in [the Roman era] . . . would strike our minds. (1981:xi)

For these reasons I ceased my efforts to compare cities in terms of disorganization and shall, instead, devote the next chapter to tracing how the acute disorganization of Greco-Roman cities in general eased the rise of Christianity.

Greco-Roman cities were covered with graffiti—this anti-Christian example (ca. 200) was found in Rome. It shows an ass-headed figure on the cross and reads, "Alexamenos worships his god."

Urban Chaos and Crisis:
The Case of Antioch

CHRISTIANITY was an urban movement,[1] and the New Testament was set down by urbanites. Indeed, many scholars believe that the Gospel of Matthew was composed in Antioch—the fourth largest city of the Roman Empire at the time.

If we want to understand how the rise of Christianity was shaped by the sociocultural environment of those who first put it into written words, we must comprehend the physical and social structures of the Greco-Roman city. Moreover, if we want to understand the immense popular appeal of the early church, we must understand how the message of the New Testament and the social relations it sustained solved acute problems afflicting Greco-Roman cities. Here too Antioch is of special interest because it was unusually receptive to the Christian movement, sustaining a relatively large and affluent Christian community quite early on (Longenecker 1985).

For these reasons, in this chapter I shall assemble some basic facts about Greco-Roman cities—with special emphasis on Antioch—in order to illuminate the physical realities of everyday life. What was it like to live there? Frankly, I was amazed to discover how difficult it is to find any answers. Even when books have titles indicating that they are about cities of the Greco-Roman era, there is usually next to nothing in them about the physical environment of the city. For example, Numa Denis Fustel de Coulanges's classic work *The Ancient City*, published in 1864 (and suggested to me as an exception to this claim) discusses nothing but the culture and customs of Greco-Roman

A preliminary version of this chapter appeared as "Antioch as the Social Situation for Matthew's Gospel," in *Social History of the Matthean Community*, ed. David L. Balch (Minneapolis: Fortress Press), 189–210.

times, and his title simply means that the setting was urban. The city per se could as well have been a figment of imagination, for there is not a word about streets, sewers, plumbing, water supplies, buildings, industry, markets, ethnic enclaves, crime, garbage, beggars, or any of the realities of urban life. In fact, the word "house" appears only in several passing references, and no houses are described.

Or consider a modern work with nearly the same title, *The City in the Ancient World*, by Mason Hammond (1972), published as part of the Harvard Studies in Urban History. This volume has an excellent index. Under "Roman citizenship," the index lists twenty-four page references. Entries also appear for Romulus, Trojan war, Borneo, and even Pleistocene period. But not one of the following words occurs in this index: aqueduct, bath(s), bathing, build, building, crime, death, disease, environment, epidemic, ethnic, feces, food, fuel, garbage, homes, house, housing, manure, pipes, plague, plumbing, privy, sewer, smoke, street, urine, washing, waste, or water. The omission of these index listings reflects the fact that this book too is about culture, and about political and military history, and is not about cities at all. Let me hasten to acknowledge that John E. Stambaugh's *The Ancient Roman City* (1988) is a fine exception to this rule. Indeed, it guided me to many valuable sources from which I could document points I initially had been forced to infer on the basis of what is known to be true of premodern cities in general. Moreover, some time after I had published the essay on which this chapter is based, I came upon Jerome Carcopino's *Daily Life in Ancient Rome*, the expanded English translation of which first appeared in 1940. The work is, of course, a classic. But, having no formal training in either early church or Roman history (or in any kind of history, for that matter), I have had to discover even the classics in a somewhat haphazard fashion. In any event, in Carcopino I discovered a kindred spirit who used his mastery of the ancient sources and of modern archaeology to explore even the grimy aspects of daily life.

Guided by Stambaugh and by Carcopino, and drawing on

the wealth of historical demography on premodern cities in other eras, I am able to reconstruct essential features of cities within which Christianity arose—the extraordinary levels of urban disorder, social dislocation, filth, disease, misery, fear, and cultural chaos that existed. In this chapter I shall depict these cities, paying special attention to Antioch, in order to set the stage for theses to be developed in the concluding chapters—that these conditions gave Christianity the opportunity to exploit fully its immense competitive advantages vis-à-vis paganism and other religious movements of the day as a *solution* to these problems.

PHYSICAL SOURCES OF CHRONIC URBAN MISERY

The first important fact about Greco-Roman cities is that they were small, in terms of both area and population. When Antioch was founded in about 300 B.C.E., its walls enclosed slightly less than one square mile, laid out along a southwest-to-northeast axis. Eventually Antioch grew to be about two miles long and about one mile wide (Finley 1977). Like many Greco-Roman cities, Antioch was small in area because it was initially founded as a fortress (Levick 1967). Once the walls were up, it was very expensive to expand.

Within so small an area, it is astonishing that the city's population was as large as it was: at the end of the first century Antioch had a total population of about 150,000 (Chandler and Fox 1974). This population total applies to inhabitants of the city proper—those living within, or perhaps immediately against, its walls. It does not apply to those living on the nearby rural estates or in the various satellite communities such as Daphne (Levick 1967). Given this population and the area of the city, it is easily calculated that the population density of Antioch was roughly 75,000 inhabitants per square mile or 117 per acre. As a comparison, in Chicago today there are 21 inhabitants per acre; San Francisco has 23, and New York City overall has 37.

Even Manhattan Island has only 100 inhabitants per acre—and keep in mind that Manhattanites are very spread out vertically, while ancient cities crammed their populations into structures that seldom rose above five stories. In Rome, it was illegal to construct private buildings higher than 20 meters (65.6 feet). Despite these height limits, buildings in Greco-Roman cities frequently collapsed. Carcopino reported that Rome "was constantly filled with the noise of buildings collapsing or being torn down to prevent it; and the tenants of an *insula* lived in constant expectation of its coming down on their heads" (1940:31–32). The tenements collapsed because they were too lightly built and because the less desirable upper floors housed the poor, who so subdivided them that the upper floors became heavier than the floors below, and heavier than the beams and foundations could carry. Given the frequent earthquakes in Antioch, it is unlikely that any of the tenements there were more than several stories tall; hence Antioch was probably functionally more crowded than Rome. Keep in mind too that modern New Yorkers do not share their space with livestock, nor are their streets fouled by horse and oxen traffic.

These density comparisons, striking as they are, still sharply underestimate the population crush because large areas of Greco-Roman cities were occupied by public buildings, monuments, and temples. In Pompeii this area amounted to 35 percent of the city's area (Jashemski 1979), in Ostia 43 percent was taken up in this way (Meiggs 1974), and in Rome the public-monumental sector occupied half of the city (Stambaugh 1988). If we assume that Antioch was average in this regard, we must subtract 40 percent of its area in order to calculate density. The new figure is 195 persons per acre. This is less dense than Stambaugh's (1988) estimate of 302 per acre in Rome, but it is very close to MacMullen's (1974) estimate of Rome's density as 200 inhabitants per acre. Both cities seem to have been somewhat denser than Corinth—I calculate the latter to have had about 137 persons per acre. As a comparison, the density in modern Bombay is 183 per acre, and it is 122 in Calcutta.

But even these figures fail to convey fully the crowded conditions of everyday life in these cities. As Michael White (1987) has noted, many writers seem to assume that everyone lived in huge atrium houses like the ones built by MGM for *Ben-Hur* (cf. Koester 1987:73); in fact, though, most people lived in tiny cubicles in multistoried tenements. Carcopino has calculated that in Rome there was "only one private house for every 26 blocks of apartments" (1940:23), and suggests that this ratio was typical of Greco-Roman cities. Within these tenements, the crowding was extreme—the tenants rarely had more than one room in which "entire families were herded together" (Carcopino 1940:44). Thus, as Stambaugh tells us, privacy was "a hard thing to find" (1988:178). Not only were people terribly crowded within these buildings, the streets were so narrow that if people leaned out their window they could chat with someone living across the street without having to raise their voices. The famous roads leading out of Rome, such as the Via Appia or the Via Latina, were from 4.8 to 6.5 meters (or 15.7 to 21.3 feet) wide! Roman law required that the actual streets of Rome be at least 2.9 meters (9.5 feet) wide (Carcopino 1940:45–46), but many parts of the city contained only footpaths. As for Antioch, consider that its main thoroughfare, admired throughout the Greco-Roman world, was only 30 feet wide (Finley 1977).

To make matters worse, Greco-Roman tenements lacked both furnaces and fireplaces. Cooking was done over wood or charcoal braziers, which were also the only source of heat; since tenements lacked chimneys, the rooms were always smoky in winter. Because windows could be "closed" only by "hanging cloths or skins blown by rain" (Carcopino 1940:36), the tenements were sufficiently drafty to prevent frequent asphyxiation. But the drafts increased the danger of rapidly spreading fires, and "dread of fire was an obsession among rich and poor alike" (Carcopino 1940:33).

Packer (1967) doubted that people could actually spend much time in quarters so cramped and squalid. Thus he concluded that the typical residents of Greco-Roman cities spent their lives mainly in public places and that the average "domicile must have served only as a place to sleep and store possessions" (Packer 1967:87).

One thing is certain when human density is high: urgent problems of sanitation arise. However, until I discovered Carcopino's volume, I found very few activities more frustrating than attempting to discover details about such matters as sewers, plumbing, garbage disposal, or even the water supply in Greco-Roman cities. One can spend an afternoon checking the indexes of scores of histories of Greece and Rome without finding any of these words listed. The aqueducts are, of course, often mentioned, as are the public baths and the public latrines often constructed next to the baths. It is all well and good to admire the Romans for their aqueducts and their public baths, but we must not fail to see the obvious fact that the human and animal density of ancient cities would place an incredible burden even on modern sewerage, garbage disposal, and water systems. Keep in mind too that there *was no soap*. Hence it is self-evident that, given the technological capacities of the time, the Greco-Roman city and its inhabitants must have been extremely filthy.

Consider the water supply. Aqueducts brought water to many Greco-Roman cities, but once there it was poorly kept and quite maldistributed. In most cities the water was piped to fountains and public buildings such as the baths. Some was also piped to the homes of the very rich. But for the rest of the residents, water had to be carried home in jugs. This necessarily greatly limited the use of water. There could have been very little for scrubbing floors or washing clothes. Nor could there have been much for bathing, and I very much doubt that the public baths truly served the public in the inclusive sense. Worse yet, the water often was very contaminated. In his exceptional study of Greek and Roman technology, K. D. White (1984) pointed out that whether their water came via aqueducts or from springs or wells, all of the larger Greco-Roman cities had to store water in cisterns. He also noted that "untreated water[,] . . . when left stagnant, encourages the growth of algae and other organisms, rendering the water malodorous, unpalatable, and after a time, undrinkable" (1984:168). No wonder Pliny advised that "all water is the better for being boiled" (quoted in White 1984:168).

Upon closer examination, the notion that Greco-Roman cities enjoyed efficient sewers and sanitation also turns out to be largely an illusion. Granted, an underground sewer carried water from the baths of Rome through the public latrines next door and on out of the city. But what about the rest of the city? Indeed, just as it is obviously silly to suppose that the wretched masses of Rome soaked nightly in the Roman baths, hobnobbing with senators and equestrians (the capacity of the baths reveals this to be a physical as well as social absurdity), it is equally silly to think that everyone jogged off to the public latrines each time that nature called. Rome, like all cities until modern times, was dependent on chamber pots and pit latrines. Indeed, Stambaugh (1988) suggests that most tenements depended entirely on pots. As for sewers, they were, for the most part, open ditches into which slops and chamber pots were dumped. Moreover, these pots were frequently emptied out the window at night from several stories up (de Camp 1966). As Carcopino described it:

> There were other poor devils who found their stairs too steep and the road to these dung pits too long, and to save themselves further trouble would empty the contents of their chamber pots from their heights into the streets. So much the worse for the passer-by who happened to intercept the unwelcome gift! Fouled and sometimes even injured, as in Juvenal's satire, he had no redress save to lodge a complaint against the unknown assailant; many passages in the *Digest* indicate that Roman jurists did not disdain to take cognisance of this offense. (1940:42)

Given limited water and means of sanitation, and the incredible density of humans and animals, most people in Greco-Roman cities must have lived in filth beyond our imagining.

Tenement cubicles were smoky, dark, often damp, and always dirty. The smell of sweat, urine, feces, and decay permeated everything; "dust, rubbish, and filth accumulated; and finally bugs ran riot" (Carcopino 1940:44). Outside, on the street, it was little better. Mud, open sewers, manure, and crowds. In fact, human corpses—adult as well as infant—were sometimes just pushed into the street and abandoned (Stambaugh 1988). And even if the wealthiest households could provide ample space and cleanliness, they could not prevent many aspects of the filth and decay surrounding them from penetrating their homes. The stench of these cities must have been overpowering for many miles—especially in warm weather—and even the richest Romans must have suffered. No wonder they were so fond of incense. Moreover, Greco-Roman cities must have been smothered in flies, mosquitoes, and other insects that flourish where there is much stagnant water and exposed filth. And, like bad odors, insects are very democratic.

The constant companion of filth, insects, and crowding is disease. This is especially so when societies lack antibiotics or, indeed, have no knowledge of germs. Here too one pages uselessly through nearly all of the books on Roman and Greek society or on the rise of Christianity, for words such as "epidemic," "plague," and even "disease" almost never appear. This seems incredible, for not only was the Greco-Roman world periodically struck by deadly epidemics, but illness and physical affliction were probably the dominant features of daily life in this era (Patrick 1967). For example, a recent analysis of decayed human fecal remains from a cesspit in Jerusalem found an abundance of tapeworm and whipworm eggs, which indicate "the ingestion of fecally contaminated foods or . . . unsanitary living arrangements in which people came into contact with human excrement" (Cahill et al. 1991:69). Although being infected with either or both of these intestinal parasites is not fatal, both can cause anemia and thus make victims more vulnerable to other illness. Moreover, where such parasitic infection was nearly universal, most people also undoubtedly suffered from "other fecal-borne bacteria and protozoal diseases."

The Greco-Roman city was a pesthole of infectious disease—because it was always thus in cities. Indeed, it was not until the twentieth century that urban mortality was sufficiently reduced that the cities of western Europe and North America could sustain their populations without additional in-migration from rural areas (Wrigley 1969). If this was true of relatively modern cities, think what must have been the case in places like Rome and Antioch. Boak noted that the cities of the Roman Empire needed such a substantial amount of in-migration in order to offset mortality that, as the rural population declined, Roman cities must have begun to shrink (1955a:14).

In chapter 5 the high mortality rates of the empire were mentioned. Historical demographers agree that "the average lifetime of the ancients was short" (Durand 1960:365). And although there have been some disagreements among those who have attempted to estimate life expectancies from Roman tomb inscriptions (Burn 1953; Russell 1958; Durand 1960; Hopkins 1966), none challenges that life expectancy at birth was less than thirty years—and probably substantially less (Boak 1955a).

It is important to realize that where mortality rates are very high, the health of those still living is very poor. The majority of those living in Greco-Roman cities must have suffered from chronic health conditions that caused them pain and some degree of disability, and of which many would soon die. Stambaugh pointed out that, compared with modern cities, sickness was highly visible on the streets of Greco-Roman cities: "Swollen eyes, skin rashes, and lost limbs are mentioned over and over again in the sources as part of the urban scene" (1988:137). As Bagnall reported, in a time before photography or fingerprinting, written contracts offered descriptive information about the parties and "generally include their distinctive

155

disfigurements, mostly scars" (1993:187). Bagnall then cited a papyrus (*P.Abinn.* 67v) that lists a number of persons owing debts, *all* of whom were scarred. Bagnall also pointed out that

> ancient letter writers are obsessed with wishes for health, reports on the sender's health, and inquiries after the health of the recipient. A modern reader might be tempted to dismiss [this] as so much polite formula. . . . But that would be quite wrong. There are many very strong statements reproaching correspondents for not writing about their health, like "I am astonished that so far you have not written me about your health." (1993:185)

Moreover, as we have seen, women in Greco-Roman times were especially afflicted because of chronic infections resulting from childbirth and abortion. Little wonder that healing was such a central aspect of both paganism and early Christianity (MacMullen 1981; Kee 1983, 1986).

Social Chaos and Chronic Urban Misery

Historians have tended to present a portrait of the Greco-Roman city as one in which most people—rich and poor alike—were descended from many generations of residents. But nothing could be further from the truth, especially during the first several centuries of the Christian era. As noted, Greco-Roman cities required a constant and substantial stream of newcomers simply to maintain their populations. As a result, at any given moment a very considerable proportion of the population consisted of *recent* newcomers—Greco-Roman cities were peopled by strangers.

It is well known that the crime rates of modern cities are highly correlated with rates of population turnover. Crime and delinquency are higher to the extent that neighborhoods or cities are filled with newcomers (Crutchfield, Geerken, and Gove 1983; Stark et al. 1983). This is because where there are large numbers of newcomers, people will be deficient in interpersonal attachments, and it is attachments that bind us to the moral order (see chapter 1). This proposition would predict that Greco-Roman cities would have been filled with crime and disorder, especially at night. And they were. As Carcopino described the situation:

> Night fell over the city like the shadow of a great danger, diffused, sinister, and menacing. Everyone fled to his home, shut himself in, and barricaded the entrance. The shops fell silent, safety chains were drawn behind the leaves of the doors. . . . If the rich had to sally forth, they were accompanied by slaves who carried torches to light and protect them on their way. . . . Juvenal sighs that to go out to supper without having made your will was to expose yourself to reproach of carelessness . . . [W]e need only turn to the leaves of the *Digest* [to discover the extent to which criminals] abounded in the city. (1940:47)

Moreover, given the immense cultural diversity of the empire, the waves of newcomers to Greco-Roman cities were of very diverse origins and therefore fractured the local culture into numerous ethnic fragments. Again, Antioch offers an instructive example.

When founded by Seleucus I, the city was laid out in two primary sections—one for Syrians and one for Greeks—and, taking a realistic view of ethnic relations, the king had the two sections walled off from one another (Stambaugh and Balch 1986). According to Downey (1963), the ethnic origins of the original settlement consisted of retired soldiers from Seleucus's Macedonian army, Cretans, Cypriotes, Argives, and Herakleidae (who had previously been settled on Mount Silipius), Athenians from Atigonia, Jews from nearby Palestine (some of whom had served as mercenaries in Seleucus's army), native Syrians, and a number of slaves of diverse origins. As the city grew, its Jewish population seems to have increased markedly (Meeks and Wilken 1978). And, of course, a substantial number of Romans were added to this mixture when the city was seized by the empire in 64 B.C.E. During the days of Roman rule, the city drew an influx of Gauls, Germans, and other "barbarians," some brought as slaves, others as legionnaires. Smith estimates that the "citizens were divided into 18 tribes, distributed locally" (1857:143). I take him to mean that there were eighteen identifiable ethnic quarters within Antioch.

Ramsay MacMullen describes the Roman world in this period as "a proper melting pot" (1981:xi). But it is not clear how much melting actually went on. What does seem clear is that the social integration of Greco-Roman cities was severely disrupted by the durability of internal ethnic divisions, which typically took the form of distinctive ethnic precincts. Ethnic diversity and a constant influx of newcomers will tend to undercut social integration, thus exposing residents to a variety of harmful consequences, including high rates of deviance and disorder. Indeed, this is a major reason why Greco-Roman cities were so prone to riots.

NATURAL AND SOCIAL DISASTERS

When we examine the magnificent ruins of classical cities, we have a tendency to see them as extraordinarily durable and permanent—after all, they were built of stone and have endured the centuries. But this is mostly an illusion. What we are usually looking at are simply the *last* ruins of a city that was turned to ruins repeatedly. And if the physical structures of Greco-Roman cities were transitory, so too were their populations; cities often were almost entirely depopulated and then repopulated, and their ethnic composition often was radically changed in the process. The renowned medical historian A. Castiglioni (1947) noted that "there were terrible epidemics which destroyed entire cities, sometimes accompanied by inundations and earthquakes, which were frequent in Italy in the first centuries of our era" (quoted in Patrick 1967:245).

These catastrophes were not limited to Italy. The cities of

Asia Minor seem to have been even more afflicted by natural disasters, to say nothing of the ravages of conquest and riot. The following summary of natural and social disasters that struck Antioch is instructive and rather typical. I have not attempted a careful survey of the sources to assemble my list but have depended primarily on Downey (1963). The totals are probably incomplete. Moreover, I skipped the many serious floods because they did not cause substantial loss of life. Still, the summary shows how extremely vulnerable Greco-Roman cities were to attacks, fires, earthquakes, famines, epidemics, and devastating riots. Indeed, this litany of disasters is so staggering that it is difficult to grasp its human meaning.

During the course of about six hundred years of intermittent Roman rule, Antioch was taken by unfriendly forces eleven times and was plundered and sacked on five of these occasions. The city was also put to siege, but did not fall, two other times. In addition, Antioch burned entirely or in large part four times, three times by accident and once when the Persians carefully burned the city to the ground after picking it clean of valuables and taking the surviving population into captivity. Because the temples and many public building were built of stone, it is easy to forget that Greco-Roman cities consisted primarily of wood-frame buildings, plastered over, that were highly flammable and tightly packed together. Severe fires were frequent, and there was no pumping equipment with which to fight them. Besides the four huge conflagrations noted above, there were many large fires set during several of the six major periods of rioting that racked the city. By a major riot I mean one resulting in substantial damage and death, as distinct from the city's frequent riots in which only a few were killed.

Antioch probably suffered from literally hundreds of significant earthquakes during these six centuries, but eight were so severe that nearly everything was destroyed and huge numbers died. Two other quakes may have been nearly as serious. At least three killer epidemics struck the city—with mortality rates probably running above 25 percent in each. Finally, there were at least five really serious famines. That comes to forty-one natural and social catastrophes, or an average of one every fifteen years.

Why in the world did people keep going back and rebuilding? One would suppose that the earthquakes alone might have caused Antioch to be abandoned. The answer is simple. Antioch was of immense strategic importance as the key stronghold for defending the border with Persia. M. I. Finley explained:

> [The] location [is] admirably suited to control the Syrian Near East. The site is at the southwest corner of the fertile Amik plain, at a point where the Orontes river (modern Nahr el 'Asi) cuts through the mountains to the sea. Antioch stands at the focal point for communications with Palestine to the south by way of the Orontes and Jordan rivers and with the Euphrates to the east by way of Aleppo. (1977:222)

Indeed, Antioch was a fortress *controlling* the Orontes—seven bridges crossed the river, and the primary site of public buildings, including the palace and the circus, was an island surrounded by two channels of the river. As Barbara Levick explained, "the Romans thought it dangerous to leave such a site unsupervised and settled veterans there as soon as they could" (1967:46). And wherever Rome planted such colonies, there was always a rush of civilian settlers in pursuit of economic opportunity. Thus Antioch continued to change hands and to be rebuilt and resettled again and again. Indeed, it lived on to be retaken from Islam several times by Byzantine forces and then by Crusaders.

Any accurate portrait of Antioch in New Testament times must depict a city filled with misery, danger, fear, despair, and hatred. A city where the average family lived a squalid life in filthy and cramped quarters, where at least half of the children died at birth or during infancy, and where most of the children who lived lost at least one parent before reaching maturity. A city filled with hatred and fear rooted in intense ethnic antagonisms and exacerbated by a constant stream of strangers. A city so lacking in stable networks of attachments that petty incidents could prompt mob violence. A city where crime flourished and the streets were dangerous at night. And, perhaps above all, a city repeatedly smashed by cataclysmic catastrophes: where a resident could expect literally to be homeless from time to time, providing that he or she was among the survivors.

People living in such circumstances must often have despaired. Surely it would not be strange for them to have concluded that the end of days drew near. And surely too they must often have longed for relief, for hope, indeed for salvation.

CONCLUSION

In this book's closing chapters I will examine how Christianity served as a revitalization movement that arose in response to the misery, chaos, fear, and brutality of life in the urban Greco-Roman world. In anticipation of those discussions, let me merely suggest here that Christianity revitalized life in Greco-Roman cities by providing new norms and new kinds of social relationships able to cope with many urgent urban problems. To cities filled with the homeless and impoverished, Christianity offered charity as well as hope. To cities filled with newcomers and strangers, Christianity offered an immediate basis for attachments. To cities filled with orphans and widows, Christianity provided a new and expanded sense of family. To cities torn by violent ethnic strife, Christianity offered a new basis for social solidarity (cf. Pelikan 1987:21). And to cities faced with epidemics, fires, and earthquakes, Christianity offered effective nursing services.

It must be recognized, of course, that earthquakes, fires, plagues, riots, and invasions did not first appear at the start of the Christian era. People had been enduring catastrophes for centuries without the aid of Christian theology or Christian social structures. Hence I am by no means suggesting that the misery of the ancient world caused the advent of Christianity. What

I am going to argue is that once Christianity did appear, its superior capacity for meeting these chronic problems soon became evident and played a major role in its ultimate triumph.

Since Antioch suffered acutely from all of these urban problems, it was in acute need of solutions. No wonder the early Christian missionaries were so warmly received in this city. For what they brought was not simply an urban movement, but a *new culture* capable of making life in Greco-Roman cities more tolerable.

CHAPTER 8

The Martyrs:
Sacrifice as Rational Choice

IN CHAPTER 1 of *The Martyrs of Palestine*, Eusebius identifies Procopius as the "first of the martyrs." Having been called before the governor, he was ordered to make libations to the four emperors. He refused and was "immediately beheaded." Soon thereafter other bishops of the church in Palestine were seized. They did not merely confront the threat of execution, for the governor was determined to break the Christian movement by using torture to force its leaders to recant. Eusebius reported:

> Some were scourged with innumerable strokes of the lash, others racked in their limbs and galled in their sides with torturing instruments, some with intolerable fetters, by which the joints of their hands were dislocated. Nevertheless they bore the event. (1850 ed.)

In chapter 2, Eusebius tells the story of Romanus, who was seized at Antioch:

> When the judge had informed him that he was to die by flames, with a cheerful countenance and a most ardent mind he received the sentence and was led away. He was then tied to the stake, and when the wood was heaped up about him, and they were kindling the pile, only waiting the word from the expected emperor, he exclaimed, "where then is the fire?" Saying this he was summoned again before the emperor, to be subjected to new tortures, and therefore had his tongue cut out, which he

---

This chapter draws heavily on the creative new theoretical work of my friend and sometime coauthor Laurence Iannaccone (1992, 1994). The theoretical propositions included in this chapter appeared previously in Stark and Iannaccone 1992 in the portion of that essay for which Iannaccone was primarily responsible.

The total number of Christians martyred by the Romans probably was fewer than a thousand. But their steadfastness greatly strengthened the faith of other Christians and impressed many pagans.

bore with the greatest of fortitude, as he proved his actions to all, showing also that the power of God is always present to the aid of those who are obliged to bear any hardship for the sake of religion, to lighten their labours, and to strengthen their ardor.

In chapter 8 we learn of the brave Valentina who was seized with other worshipers in Gaza and brought before Maximinus. As the executioners brutally tortured another Christian woman,

> unable to bear the merciless, cruel, and inhuman scene before her, and with courage exceeding all [Greek heros], she exclaimed against the judge from the midst of the crowd, "And how long, then, will you thus cruelly torture my sister?" He [Maximinus], the more bitterly incensed by this, ordered the woman immediately to be seized. She was then dragged into the midst . . . and attempts were first made to bring her over to sacrifice by persuasion. But when she refused she was dragged to the altar by force . . . [W]ith intrepid step, she kicked the altar, and overturned all on it, together with the fire. Upon this, the judge, exasperated, like a savage beast, applied tortures beyond all that he had done before.

To Eusebius, the bravery and steadfastness of the martyrs was proof of Christian virtue. Indeed, many pagans were deeply impressed. Galen, the distinguished Greek physician to Roman emperors, wrote of Christians that "their contempt of death (and of its sequel) is patent to us every day" (quoted in Benko 1984:141). But that is not the way modern social scientists have reacted. In their eyes, such sacrifices are so unthinkable as to be obvious symptoms of psychopathology. Several have attributed the ability of early Christians to endure as rooted in *masochism* (Riddle 1931; Menninger 1938; Reik 1976). That is, we are expected to believe that the martyrs defied their accusers because they loved pain and probably gained sexual pleasure from it.

Thus in his monograph *The Martyrs: A Study in Social Control*, written under the supervision of Shirley Jackson Case at the University of Chicago Divinity School, Donald W. Riddle claimed:

> One of the elements of the morbid desire for martyrdom was the abnormal enjoyment of the pain which it involved. . . . Clearly, the voluntary surrender of one's self to the experience of martyrdom, when it was known that the most exquisite tortures were involved, is *prima facie* evidence of the presence of the tendency towards masochism. (1931:64)

In later passages Riddle discovered unmistakable evidence of masochism whenever Christians were able to endure their tortures with composure or dignity, and diagnosed acute cases of masochism whenever anyone defied the state by voluntary acceptance of martyrdom.

Views such as this are not unusual among social scientists. Rather, from the beginning, social scientific studies of religion have been shaped by a single question: *What makes them do it?* How *could* any rational person make sacrifices on behalf of unseen supernatural entities? The explicit answer to this question nearly always has been that religion is rooted in the *irrational.* Keep in mind that the imputation of irrational religious behavior by social scientists is not limited to extraordinary actions such as martyrdom. Rather, they have been content to apply the irrationalist argument to such ordinary activities as prayer, observance of moral codes, and contributions of time and wealth. For whether it be the imputation of outright psychopathology, of groundless fears, or merely of faulty reasoning and misperceptions, the irrationalist assumption has dominated the field. The notion that normal, sophisticated people could be religious has been limited to a few social scientists willing to allow their own brand of very mild, "intrinsic," religiousness to pass the test of rationality.

Thus, until recently, the social *scientific* study of religion was nothing of the sort. The field was far more concerned with discrediting religion than with understanding it. This is clear when it is realized that *only* in the area of religious belief and behavior have social scientists not based their theories on a rational choice premise. Indeed, my colleagues and I recently showed that antagonism toward all forms of religion and the conviction that it soon must disappear in an enlightened world were articles of faith among the earliest social scientists, and that today social scientists are far less likely to be religious than are scholars in other areas, especially those in the physical and natural sciences (Stark, Iannaccone, and Finke 1995).

Nevertheless, despite the enormous weight of learned opinion that created and sustained it, the irrationalist approach to religion recently has fallen upon evil times—beset by contrary evidence and by the unanticipated theoretical power of rational choice theories imported from microeconomics and modified appropriately. This chapter represents another step in that direction and extends my efforts to establish a scientific, rather than a polemical and political, basis for studies of religion. In it I shall attempt to show that, when analyzed properly, religious sacrifices and stigmas—even when acute cases are considered—usually turn out to represent rational choices. Indeed, the more that people must sacrifice for their faith, the greater the value of the rewards they gain in return. Put in conventional economic language, in terms of the ratio of costs to benefits, within limits the more expensive the religion, the better bargain it is.

To proceed, I will introduce a series of propositions drawn from rational choice theory (Iannaccone 1992, 1994; Stark and Iannaccone 1992, 1994). When applied to early Christianity, these propositions yield the conclusion that sacrifice and stigma were the dynamo behind the rise of Christianity—the factors that created strong organizations filled with highly committed members ready to do what needed to be done. For the fact is that Christianity was by far the best religious "bargain" around.

RELIGION AND RATIONALITY

Let us begin with a theoretical proposition: *Religion supplies compensators for rewards that are scarce or unavailable.*

A reward is *scarce* if its supply is sufficiently limited that not everyone (and perhaps not anyone) can have as much of it as they desire. The scarcest of all rewards are those that simply are not available in the here and now. Since these scarcest of rewards are among those most highly valued by most human beings, religions offer alternative means for gaining them: religious compensators are a sort of substitute for desired rewards.

Compensators, as noted in chapter 2, provide an explanation of how the desired reward (or an equivalent alternative) actually can be obtained, but propose a method for attaining the reward that is rather elaborate and lengthy: often the actual attainment will be in the distant future or even in another reality, and the truth of the explanation will be very difficult, if not impossible, to ascertain in advance. When a child asks for a bike and a parent proposes that the child keep his or her room clean for a year and get no grade below B during the same period, whereupon the bike will appear, a compensator has been issued in lieu of the desired reward. We can distinguish compensators from rewards because the latter is the thing wanted, the former a proposal about gaining the reward.

As reward-seeking beings, humans will always prefer the reward to the compensator, but they will often have no choice because some things we want cannot be had in sufficient supply by some people and some rewards cannot be had, here and now, by anyone. Compensators abound in all areas of life, but our interest here is in religious compensators. Let me note only the most obvious instance. Most people desire immortality. No one knows how to achieve that here and now—the Fountain of Youth remains elusive. But many religions offer instructions about how that reward can be achieved over the longer term. When one's behavior is guided by such a set of instructions, one has accepted a compensator. One is also exhibiting religious commitment, since the instructions always entail certain requirements vis-à-vis the divine. Indeed, it is usually necessary to enter into a long-term exchange relationship with the divine and with divinely inspired institutions in order to follow the instructions: effective religious organizations rest upon these underlying exchange relationships.

I want it to be clear that I imply nothing about the truth or falsity of religious compensators. My interest is limited to the process of rational choices by which humans value and exchange these compensators.

Religious compensators are imbued with unique advantages and disadvantages. On the one hand, they offer the prospect of huge rewards, rewards that are otherwise not plausibly obtainable from any other source. Only by evoking supernatural powers can religious compensators promise eternal life, reunion with the departed, a perfected soul, or unending bliss. The persistence of death, war, sin, and human misery need not invalidate these promises, since their truth and fulfillment are rooted in another reality. An individual may one day arrive at the conclusion that, in this life, virtue must be its own reward. But no one can know that virtue is not rewarded in the world to come, where the first shall be last and the last shall be first. On the other hand, neither can anyone know that virtue *is* rewarded in the world to come, or indeed whether such a world exists. Hence because these and other religious compensators are beyond the possibility of evaluation, they are inherently risky.

Let us now analyze how humans behave when confronted with risk and choice. The initial proposition is fundamental to the whole of social science: *Individuals choose their actions rationally, including those actions which concern compensators.*

Rational choice involves weighing the anticipated costs and benefits of actions and then seeking to act so as to maximize net benefits.

The assumption of rationality has numerous expressions in the social sciences. Economists speak of utility maximization; exchange theorists postulate that "people are more likely to perform an activity the more valuable they perceive the reward of that activity to be" (Homans 1964). Elsewhere I have proposed that "humans seek to maximize rewards and to minimize costs" (Stark 1992). But there is probably no reason to insist on one expression over another.

Many object to the rational choice proposition on the grounds that it is reductionistic. Assuredly, it is. Reductionism is the primary scientific task—to explain as much of the world as possible by reference to as little as possible. Moreover, surely it is not more reductionistic to attribute religious behavior to rational choices than to blame it on "false consciousness," "neurosis," or "masochism." Furthermore, the rational actor proposition does not assume that the actor necessarily has, or must obtain, complete information concerning optional actions. Later in this chapter I examine means humans use to seek more complete information about the validity of religious compensators, and how they rate sources as to the most "conclusive" validations. Because it is quite impossible to gain full knowledge about the ultimate fulfillment of many religious compensators, actors must select on the basis of incomplete information. But, as Gary S. Becker explained:

> Incomplete information ... should not, however, be confused with irrational or volatile behavior. The economic approach has developed a theory of the optimal or rational accumulation of costly information that implies, for example, greater investment in information when undertaking major than minor decisions. ... The assumption that information is often seriously incomplete because it is costly to acquire is used in the economic approach to explain the same kind of behavior that is explained by irrational and ... "non rational" behavior in other discussions. (1976:6–7)

That is, it often would be irrational, given the costs, to seek more complete information, and often it would be equally irrational to fail to act for want of more complete information since the costs of being wrong are much less than the costs of better information, and the potential gains from acting far outweigh the costs of acting.

But if humans seek to maximize, why is it that they do not all act alike? Here the preference axiom is vital: *People differ greatly in their relative evaluations of specific rewards or benefits.* Were I to stick closely to formulations from economic theory, I would have worded this to note that people have different "preference schedules" and therefore some people will evaluate any given reward or benefit more highly than will some other people. There is a considerable literature in the sociology of religion to demonstrate that people have decidedly different tastes in things religious,[1] some of which can be traced to variations in their existential circumstances (Argyle 1958; Glock and Stark 1965; Stark and Bainbridge 1985, 1987; Iannaccone 1988, 1990). At the most general level this proposition clarifies how it is possible for people to engage in exchanges.

I include this proposition here in large part to counter critics who claim that by postulating the rationality of religious behavior, I exclude all behavior that is not selfish or hedonistic, and that I thereby dismiss the power of religion to animate those altruists and ascetics who people the community of saints. This is simply wrong and trivializes the very behavior it ostensibly praises. To say that people differ in terms of their preference schedules is simply an uninspired way of saying that Mother Teresa may well be elevated to sainthood one day, not because she avoids rewards and pursues costs, but because of *what* she finds rewarding. To call Mother Teresa an altruist and thus classify her behavior as nonrational is to deny the finest of human capacities, our ability to love. Thus although rational choice theories restrict behavior to that which is consistent with a person's definitions of rewards, it has very little to say about the actual content of those rewards. This leaves all the room needed for people to be charitable, brave, unselfish, reverent, and even silly.

In combination, the first three propositions claim that individuals will evaluate religious compensators in essentially the same way that they evaluate all other objects of choice. They will evaluate their costs and benefits (including the "opportunity costs" that arise when one action can be undertaken only if others are forgone) and will "consume" those compensators which, together with their other actions, maximize net benefits. In particular, they will weigh the tremendous rewards posited by many religious compensators both against the cost of meeting the conditions that compensators always entail and against the risk that the posited rewards will not be forthcoming.

However, since people avoid risk just as surely as they seek rewards, compensators present people with classic *approach/avoidance* dilemmas. Individuals must somehow weigh the costs of a compensator against the value of the rewards to be received, allowing for the risk of getting nothing, or at least much less than was promised. However, since no probability of risk can be known directly, individuals must seek other sources of confidence—that is, humans will seek more complete information about the compensators they might select.

THE CREDIBILITY PROBLEM

But if the value of religious compensators cannot be known with certainty in this world, how *can* humans estimate the risk of investing in them? Five propositions explain how. The first two are these:

The perceived value of a religious compensator is established through social interactions and exchanges.

Individuals perceive a religious compensator as less risky, and hence more valuable, when it is promoted, produced, or consumed collectively.

Here we discover why religion is above all a social phenomenon. Those who attempt to practice a private, purely personal religion lack means for assessing its value. For them to place a high value on religious compensators would at least border on the irrational. Moreover, the religious activities of truly solitary religionists will receive little if any reinforcement and should therefore tend to be extinguished (ascetic religious "hermits" in fact are situated in a supportive social setting). But those who practice a religion within a group have a natural basis for estimating the value of their religious compensators. Such persons will tend to accept a value that is an average of the levels of confidence expressed by those with whom they interact (undoubtedly weighted by his or her confidence in each source). As we shall see shortly, this helps explain high levels of commitment—which can be analyzed as high levels of investment to keep compensators in force—sustained by congregations that are very strict about their confessional requirements of membership. Doubters lower the value assigned to compensators.

Thus religion is almost always a social phenomenon. Or, as an economist would put it, religion is a *collectively produced commodity*. It is obvious enough that many religious activities require group participation—liturgies and testimony meetings, congregational prayers and responsive readings, sermons and songs. But it is no less true that religious faith itself is a social product, collectively produced and maintained. Collective production is no less central to providing safeguards against fraud—a chronic problem of client cults where people obtain religious commodities from self-employed practitioners on a one-to-one basis (Stark and Bainbridge 1985).

Now, let us consider another proposition: *A religion's compensators are perceived as less risky, and hence more valuable, when there is credible evidence that participation in the religion generates tangible benefits that are not readily explained in secular terms.*

Testimonials are a common means of promoting secular products. Within religion, they rank as the primary technique by which religious groups act collectively to generate faith in their compensators. Of course, no testimony suffices to *prove* that a religion's otherworldly promises are true. But testifiers can and usually do convey their personal certainty that such is the case. Moreover, religious testimonials can enumerate the tangible benefits that a testifier attributes to his or her religious commitment. They can recount experiences of personal regeneration that followed conversion or renewal—victory over alcoholism, drug dependency, or marital infidelity. In more dramatic fashion some testifiers can claim to have benefited from miracles—supernatural interventions that averted catastrophe or provided inexplicable healing. In this way people offer evidence that a religion "works" and that its promises must therefore be true.

Testimonials are especially persuasive when they come from a trusted source, such as a personal acquaintance. Here again we see why successful religions gravitate toward collective production. Fellow members are much more trustworthy than strangers. Testimonials are also more persuasive when the testifiers have relatively little to gain (or better yet, much to lose) from having their claims heard and believed. Friends and fellow congregants have fewer incentives to overstate the benefits of the religion than do clergy, whose livelihood may depend on keeping the flock faithful. Hence: *Religious leaders have greater credibility when they receive low levels of material reward in return for their religious services.*

Put most bluntly, affluent clergy are never a match for lay preachers and impoverished ascetics in head-to-head credibility contests. It is as Walter Map observed, after seeing Waldensian representatives come to Rome in 1179: "They go about two by two, barefoot, clad in woolen garments, owning nothing, holding all things in common like the Apostles . . . [I]f we admit them, we shall be driven out" (quoted in Johnson 1976:251). In short, the powerful ascetic current that persists in all religious traditions is a natural response to the problem of religious risk. Moreover, by the same logic we can conclude: *Martyrs are the most credible exponents of the value of a religion, and this is especially true if there is a voluntary aspect to their martyrdom.*

By voluntarily accepting torture and death rather than defecting, a person sets the highest imaginable value upon a religion and communicates that value to others. Indeed, as will be reported later in this chapter, Christian martyrs typically had the opportunity to display their steadfastness to large numbers of other Christians, and the value of Christianity they thereby communicated often deeply impressed pagan observers as well.

THE FREE-RIDER PROBLEM

Free-rider problems are the Achilles' heel of collective activities. Michael Hechter summarizes the free-rider problem as follows. "Truly rational actors will not join a group to pursue common ends when, without participating, they can reap the benefit of other people's activity in obtaining them. If every member of the relevant group can share in the benefits ... then the rational thing is to free ride ... rather than to help attain the corporate interest" (1987:27). The consequence is, of course, that insufficient collective goods are created because too few contribute. Everyone suffers—but those who give most generously suffer the most. Let me state this as a proposition: *Religion involves collective action, and all collective action is potentially subject to exploitation by free riders.*

One need not look far to find examples of anemic congregations plagued by free-rider problems—a visit to the nearest liberal Protestant church usually will suffice to discover "members" who draw upon the group for weddings, funerals, and (perhaps) holiday celebrations, but who provide little or nothing in return. Even if they do make substantial financial contributions, they weaken the group's ability to create collective religious goods because their inactivity devalues the compensators and reduces the "average" level of commitment.

However, far more striking examples are found in sects and cults. In such groups, which can survive only with high levels of commitment, the costs of free riding are laid bare. Consider, for example, the Shakers' problems with transient members. These so-called winter Shakers would join Shaker communities in the late fall, obtain food and shelter throughout the winter, and then leave when employment opportunities had improved (Bainbridge 1982).

During the time Lofland and I observed them (see chapter 1), the Moonies encountered similar difficulties with "exploiters" whose motives for joining conflicted with or undermined the goals of the movement. Some merely "attempted to extract some nonreligious benefit from the [Moonies], such as inexpensive room and board, money, ... or sex" (Lofland 1977:152). Others actually attempted to use participation in the group as a base from which to recruit customers for their own, competing, spiritualist churches.

Free riding was by no means unique to the Shakers and Moonies. Most of the nineteenth-century communes studied by

Hine (1983) and Kanter (1972) were afflicted with "commitment problems." This perverse dynamic threatens all groups engaged in the production of collective goods, and it pertains to social and psychic benefits such as enthusiasm and solidarity no less than to material resources. It would seem that religions are caught on the horns of a dilemma. On the one hand, a congregational structure that relies on the collective action of numerous volunteers is needed to make the religion credible. On the other hand, that same congregational structure threatens to undermine the level of commitment and contributions needed to make a religious group effective. However, costly demands offer a solution.

SACRIFICE AND STIGMA

The costly demands in question are not simply monetary costs analogous to the purchase price of secular goods. They are instead what at first glance would seem to be gratuitous costs, the *stigmas* and *sacrifices* common to sects, cults, and other "deviant" religious groups. Religious *stigmas* consist of all aspects of social deviance that attach to membership in the group. A group may prohibit some activities deemed normal in the external society (drinking, for example), or it may require other activities deemed abnormal by the world (shaving one's head, for example). By meeting these demands, members deviate from the norms of the surrounding society. *Sacrifices* consist of investments (material and human) and forgone opportunities required of those who would gain and retain membership in the group. Clearly, stigma and sacrifice often go hand in hand, as when the stigma of highly unusual dress prevents normal career development.

Stated in terms more familiar to sociologists of religion, sacrifices and stigmas both generate and reflect the "tension" between the religious group and the rest of society (Johnson 1963; Stark and Bainbridge 1985, 1987; Iannaccone 1988).

They distinguish mainstream "churches" from deviant "sects" or "cults."

At first glance it would seem that costly demands must always make a religion less attractive. And indeed, the economists' law of demand predicts just that, *other things remaining equal.* But it turns out that other things do not remain equal when religions impose these kinds of costs on their members. To the contrary, costly demands strengthen a religious group by mitigating "free-rider" problems that otherwise lead to low levels of member commitment and participation: *Sacrifice and stigma mitigate the free-rider problems faced by religious groups.*

They do so for two reasons. First, they create a barrier to group entry. No longer is it possible merely to drop in and reap the benefits of membership. To take part at all, you must qualify by accepting the stigmas and sacrifices demanded from everyone. Thus high costs tend to *screen out* free riders—those potential members whose commitment and participation would otherwise be low. The costs act as nonrefundable registration fees that, as in secular markets, measure seriousness of interest in the product. Only those willing to pay the price qualify.

Second, high costs tend to *increase* participation among those who do join. Group members find that the temptation to free ride is weaker, not because their human nature has somehow been transformed, but rather because the opportunities to free ride have been reduced and (in equilibrium) the payoff to involvement has been substantially increased. If we may not attend dances or movies, play cards, go to taverns, or join fraternal organizations, we will eagerly await the Friday church social.

The dynamics of stigma and sacrifice have the following direct and formal consequences (Iannaccone 1992). First: *By demanding higher levels of stigma and sacrifice, religious groups induce higher average levels of member commitment and participation.* Second: *By demanding higher levels of stigma and sacrifice, religious groups are able to generate greater material, social, and religious benefits for their members.*

At first glance it seems paradoxical that when the cost of

membership increases, the net gains of membership increase too. But this is necessarily the case with collectively produced goods. Some examples may be helpful. The individual's positive experience of a worship service increases to the degree that the church is full, the members participate enthusiastically (everyone joins in the songs and prayers), and others express very positive evaluations of what is taking place. Thus as each member *pays* the costs of membership, each *gains* from higher levels of production of collective goods.

Furthermore, for a religious group, as with any organization, *commitment is energy*. That is, when commitment levels are high, groups can undertake all manner of collective actions, and these are in no way limited to the psychic realm. For example, because Mormons are asked to contribute not only 10 percent of their incomes, but also 10 percent of their time to the church, they are thereby enabled to lavish social services upon one another—many of the rewards for being a Mormon are entirely tangible.

These propositions lead to a critical insight, perhaps *the* critical insight: Membership in an expensive religion is, for many people, a "good bargain."[2] Conventional cost-benefit analysis alone suffices to explain the continued attraction of religions that impose sacrifices and stigmas upon their members. This conclusion is, of course, in extreme contrast with the conventional social science view that to pay high religious costs can only reflect irrationality, or at least woeful ignorance. However, more sophisticated analysis reveals that members of strict religious organizations have substantial reason to believe that their information about compensators is sufficient and thus their behavior fulfills the rational choice proposition. This suggests why the recent introduction of rational choice theories into the social scientific study of religion has been recognized as a major shift in paradigms (Warner 1993)—the irrationalist position is in full retreat.

Against this theoretical background, I should like to reexamine early Christianity. How much did it cost to be a Christian? Is it plausible that these costs strengthened the commitment of the group? Was Christian commitment translated into this-worldly rewards to the faithful? In short, was Christianity a "good deal?"

CHRISTIAN SACRIFICES

Christians were expected to do much for their faith. A substantial list of "do nots" departed from pagan norms and practices, many of which have been discussed in chapter 5. But equally costly were the things Christian were expected to do, and, it was hoped, to do gladly—care for the sick, infirm, and dependent, for example. Later in this chapter we will see how these sacrifices typically came back as rewards. But there is no need here to expand the list of what might be called the many smaller sacrifices of Christian membership. Rather, now it is time to confront the most difficult possible task for any attempt to apply rational choice theory to religion.

ULTIMATE SACRIFICES

Perhaps rational people are willing to give money and time to social service and observe strict norms governing sex and marriage because of religion. But how could a rational person accept grotesque torture and death in exchange for risky, intangible religious rewards?

First of all, many early Christians probably could not have done so, and some are known have recanted when the situation arose. Eusebius reported that when the first group of bishops was seized, "some indeed, from excessive dread, broken down and overpowered by their terrors, sunk and gave way immediately at the first onset" (*The Martyrs of Palestine* 1, 1850 ed.).

Second, persecutions rarely occurred, and only a tiny number of Christians ever were martyred—only "hundreds, not thousands" according to W.H.C. Frend (1965:413). Indeed, commenting on Tacitus's claim that Nero had murdered "an immense multitude" of Christians, Marta Sordi wrote that "a few hundred victims would justify the use of this term, given the horror of what happened" (1986:31). The truth is that the Roman government seems to have cared very little about the "Christian menace." There was surprisingly little effort to persecute Christians, and when a wave of persecution did occur, usually only bishops and other prominent figures were singled out. Thus for rank-and-file Christians the threat of persecution was so slight as to have counted for little among the potential sacrifices imposed on them.

But even if their numbers were few, some Christians went unhesitatingly to terrible deaths rather than recant. How could this have been the rational choice? In most of the reported instances the ability to face martyrdom was an extraordinary instance of the collective creation of commitment as a result of which prominent members built up an immense stake in martyrdom.

Martyrdom not only occurred in public, often before a large audience, but it was often the culmination of a long period of preparation during which those faced with martyrdom were the object of intense, face-to-face adulation. Consider the case of Ignatius of Antioch. Sometime late in the first century, Ignatius became bishop of Antioch. During the reign of the emperor Trajan (98–117)—the precise year is unknown—Ignatius was condemned to death as a Christian. But instead of being executed in Antioch, he was sent off to Rome in the custody of ten Roman soldiers. Thus began a long, leisurely journey during which local Christians came out to meet him all along the route, which passed through many of the more important sites of early Christianity in Asia Minor on its way to the West. At each stop Ignatius was allowed to preach to and meet with those who gathered, none of whom was in any apparent danger although their Christian identity was obvious. Moreover, his guards allowed Ignatius to write letters to many Christian congregations in cities bypassed along the way, such as Ephesus and Philadelphia. Ignatius's surviving seven letters have been much studied for their theological and historical content (Schoedel 1985; Grant 1966). What is important here, however, is what they tell us about the spiritual and psychological preparation for martyrdom.

Here was a man who truly believed that he had an appointment with immortality in *this world* as well as the next. Robert Grant has remarked upon the "regal-imperial style" of the letters and how they convey that the author was engaged in a triumphal journey (1966:90). Or, as William Schoedel remarked,

> It is no doubt as a conquering hero that Ignatius thinks of himself as he looks back on part of his journey and says that the churches who received him dealt with him not as a "transient traveller," noting that "even churches that do not lie on my way according to the flesh went before me city by city." (1991:135)

What Ignatius feared was not death in the arena, but that well-meaning Christians might gain him a pardon. Thus he wrote ahead to his fellow Christians in Rome adjuring that they in no way interfere to prevent his martyrdom:

> The truth is, I am afraid it is your love that will do me wrong. For you, of course, it is easy to achieve your object; but for me it is difficult to win my way to God, should you be wanting in consideration of me. . . . Grant me no more than that you let my blood be spilled in sacrifice to God. . . .
>
> I am writing to all the Churches and state emphatically to all that I die willingly for God, provided you do not interfere. I beg you, do not show me unseasonable kindness. Suffer me to be the food of wild beasts, which are the means of making my way to God. God's wheat I am, and by the teeth of wild beasts I am to be ground that I may prove Christ's pure bread. (*Epistle to the Romans*, 1946 ed.)

Ignatius was reaching for glory, both here and beyond. He expected to be remembered through the ages and compares himself to martyrs gone before him, including Paul, "in whose footsteps I wish to be found when I come to meet God."

We thus encounter what is known as the cult of the saints, most of whom were martyrs (Droge and Tabor 1992; Brown 1981). It soon was clear to all Christians that extraordinary fame and honor attached to martyrdom. Nothing illustrates this better than the description of the martyrdom of Polycarp, contained in a letter sent by the church in Smyrna to the church in Philomelium (collected in Fremantle 1953:185–192). Polycarp was the bishop of Smyrna who was burned alive in about 156. After the execution his bones were retrieved by some of his followers—an act witnessed by Roman officials, who took no action against them. The letter spoke of "his sacred flesh" and described his bones as "being of more value than precious stones and more esteemed than gold." The letter-writer reported that the Christians in Smyrna would gather at the burial place of Polycarp's bones every year "to celebrate with great gladness and joy the birthday of his martyrdom." The letter concluded, "The blessed Polycarp . . . to whom be glory, honour, majesty, and a throne eternal, from generation to generation. Amen." It also included the instruction: "On receiving this, send on the letter to the more distant brethren that they may glorify the Lord who makes choice of his own servants."

In fact, today we actually know the names of nearly all of the Christian martyrs because their contemporaries took pains that they should be remembered for their very great holiness. Indeed, as Peter Brown pointed out, the sufferings of the martyrs "were miracles in themselves" (1981:79). Brown quoted the *Decretrum Gelasianum*:

> We must include also [for public reading] the deeds of the saints in which triumph blazed forth through the many forms of torture that they underwent and their marvelous confession of faith. For what Catholic can doubt that they suffered more than is possible for human beings to bear, and did not endure this by their own strength, but by the grace and help of God?

Moreover, martyrdom did not merely earn rewards in the world to come, while promising only posthumous honor in this world. Instead, martyrs were often very highly rewarded prior to their final ordeal. For example, just as Christians flocked to meet and to venerate Ignatius on his journey, so too did they flock to prisons to adore and shower food and services on many others the Romans selected for martyrdom. Athanasius's *The Life of Saint Antony* offers a revealing portrait.

During the last persecution in 311, some Christians were arrested in Egypt and taken to Alexandria. As soon as they heard about it, a number of ascetic monks, including Antony, left their cells and went to Alexandria in support of the martyrs-to-be. Once there, Antony "was busy in the courtroom stimulating the zeal of the contestants as they were called up, and receiving and escorting them as they went to their martyrdom and remaining with them until they had expired" (*Life of Saint Antony*, 1950 ed.). Eventually, the "zeal" of the monks grew too much for the judge, who "gave orders that no monk was to appear in court." Because Antony "had a yearning to suffer martyrdom" but felt it wrong to volunteer, he disobeyed the order and made himself quite visible in court the next day. But it was not to be. The judge ignored him. So, after the last execution, Antony "left and went back to his solitary cell; and there he was a daily martyr to his conscience."

Eugene and Anita Weiner present as clear a picture as we have of martyrdom as a group phenomenon:

> Every effort was made to ensure that the group would witness the events leading up to the martyrdom. It was not uncommon for fellow Christians to visit the accused in their cells and to bring food and clothing to make the imprisonment more bearable. There were even celebrations to dramatize the forthcoming test of faith. These supportive efforts both brought comfort and help in a most trying situation, and had a latent message for the martyr-designate, "what you do and say will be observed and recorded." In a word, it will be significant and passed down in ritual form and celebration.
>
> All martyrs were on stage. Some suffered remorse and recanted but those who could take the pressure were assured of eternity, at least in the memories of the survivors. What was dis-

tinctive about martyrdom was not only promise of reward in the hereafter, but the certainty of being memorialized in this world. The martyr saw before dying that he or she had earned a place in the memories of the survivors and in the liturgy of the church. (1990:80–81)

For many Christians, especially for those sufficiently prominent to have been accused, these were big stakes. It is hardly surprising that many of them thought it worthwhile to make the supreme sacrifice.

MARTYRDOM AND CHRISTIAN CONFIDENCE

Their faith in life everlasting made it possible for Christians to face death bravely; nevertheless, death presented the early church with a severe crisis of credibility. The promise that most converts would live to see the Lord's return was stressed by the apostles. As Mark 13:30 tells us: "Truly, I say to you, this generation will not pass away before these things take place." Within a few years, however, many converts did begin to pass away without having seen "the Son of man coming in clouds with great power and glory" (Mark 13:26). By "the 60s a whole generation *had* elapsed," as John A. T. Robinson (1976:180) pointed out. Although Robinson acknowledged that the problem of the delayed Parousia persisted for a long time, he suggested that "the question must have been at its most acute" in the sixties.

Most who have written on this topic stress that the destruction of Jerusalem in the year 70 was widely regarded as the beginning of the "Last Days" and thus served to at least postpone the crisis concerning the Second Coming. Even if this is correct, there existed an acute potential crisis of Christian confidence in the sixties regardless of the promise of an early return by Jesus. Elsewhere I have written at some length about the problems presented to movements by the "dismal arithmetic of first generation growth" and how this often "crushes the confidence" out of new religious movements (Stark 1987:21). That is, most new religious movements begin very small and grow no faster than did early Christianity. Having surveyed a large number of such movements, I noticed that it was typical for the founding generation to apparently lose hope of saving the world, and to turn their movements inward, as they neared the end of their lives. That is, unless something comes along to renew hope and commitment, as the first generation evaluate the results of thirty or forty years of conversion efforts and see that they have succeeded in attracting only two or three thousand members (if that many), they are inclined to lose heart. As this takes place, often a new rhetoric is voiced; this de-emphasizes the importance of growth and explains that the movement has succeeded in gathering a saving remnant, which is all that was ever intended, actually.

Islam never faced this problem because its rapid growth during the Prophet's lifetime, more often by conquest and treaty than by personal conversion, gave no occasion for disappointment. And the Mormons overcame the problem by withdrawing to their own Mormon society, where they amassed confidence from being a majority faith—even if in only one place. Neither solution applies to the early church. When Paul, Peter, and other members of the founding generation looked around in the sixties, they could have counted only something less than three thousand Christians. Not only had Jesus not returned, three decades of missionizing had yielded only these slim results. The New Testament gives us no basis for believing that these men were immune to doubt, and it would be strange had they not sometimes despaired. If they did, how was the problem solved?

It is all well and good to suggest that religions are often able to rationalize failed prophecies and to modify their belief systems sufficiently to overcome such difficulties.[3] But such statements are only descriptive—they do not tell how the shift was accomplished without loss of credibility, how faith was reinforced sufficiently so that revisions in a core doctrine could be accepted. Moreover, how did the Christians avoid doctrinal shifts away from hopes of converting the multitudes—shifts that similar groups have so often made? How did they gain the moral strength to keep going until eventually their arithmetic of growth ceased to be dismal?

If it is true that a twofold crisis of confidence became most acute in the sixties, then I think it extremely important to note that three rather extraordinary incidents of martyrdom occurred in that same decade.

First, in about 62, James, the brother of Jesus and the head of the church in Jerusalem, was seized along with some of his followers by Ananus, the new high priest. Exploiting the interim between the death of the Roman governor of Judea and the arrival of his replacement, Ananus brought James and the others before the Sanhedrin where they were condemned for breaking Jewish law, then taken out and stoned to death.

Second, after spending several years under arrest in Caesarea Maritima and then being transported to Rome to await the outcome of his appeal to Caesar, the apostle Paul was executed in Rome during 64 or 65. Third, either late in 65 or in 66 (Robinson 1976), Nero launched his persecution of Christians, causing some of them to be torn to pieces in the arena by wild dogs and having others crucified in his garden, sometimes setting the latter on fire "to illuminate the night when daylight failed" (Tacitus, *Annals* 15.44, 1989 ed.). Among those who died during this first official Roman persecution of Christians was the apostle Peter.

Not only did the three most admired and holy figures of the time die for their faith, undaunted either by the delay of the Second Advent or by the small number of their followers, it would appear that Paul and Peter could have avoided their fates, Paul by recanting and Peter by flight. Moreover, the *Quo Vadis?* story, widely circulated among early Christians (even if it failed eventually to be included in the official canon), provided vivid details about how Peter embraced martyrdom after meeting Jesus on the road out of Rome. It is worth recounting here.

In the *Acts of Peter* we read that an upper-class Roman wife and convert sent word that Peter should flee Rome as he was to be seized and executed. For a time Peter resisted pleas that he should leave:

> "Shall we act like deserters, brethren?" But they said to him, "No, it is so that you can go on serving the Lord." So he assented to the brethren and withdrew himself, saying, "Let none of you retire with me, but I shall retire by myself in disguise." And as he went out the gate he saw the Lord entering Rome; and when he saw him he said, "Lord, where are you going (*quo vadis*)?" And the Lord said to him, "I am going to be crucified." And Peter said to him, "Lord, are you being crucified again?" He said to him, "Yes, Peter, I am being crucified again." And Peter came to himself; and he saw the Lord ascending into Heaven; then he returned to Rome, rejoicing and giving praise to the Lord, because he said, "I am being crucified"; since this was to happen to Peter. (Stead's translation, reprinted in Barnstone 1984:442)

Back among his followers, Peter told them what had taken place and of his new resolve to be crucified. They again tried to dissuade him, but he explained that they were now to serve as the "foundation" so that they might "plant others through him." In the crucifixion account that follows, Peter (crucified upside down at his own request) speaks at length from the cross to a crowd of onlooking Christians about the power of faith in Christ.

Edmondson noted that the encounter with Jesus, "which had caused Peter to turn back and welcome martyrdom, would strike home to the hearts and consciences of any waverers that heard them" ([1913] 1976:153). I think so too. That Peter could gladly follow his Savior to the cross, despite the fact that the end of times was delayed, must have been a powerful reinforcement of faith for Christians not asked to pay such a price for belonging.

In my judgment it was the martyrs of the sixties who eased the crisis of failed prophecy and small numbers, by adding their suffering to that of Jesus as proof of atonement. In the context of this chapter's earlier discussion of credibility, it seems appropriate to ask how much more credible witnesses could be found than those who demonstrate the worth of a faith by embracing torture and death.

Christian Rewards

But Christianity was not about sacrifice and stigma alone. The fruits of this faith were equally substantial. As a direct result of their sacrifice and stigma, Christians were largely immune to the free-rider problem. Consequently, they were able to produce a very potent religion. The services conducted in those early house churches must have yielded an immense, shared emotional satisfaction.

Moreover, the fruits of this faith were not limited to the realm of the spirit. Christianity offered much to the flesh, as well. It was not simply the promise of salvation that motivated Christians, but the fact that they were greatly rewarded here and now for belonging. Thus while membership was expensive, it was, in fact, a bargain. That is, because the church asked much of its members, it was thereby possessed of the resources to *give* much. For example, because Christians were expected to aid the less fortunate, many of them received such aid, and all could feel greater security against bad times. Because they were asked to nurse the sick and dying, many of them received such nursing. Because they were asked to love others, they in turn were loved. And if Christians were required to observe a far more restrictive moral code than that observed by pagans, Christians—especially women—enjoyed a far more secure family life.

In similar fashion, Christianity greatly mitigated relations among social classes—at the very time when the gap between rich and poor was growing (Meeks and Wilken 1978). It did not preach that everyone could or should become equal in terms of wealth and power in *this* life. But it did preach that all were equal in the eyes of God and that the more fortunate had a God-given responsibility to help those in need.

As William Schoedel (1991) has noted, Ignatius stressed the responsibility of the church to care for widows and children. Indeed, Ignatius made it clear that he was not simply discussing doctrines about good works but was affirming the reality of a massive structure of Christian voluntarism and charity. Tertullian noted that members willingly gave to the church, which, unlike the pagan temples, did not spend the donations on gluttony:

> For they [the funds] are not taken thence and spent on feasts, and drinking bouts, and eating houses, but to support and bury poor people, to supply the wants of boys and girls destitute of means and parents, and of old persons confined to the house; such too as have suffered shipwreck; and if there happen to be any in the mines, or banished to the islands, or shut up in the prisons for nothing but their fidelity to the cause of God's Church, they become nurslings of their confession. (*Apology* 39, 1989 ed.)

Recall from chapter 4 that the apostate emperor Julian agreed that Christians "devoted themselves to philanthropy" and urged pagan priests to compete. But Julian soon discovered that the means for reform were lacking. Paganism had failed to develop the kind of voluntary system of good works that Christians had been constructing for more than three centuries; moreover, paganism lacked the religious ideas that would have made such organized efforts plausible.

But did it matter? Did Christian good works really change the quality of life in Greco-Roman times? Modern demographers regard life expectancy as the best summary measure of the quality of life. It is thus significant that A. R. Burn (1953) found, based on inscriptions, that Christians had longer life expectancies than pagans. If he is correct, then Q.E.D.

The goddess Isis (shown in this statue from Hadrian's villa) was one of the many eastern additions to the Greco-Roman pantheon. Eventually there were more pagan gods than most people could name.

Opportunity and Organization

It is time to more clearly place the early church in its social and cultural environment and to examine the interplay between the church and the Greco-Roman world. This chapter consists of two major parts. In the first I will assess the opportunity for a major new faith to emerge at this particular place and time. The second part of the chapter will focus on organizational features of the Christian movement that made it such a formidable challenger—many of these are the same features that brought about its persecution.

OPPORTUNITY

Typically, the fate of new religious movements is largely beyond their control, depending greatly on features of the environment in which they appear. Here, two important factors are involved. The first is the degree of state regulation of religion. Where the state is prepared to vigorously persecute any challengers to the conventional faith(s), it will be extremely difficult for new religions to grow. The second is the vigor of the conventional religious organization(s) against which new religions must compete. Usually, there is no significant market niche for a new religion to fill because most people are already reasonably satisfied participants in the "older" religion(s). However, once in a while the conventional religious organization(s) are sufficiently weak to provide an opportunity for something truly new to arise and flourish.

Roman Regulation of Religion

In many respects Rome provided for a greater level of religious freedom than was seen again until after the American Revolution. But just as deviant religious groups have often discovered limits to the scope of freedom of religion in America, so too in Rome not just anything was licit. In particular, from time to time Jews and then Christians were deemed to be "atheistic" for their condemnation of false gods. I shall pursue this matter later in the chapter when I distinguish between religious economies based on the principle of religious portfolios and those based on exclusive commitment. Here I merely want to suggest briefly that although Christians stood in formal, official disrepute for much of the first three centuries, informally they were free to do pretty much as they wished, in most places, most of the time.

As was established in the previous chapter, dreadful as the persecutions were, they were infrequent and involved very few people. Hence the early Christians may have faced some degree of social stigma but little actual repression. Henry Chadwick reported that when a Roman governor in Asia Minor began a persecution of Christians during the second century, "the entire Christian population of the region paraded before his house as a manifesto of their faith and as a protest against injustice" (1967:55). The more significant part of this story is not that the Christians had the nerve to protest, but that they went unpunished.

In similar fashion, archaeological evidence shows that from very early days, house churches were clearly identifiable—the neighbors would have been entirely aware that these were Christian gathering places (White 1990). In addition, soon many Christians began to take names that were distinctively Christian—scholars have no difficulty identifying them as such today (Bagnall 1993), and surely non-Christians in antiquity were sufficiently perceptive to have done so too. Funerary inscriptions also often bore clearly Christian identifications (Meyers 1988; Finegan 1992).

That Christians were not a secret sect is, of course, patent in the fact that they grew. If a group is to attract outside members, potential converts must, at the very least, be able to find it. Moreover, for a group to grow as rapidly as Christians did, it must maintain close ties to nonmembers—it must remain an open network. Thus had Roman repression been so consistent and severe that the Christians actually had become a hidden underground movement, this book would not have been written. A truly underground Christianity would have remained insignificant.

Pluralism

In his superb study *Paganism in the Roman Empire*, Ramsay MacMullen chided Harnack for paying no attention to the opposition in his massive study of the expansion of Christianity:

> Among his thousands of references to sources, however, I can find not one to a pagan source and hardly a line indicating the least attempt to find out what non-Christians thought and believed. Thus to ignore the prior view of converts [to Christianity] or to depict the Mission as operating on a clean slate is bound to strike the historian as very odd indeed. (1981:206)

Indeed! To know how Christianity arose it is crucial to see how it was given the opportunity to do so, to learn why it was not limited to obscurity by an incredibly diverse and entrenched paganism.

If we are to approach this question efficiently, it will be helpful to draw upon some new social scientific tools. In my most recent theoretical work, the concept of religious economies plays a central role. A *religious economy* consists of all the religious activity going on in any society. Religious economies are like commercial economies in that they consist of a market of current and potential customers, a set of *religious firms* seeking to serve that market, and the religious "product lines" offered by the various firms. The use of market language to discuss things often thought to be sacred was not, and is not, meant to offend, but to enable me to import some basic insights from economics to help explain religious phenomena (Stark 1985a, 1985b; Stark and Bainbridge 1985, 1987; Stark and Iannaccone 1992, 1994; Finke and Stark 1992).

Among the many innovations made possible by this approach is the capacity to focus on the behavior of religious *firms* rather than only upon religious *consumers.* Let me give an example of what this shift in focus offers. If levels of religious participation decline in a society, social scientists have postulated that this was caused by a decline in the *demand* for religion, and conversely that increases in religiousness reflect increased individual "needs." But if one examines such changes within the context of a religious economy, attention is directed toward religious *suppliers.* Under what conditions are religious firms able to *create a demand?* And what happens when only lazy or dispirited religious firms confront the potential religious consumer?

As I pondered the workings of religious economies, I soon recognized that the most decisive factor involved is whether they are free markets or markets in which the government regulates the economy in the direction of monopoly. This led me to a set of theoretical propositions, three of which are useful here. The first is: *The capacity of a single religious firm to monopolize a religious economy depends upon the degree to which the state uses coercive force to regulate the religious economy.* The second is: *To the degree that a religious economy is unregulated, it will tend to be very pluralistic.*

By *pluralistic* I refer to the number of firms active in the economy; the more firms having a significant market share, the greater the degree of pluralism.

By the same logic, it becomes clear that religious economies can never be fully monopolized, even when backed by the full coercive powers of the state. Indeed, even at the height of its temporal power, the medieval church was surrounded by heresy and dissent. Of course, when the repressive efforts of the state are sufficiently intense, religious firms competing with the state-sponsored monopoly will be forced to operate underground. But whenever and wherever repression eases, pluralism will begin to develop.

Once pluralism is in full bloom, however, a third proposition applies: *Pluralism inhibits the ability of new religious firms to gain a market share.* That is, new firms must struggle for a place in the economy against the opposition of efficient and successful firms. Under these conditions, successful new firms will simply be variants on the standard religious culture—as Protestant firms grown lazy or worldly are so often overtaken by upstart sects (Finke and Stark 1992). But for something truly new to make headway—Hindu groups in the United States, for example—is extremely rare and depends on something's having gone wrong in the process by which pluralism maintains market equilibrium.

We have seen that the Greco-Roman religious economy was little regulated, and, as predicted, it sustained extensive pluralism. It is difficult to say how many different cults flourished in the major Greco-Roman cities. Ramsay MacMullen noted that there were ten or fifteen major gods with temples nearly everywhere "atop a mass" of others, many of them peculiar to particular places (1981:7). But whatever the number, it was large and the mix very complex.

There is considerable controversy over just how the gods of Rome became so numerous and diverse. Everyone agrees that as the dominion of Rome spread, gods from the new territories found their way back to Rome as well as to other major trade and population centers. And everyone agrees that these new faiths were spread by migrants—traders, sailors, slaves—and sometimes by soldiers returning from long tours of duty in foreign lands. But there is disagreement about what happened next. Franz Cumont ([1929] 1956) stressed successful recruitment as the basis for the new cults, such as that of Isis. Jules Toutain denied this, claiming that Isis worship remained "an exotic cult, taking no root in provincial soil" (quoted in MacMullen 1981:116)—and MacMullen agreed. From examination of collections of inscriptions, the latter concluded that "we can explain what favor the cult did enjoy by supposing it to have been passed on within families, whose members moved about, rather than communicated to new recruits" (1981:116).

On the other hand, MacMullen does agree that the cults of Jupiter of Doliche and of Mithraism grew and spread "entirely through conversions" (1981:188). I find it difficult to see how faith could be so solidly ancestral in origin as to preclude conversions to Isis, yet that these ties should fail in comparable instances. But perhaps we should attend to Arthur Darby Nock's (1933) caution that the modern notion of conversion does not represent the phenomenology involved in the acceptance of new cults in Greco-Roman times. Rather, these religions "were as a rule supplements rather than alternatives to ancestral piety" (1933:12). Nock argued further that "genuine conversion to paganism will appear in our inquiry only when Christianity had become so powerful that its rival was, so to speak, made an entity by opposition and contrast" (1933:15).

The Weakness of Paganism

Henry Chadwick assured his readers that "Paganism was far from being moribund when Constantine was converted to Christianity" (1967:152), and E. R. Dodds noted that in the fourth century paganism began "to collapse the moment the supporting hand of the State [was] withdrawn from it" ([1965] 1970:132). I quote these two distinguished scholars to illustrate the general agreement among historians that paganism was brought down by Christianity and that the conversion of Constantine was the killing blow—that paganism declined precipitously during the fourth century when Christianity replaced it as the state religion, thus cutting off the flow of funds to the pagan temples.

No one can doubt the evidence of the dismantling of paganism in the fourth and fifth centuries, as countless temples were torn down or converted to other uses. MacMullen noted:

> The renewed and relentless pillage of a once glorious non-Christian Establishment—with all the claims of temples on local taxes, the temple estates, the investments set aside by devoted and boastful donors to pay the priests and cover the costs of worship—all this accumulated fat of centuries of piety was essentially torn away. There can have been nothing much left by A.D. 400. (1984:53)

Nevertheless, the idea that paganism's weakness was caused by Christian political power fails to explain how Christianity managed to be so successful that it could *become* the state church. As outlined above, on theoretical grounds I must propose that Christianity would have remained an obscure religious movement had the many firms making up Roman pluralism been vigorous. That Christianity was able to wedge out a significant place for itself against the opposition of paganism directs our attention to signs of weakness in paganism.

Let us begin with pluralism per se. However new gods traveled the empire and gained adherents, it seems to me that by the first century the empire had developed *excessive* pluralism—that the massive influx of various new gods from other parts of the empire had by then created what E. R. Dodds called "a bewildering mass of alternatives. There were too many cults, too many mysteries, too many philosophies of life to choose from" ([1965] 1970:133). Faced with this array, people are likely to have been somewhat overwhelmed by their options and therefore to have been somewhat unwilling to stake very much on any given cult. Moreover, since the population was not expanding, more temples to more gods ought to have reduced the resources—both material and subjective—available to each. If this is true, then we ought to be able to detect some signs of decay. Indeed, any significant decline in support for paganism should have registered rather soon. After all, paganism was expensive to maintain, since it was embodied in elaborate temples, was served by professional priests, and depended on lavish festivals as the primary mode of participation. I must quote Tertullian, *Apology* 39:

> The Salii cannot have their feast without going into debt; you must get the accountants to tell you what the tenths of Hercules and the sacrificial banquets cost; the choicest cook is appointed for the Apaturia, the Dionysia, the Attic mysteries; the smoke from the banquet of Serapis will call out the firemen. (1989 ed.)

The funds for all of this came from the state and from a few wealthy donors, rather than from a rank and file (MacMullen 1981:112). If funding ever declined seriously, the decline ought to have been visible immediately.

In fact, there are abundant signs of pagan decline. In his remarkable study *Egypt in Late Antiquity*, Roger S. Bagnall reported a rapid decline in "inscriptions dedicating sacred architecture." He continued:

> It is difficult to avoid the conclusion that imperial support for the construction, renovation, and decoration of buildings in Egyptian temples declined markedly after Augustus, shrank gradually through the reign of Antoninus, fell off precipitously after that, and disappeared altogether in the middle of the third century. (1993:263)

Bagnall reported similar results from surveys of papyri, noting that they "are remarkably stingy with information about temples and priests after the middle of the third century" (1993:264). Bagnall summed up the evidence as showing that paganism in Egypt "declined markedly in the third century; but . . . [was] already in decline in the first century" (1993:267). As a final "outward sign" of the decline, Bagnall noted that Amesysia, a festival of Isis, was last known to have been held in

257 (1993:267). J. B. Rives (1995) has documented a similar decline in the influence of traditional paganism in Carthage, also beginning in the first century.

Bagnall's mention of Isis raises a second kind of evidence of decline: the religious economy had become extremely volatile. Faiths from the "Orient" did seem to come into sudden vogue and attract many participants. The cult of Isis (or, more correctly, the cult of Isis and Serapis) seems to have originated in Egypt in about the third century B.C.E.—reworked from older traditions (Solmsen 1979). From Alexandria, the Isis cult spread across the empire. But not everywhere, and not at a constant rate.

Tim Hegedus (1994) has coded a scale of the spread of Isis, and from his work I am able to assign scores as to when the Isis cult arrived (if it did) in most of the twenty-two Greco-Roman cities discussed in chapter 6.[1] It has been suggested that the spread of new cults such as that of Isis demonstrated religious needs unmet, or not well met, by the traditional pagan temples and shrines. In a sense, then, examination of the expansion of Isis worship might map market opportunities and thereby anticipate the expansion of Christianity. It is with some satisfaction that I can report a highly significant correlation of .67 between the expansion of Isis and the expansion of Christianity. Where Isis went, Christianity followed.

A third aspect of the weakness of paganism has to do with the lack of public reverence. This may have been another consequence of such a crowded pantheon, and it may also have to do with pagan conceptions of the gods themselves. Before making any attempt to demonstrate this claim, I must express my respect for Ramsay MacMullen's warning that it is extremely hard to discover the religious situation in our own time, let alone in such "a remote and ill-documented period" (1981:66). In demonstration of this point, MacMullen assembled a set of contradictory quotations from the sources as to the general state of pagan piety: for instance, the assertion that the Romans "in Juvenal's day . . . laughed at anyone professing faith in an altar or

temple," as contrasted with Lucian's claim that "the great majority of Greeks" and all Romans "are believers." Which? Moreover, I fully share MacMullen's disdain for historical psycholo-
gisms, such as the view that this was an age of "anxiety," or that
in this era occurred "a failure of nerve," or that it was a time of
"enthusiasm." As an experienced opinion pollster I also share
his skepticism about characterizing the "feelings and thoughts
of fifty million people" on the basis of some literary quotations
or a few inscriptions.

Nevertheless, I think there may be a substitute for an opinion
poll of religious belief in antiquity. What is wanted is a sample
of unfiltered public attitudes. Consider, then, the archaeological discovery that the walls of Pompeii abound in extremely
blasphemous graffiti and drawings, some of them very obscene
as well. While I harbor no thoughts that these were connected
to the city's fate, they arouse my deepest suspicions about the
overall state of reverence—not simply because some residents
were prompted to create them, but because no one was
prompted to remove or cover them. MacMullen commented
that "we may take [the existence of similar graffiti] for granted
elsewhere, if there were other sites so well preserved"
(1981:63). I may be leaping to unjustified conclusions, but
these data speak to me of widespread irreverence.

Blasphemous graffiti may also reflect that pagan gods were
not entirely godlike as we understand that term today (or as the
early Christians understood it). While I reserve extended discussion of pagan conceptions of the gods for chapter 10, we
may usefully anticipate that discussion here. E. R. Dodds
pointed out that in "popular Greek tradition a god differed
from a man chiefly in being exempt from death and in the supernatural power which this exemption conferred on him"
([1965] 1970:74). Moreover, while people often appealed to
various gods for help, it was not assumed that the gods truly
cared about humans—Aristotle taught that gods could feel no
love for mere humans. Classical mythology abounds in stories
in which the gods do wicked things to humans—often for the

sport of it. Arthur Darby Nock noted that worship of such gods need not have inspired sincere belief (1964:4). So perhaps what the walls of Pompeii really communicate is a rather casual, utilitarian, and even resentful view of the gods.

Toward Monotheism?

Many writers suggest that by the time Christianity appeared, the world of antiquity was groping toward monotheism, having been inspired by the example of Judaism. In light of recent social scientific theorizing, that should indeed have been the case—subject to several important qualifications. Therefore, I pause again to introduce some theoretical propositions, this time concerning the evolution of the gods. The specific propositions to be introduced were deduced in the formal theory of religion I developed with William Sims Bainbridge (1987).

Many scholars have noted the tendency for religions to evolve in the direction of monotheism (e.g., Swanson 1960; Bellah 1964). Stated as a more formal proposition: *As societies become older, larger, and more cosmopolitan,*[2] *they will worship fewer gods of greater scope.* Here, however, is an instance when the logical processes of deduction produced novelty. For it turned out that within our theoretical system, the end product of this evolution is not *monotheism,* defined as belief in only one god (or supernatural being) of infinite scope. In the context of our system such a god would necessarily be conceived of either as almost wholly remote from human concerns and affairs (as exemplified by Unitarianism and the versions of Buddhism sustained by Chinese court philosophers) or as dangerously capricious in the manner of the Greek pantheon. Here the issue is rationality, not only on the part of believers, but on the part of the gods.

A major result was our deduction that evil supernatural forces (such as Satan) are essential to the most rational conception of divinity. Defining *rationality* as marked by consistent goal-oriented activity, we can state that *Distinguishing the supernatural into two classes—good and evil—offers a rational portrait of the gods.* In our system *good* and *evil* refer to the intentions of the gods in their exchanges with humans. *Good* consists of the intention to allow humans to profit from exchanges. *Evil* consists of the intention to inflict coercive exchanges or deceptions upon humans, leading to losses for the humans.

Thus we deduced the necessity either to conceive of a single god who is above the question of good or evil by virtue of being remote from any exchanges with humans (the Tao is not a fit exchange partner), or to admit the existence of more than one supernatural being. Good and evil reflect the possible goal-orientations of the gods—to give more than they take, or to take more than they give. A god holding either of these intentions is more rational than a god who holds both intentions. Note that these deductions about the need for a separation of good and evil are entirely consistent with millennia of theological thought. We further deduced that *The older, larger, and more cosmopolitan societies become, the clearer the distinction drawn between good and evil gods.*

These theoretical predictions jibe nicely with the historical record. In the words of Ramsay MacMullen:

> Something close to monotheism, by one approach or another, had long been talked about and attracted adherents among Romans and Greeks alike. That He should be envisioned as a monarch enthroned on high was familiar; that He should have his angels and other supernatural beings to do his work, just as Satan had *his* throngs—that was familiar too. (1984:17)

The God-Fearers are a clear reflection of a growing preference for fewer gods of greater scope. Such a trend can only be taken as an indication of a decline in the plausibility of paganism.

Social Disorganization

In many previous chapters I have stressed the extent to which the Greco-Roman world, and especially the cities, suffered from chronic social disorganization and periodic extreme crises. I have also noted how these overloaded pagan institutions and doctrines compared with the Christian response. There is no need to reprise these points here—but let us bear them in mind.

In summary, Christianity found a substantial opportunity to expand because of the incapacities of paganism, weaknesses quite outside of Christian control. If Christianity ultimately buried paganism, it was not the source of its terminal illness.

But if there are many factors religious movements cannot control, there are some things that movements *can* control. In the remainder of this chapter we examine the religious firm known as early Christianity and see what made it so effective.

ORGANIZATION

Let us return to the topic of pluralism. It turns out that there are two very different and basic kinds of religious firms and hence two very different styles of pluralism with very different social implications.

One kind of religious firm—the one most familiar to us in the Western world—demands *exclusive commitment*. Members are not free to go to church in the morning, to visit the mosque at noon, and to devote the evening to the synagogue. The other variety of firm is *nonexclusive* and takes multiple religious involvements for granted. Such firms are familiar in Asia. In Japan, for example, most people report more than one religious preference; religious membership statistics equal 1.7 times the total population (Morioka 1975). Pluralistic religious economies made up of firms demanding exclusive commitments have a high potential for intergroup conflict, while those made up of nonexclusive firms will generate little religious conflict.

When we look more closely at each kind of firm, a very basic difference comes to light. Exclusive firms engage in the *collective production* of religion, a process discussed at length in the previous chapter. Nonexclusive firms cannot sustain collective production and therefore specialize in *privately produced* religious goods. As defined by Laurence Iannaccone (1995), privately produced religious commodities can be transferred from the individual producer to an individual consumer without involvement by a mediating group. New Age crystals are a current example of a privately produced religious commodity, as are astrological charts, or psychic healing.

In chapter 8, following Iannaccone, I explained how religious compensators are inherently risky and how collective production helps to greatly reduce the perceived risks that the compensators are false. But we also ought to recognize that, other things being equal, people will respond to religious risk in the same fashion as they respond to other risks, such as those entailed in financial investment: they will seek to *diversify*. If I am not able to determine which of an array of religious investments is the most secure, my most rational strategy would be to include all, or many, of them in my portfolio. And that is precisely what people do when confronted with nonexclusive firms. However, often other things are not equal, and often people are not free to diversify their religious holdings.

Two theoretical propositions developed by Laurence Iannaccone (1995) clarify the issues. The first is: *Whenever religious firms exist to provide private commodities, competitive forces and risk aversion will lead consumers to patronize multiple firms, thereby diversifying their religious portfolios.* The second proposition states: *Whenever religious firms exist to facilitate the production of collective goods, the firm and its patrons will demand exclusivity to mitigate free-rider problems.*

Obviously, the religious firms constituting Greco-Roman paganism were nonexclusive, while Judaism and Christianity were of the latter variety. And herein lies a major aspect of the eventual triumph of Christianity: exclusive firms are far stronger organizations, far better able to mobilize extensive resources and to provide highly credible religious compensators, as well as substantial worldly benefits. To understand these differences, let us look more closely at nonexclusive firms.

Client Cults

In 1979 William Sims Bainbridge and I first introduced the concept of a client cult to characterize nonexclusive religious firms. The terminology was meant to emphasize that the relationship between the producer and the consumer far more closely resembled that between practitioners and clients than that between clergy and church members. Or, as Emile Durkheim pointed out about magic:

> Between the magician and the individuals who consult him, as between these individuals themselves, there are no lasting bonds. . . . The magician has a clientele and not a church, and it is very possible that his clients have no other relations between each other, or even do not know each other; even the relations which they have with him are generally accidental and transient; they are just like those of a sick man with his physician. (1915:44)

Durkheim summed up the matter by asserting, "There is no Church of magic." That is, a church rests on people's maintaining long-term, stable, and exclusive commitments. But when people construct a religious portfolio, their commitment to any given stock is weak and subject to constant reappraisal.

Thomas Robbins pointed out that one was "*converted* to the intolerant faiths of Judaism and Christianity while one merely *adhered* to the cults of Isis, Orpheus, or Mithra" (1988:65). MacMullen made much the same point: "At the very towering peak of their appalling rage and cruelty against Christians, pagans never sought to make converts *to* any cult—only *away* from atheism, as they saw it. Toleration gone mad, one may say" (1981:132). In similar fashion, when there exists an array of nonexclusive faiths, the perceived value of any given selection will be low; this helps explain the disrespect so openly displayed toward the sacred. In Taiwan, for example, statues of the traditional folk gods are sometimes beaten with sticks for failing to deliver. In Greco-Roman times, Livy noted that "people attack the gods with headstrong words" (*History* 45.23.19, 1959 ed.), and Libanius claimed that many people slandered the gods daily "whenever any of their affairs go amiss" (*Orations* 19.12, 1969 ed.). Recall the walls of Pompeii.

When people typically shop around seeking to improve their religious portfolios, start-up costs for new religious firms will be very low; this too will result in a glutted marketplace, and the price of religious goods will be correspondingly reduced. Moreover, as Iannaccone pointed out, competition will force nonexclusive firms to specialize, and over time they will "come to resemble highly specialized boutiques" (1995:289).

Nonexclusive religious firms will consist primarily of priests, and it will be obvious that they benefit from convincing clients of the efficacy of their gods—they typically ate the "sacrificial" animals, for example (Baird 1964:91). Therefore, the religious compensators offered by such firms will lack credibility, further reducing their value. Simply put, pagan cults were not able to get people to *do* much of anything. As Lactantius said about paganism, it "is no more than worship by the fingertips" (*Divine Institutes* 5.23, 1964 ed.). And at the bottom of this weakness is the inability of nonexclusive faiths to generate *belonging*.

A religious portfolio can serve well enough when full-service religious firms are missing. But history suggests that when nonexclusive faiths are challenged by exclusive competitors, in a relatively unregulated market, the exclusive firms win.[3] They win because they are the better bargain, despite their higher costs.

In chapter 8 we saw that things are very different when religion is produced by collective actions. Such groups, as Iannaccone noted, can and do demand exclusive commitment. If they are to do so, of course, they cannot limit themselves but must be full-service firms taking what Iannaccone called "a department store approach to religion" (1995:289). They must offer a comprehensive belief system and spiritual and social activities appropriate for all ages. Involvement in an exclusive religious group does not necessarily cause people to lose the urge to diversify, but it denies them the opportunity to do so *if* they are to share in the potent religious rewards of such involvement. And just as the weakness of paganism lay in its inability to generate belonging, the fundamental strength of an exclusive faith is its strength as a group.

E. R. Dodds has put this as well as anyone:

> A Christian congregation was from the first a community in a much fuller sense than any corresponding group of Isiac or Mithraist devotees. Its members were bound together not only by common rites but by a common way of life. . . . Love of one's neighbour is not an exclusively Christian virtue, but in [this] period Christians appear to have practised it much more effectively than any other group. The Church provided the essentials of social security. . . . But even more important, I suspect, than these material benefits was the sense of belonging which the Christian community could give. ([1965] 1970:136–137)

Central to this sense of community and belonging, one common to all exclusive religious groups, were the strong bonds between the clergy and the rank and file (Banks 1980). You did not approach Christian clergy to purchase religious goods, but to be guided in fulfilling the Christian life. Nor were the clergy distanced from their flocks—they were not an initiated elite holding back arcane secrets, but teachers and friends, selected, as Tertullian explained, "not by purchase, but by established character" (*Apology* 39, 1989 ed.). Moreover, the church depended on the rank and file for its resources. According to Tertullian:

> There is no buying and selling of any sort in the things of God. Though we have our treasure chest, it is not made up of purchase-money, as of a religion that has its price. On the monthly day, if he likes, each puts in a small donation; but only if it be his pleasure, and only if he is able; for there is no compulsion; all is voluntary. These gifts are, as it were, piety's deposit fund.

Not only did this free Christianity from any dependence on state support, it also gave a greatly reduced role to the wealthy—small donations rapidly added up. Consequently, the early church was a mass movement in the fullest sense and not simply the creation of an elite. Ramsay MacMullen recognized that the failure of Roman authorities to understand this fact accounts for the strange aspect of the persecutions: that only leaders were seized, while crowds of obvious Christians went unpunished (1981:129). That is, when the Romans decided to destroy Christianity, "they did so from the top down, evidently taking it for granted that only the Church's leaders counted." This mistaken judgment was, according to MacMullen, based on the fact that paganism was utterly dependent on the elite and could easily have been destroyed from the top.

It is worth mention too that the early church abounded in ascetics whose testimony as to the worth of faith would have been extremely credible, as noted in chapter 8. Finally, because Christianity was a mass movement, rooted in a highly committed rank and file, it had the advantage of the best of all marketing techniques: person-to-person influence.

CONCLUSION

Christianity *did not* grow because of miracle working in the marketplaces (although there may have been much of that going on), or because Constantine said it should, or even because the martyrs gave it such credibility. It grew because Christians constituted an intense community, able to generate the "invincible obstinacy" that so offended the younger Pliny but yielded immense religious rewards. And the primary means of its growth was through the united and motivated efforts of the growing numbers of Christian believers, who invited their friends, relatives, and neighbors to share the "good news."

A Brief Reflection on Virtue

I N CONTRAST with times past, historians today are more than willing to discuss how social factors shaped religious doctrines. Unfortunately, at the same time they have become somewhat reluctant to discuss how doctrines may have shaped social factors. This shows up with particular frequency in the form of allergic reactions to arguments that attribute the rise of Christianity to superior theology. For some historians, this allergy reflects their having been too much influenced by out-of-date, and always absurd, Marxist claims that ideas are mere epiphenomena. But for others, their position seems to reflect an underlying discomfort with religious faith per se, and especially with all hints of "triumphalism." It is deemed bad taste nowadays to suggest that any religious doctrines are "better" than any others.[1] Harnack is frequently disparaged on these grounds, as both L. Michael White (1985) and Jaroslav Pelikan (1962) have noted.

It is true, of course, that the Christian commitment of historians in earlier generations often did make the rise of Christianity seem to be the inevitable triumph of virtue via divine guidance. Indeed, as White noted, for Harnack and his circle, "the term 'expansion' comes to be used . . . as a virtual synonym for 'triumph of the gospel message'" (1985:101). But if these excesses prevented more thorough scholarship (although it is difficult to imagine someone more thorough than Harnack), that is not sufficient justification for dismissing theology as irrelevant. Indeed, in a number of earlier chapters it has been evident that doctrines often were of immense importance. Surely doctrine was central to nursing the sick during times of plague, to the rejection of abortion and infanticide, to fertility, and to organizational vigor. Therefore, as I conclude this study, I find

The victor of a battle of gladiators stands over his last living opponent waiting for the crowd to signal whether he should spare him or kill him too—the thumbs-down signal means death.

it necessary to confront what appears to me to be *the ultimate factor* in the rise of Christianity.

Let me state my thesis: *Central doctrines of Christianity prompted and sustained attractive, liberating, and effective social relations and organizations.*

I believe that it was the religion's particular doctrines that permitted Christianity to be among the most sweeping and successful revitalization movements in history. And it was the way these doctrines took on actual flesh, the way they directed organizational actions and individual behavior, that led to the rise of Christianity. My treatment of these two points will be brief since they have always been implicit, and very often explicit, in the previous nine chapters.

The Words

To anyone raised in a Judeo-Christian or Islamic culture, the pagan gods seem almost trivial. Each is but one of a host of gods and godlings of very limited scope, power, and concern. Moreover, they seem quite morally deficient. They do terrible things to one another, and sometimes they play ugly pranks on humans. But, for the most part, they appear to pay little attention to things "down below."

The simple phrase "For God so loved the world . . ." would have puzzled an educated pagan. And the notion that the gods care how we treat one another would have been dismissed as patently absurd.

From the pagan viewpoint, there was nothing new in the Jewish or Christian teachings that God makes behavioral demands upon humans—the gods have always demanded sacrifice and worship. Nor was there anything new in the idea that God will respond to human desires—that the gods can be induced to exchange services for sacrifices. But, as I noted in chapter 4, the idea that God loves those who love him was entirely new.

211

Indeed, as E. A. Judge has noted in detail, classical philosophers regarded mercy and pity as pathological emotions—defects of character to be avoided by all rational men. Since mercy involves providing *unearned* help or relief, it was contrary to justice. Therefore "mercy indeed is not governed by reason at all," and humans must learn "to curb the impulse"; "the cry of the undeserving for mercy" must go "unanswered" (Judge 1986:107). Judge continued: "Pity was a defect of character unworthy of the wise and excusable only in those who have not yet grown up. It was an impulsive response based on ignorance. Plato had removed the problem of beggars from his ideal state by dumping them over its borders."

This was the moral climate in which Christianity taught that mercy is one of the primary virtues—that a merciful God requires humans to be merciful. Moreover, the corollary that *because* God loves humanity, Christians may not please God unless they *love one another* was something entirely new. Perhaps even more revolutionary was the principle that Christian love and charity must extend beyond the boundaries of family and tribe, that it must extend to "all those who in every place call on the name of our Lord Jesus Christ" (1 Cor. 1:2). Indeed, love and charity must even extend beyond the Christian community.

Recall Cyprian's instructions to his Carthaginian flock, quoted at length in chapter 4, that

> there is nothing remarkable in cherishing merely our own people with the due attentions of love, but that one might become perfect who should do something more than heathen men or publicans, one who, overcoming evil with good, and practicing a merciful kindness like that of God, should love his enemies as well. . . . Thus the good was done to all men, not merely to the household of faith. (Quoted in Harnack 1908: 1:172–173)

This was revolutionary stuff. Indeed, it was the cultural basis for the revitalization of a Roman world groaning under a host of miseries.

THE FLESH

In his fine recent work *The Origins of Christian Morality*, Wayne Meeks reminded us that when we are talking about "morality or ethics we are talking about people. Texts do not have an ethic; people do" (1993:4). It was only as Christian texts and teach-ings were acted out in daily life that Christianity was able to transform the human experience so as to mitigate misery.

Chief among these miseries was the cultural chaos produced by the crazy quilt of ethnic diversity and the blazing hatreds entailed thereby. In uniting its empire, Rome created economic and political unity at the cost of cultural chaos. Ramsay MacMullen has written of the immense "diversity of tongues, cults, traditions and levels of education" encompassed by the Roman Empire (1981:xi). But it must be recognized that Greco-Roman cities were microcosms of this cultural diversity. People of many cultures, speaking many languages, worshiping all manner of gods, had been dumped together helter-skelter.

In my judgment, a major way in which Christianity served as a revitalization movement within the empire was in offering a coherent culture that was *entirely stripped of ethnicity*. All were welcome without need to dispense with ethnic ties. Yet, for this very reason, among Christians ethnicity tended to be submerged as new, more universalistic, and indeed cosmopolitan, norms and customs emerged. In this way Christianity first evaded and then overwhelmed the ethnic barrier that had prevented Judaism from serving as the basis for revitalization. Unlike the pagan gods, the God of Israel did indeed impose moral codes and responsibilities upon his people. But to embrace the Jewish God, one had also to don Jewish ethnicity, albeit that, as Alan Segal (1991) suggests, the Judaism of the first century may have been more inclusive than has been recognized. I agree with Segal that the existence of the God-Fearers demonstrates this inclusiveness, but it also seems clear that the God-Fearers were limited to the social fringes of the diasporan Jewish communities precisely because of their failure to fully embrace the Law, and hence the Law remained the primary ethnic barrier to conversion. Indeed, as I argued in chapter 3, many Hellenized Jews of the diaspora found Christianity so appealing precisely because it freed them from an ethnic identity with which they had become uncomfortable.

Christianity also prompted liberating social relations between the sexes and within the family—to which much of chapter 5 was devoted. And, as noted in chapter 7, Christianity also greatly modulated class differences—more than rhetoric was involved when slave and noble greeted one another as brothers in Christ.

But, perhaps above all else, Christianity brought a new conception of humanity to a world saturated with capricious cruelty and the vicarious love of death (Barton 1993). Consider the account of the martyrdom of Perpetua. Here we learn the details of the long ordeal and gruesome death suffered by this tiny band of resolute Christians as they were attacked by wild beasts in front of a delighted crowd assembled in the arena. But we also learn that had the Christians all given in to the demand to sacrifice to the emperor, and thereby been spared, *someone else* would have been thrown to the animals. After all, these were games held in honor of the birthday of the emperor's young son. And whenever there were games, people had to die. Dozens of them, sometimes hundreds (Barton 1993).

Unlike the gladiators, who were often paid volunteers, those thrown to the wild animals were frequently condemned criminals, of whom it might be argued that they had earned their fates. But the issue here is not capital punishment, not even very cruel forms of capital punishment. The issue is spectacle— for the throngs in the stadia, watching people torn and devoured by beasts or killed in armed combat was the ultimate spectator sport, worthy of a boy's birthday treat. It is difficult to comprehend the emotional life of such people.[2]

In any event, Christians condemned both the cruelties and the spectators. Thou shalt not kill, as Tertullian (*De Spectaculis*) reminded his readers. And, as they gained ascendancy, Christians prohibited such "games." More important, Christians effectively promulgated a moral vision utterly incompatible with the casual cruelty of pagan custom.

Finally, what Christianity gave to its converts was nothing less than their humanity. In this sense virtue *was* its own reward.

CHAPTER 1
CONVERSION AND CHRISTIAN GROWTH

1. Paul Johnson makes the perceptive point that the Decian persecution, which began around the year 250, was a reaction to the fact that "Christians were now far more numerous" and that their numbers seemed to be increasing rapidly (1976:73).

2. Within the movement she was invariably referred to as "Miss."

3. Reading the New Testament, especially the letters written by various apostles, one can easily conclude that almost from the start the Christian movement was a very large and flourishing undertaking. Thus when Peter includes in the salutation of his first epistle "the exiles of the Dispersion in Pontus, Galatia, Cappadocia, Asia, and Bithynia," the intended audience seems imposingly numerous. Indeed, in Romans 16, Paul names more than two dozen Christians to whom he sends his greetings. My colleague Michael Williams has sometimes asked students in his seminars about the total size of the intended audience for such letters. Invariably, students think it numbers into many thousands. In contrast, I calculate that there would only have been a total of between two thousand and three thousand Christians during the 60s, the decade during which Paul was executed and Peter was crucified. In defense of my projections we must note that whatever the size of the congregations in various cities at this time, they still held their services in private homes—even in Rome. Moreover, a brief return to my experiences with the Moonies may prove instructive here.

Early in the 1960s, after several years of missionizing in San Francisco, Miss Kim decided that the group needed to split into small mission teams, each taking on a new a city. She was concerned that members spent too much of their time with one another and that perhaps more fertile mission fields awaited elsewhere. So in twos and threes her young members struck out on their own—to Dallas, Denver, Berkeley, and elsewhere. And once her teams were established in their new cities, Miss Kim's expectations were partially met as a trickle of new converts began to come in. Like Paul, Miss Kim wrote many letters—often devoting considerable space to matters of doctrine and interpretation. Moreover, Miss Kim's letters abounded in greetings. Were I possessed of a selection of these letters, I think they would precisely compare with New Testament letters in terms of the apparent size of the audience. The following fictitious salutation is typical of Miss Kim's correspondence as I remember it: *To sister Ella, to brother Howard, to Dorothy visiting from Dallas, and to all who now partake of the Unification Church in San Jose, greetings in Father's name.* But the fact is that there probably were not yet two hundred members in the whole United States when letters like that were being sent by Miss Kim. Ella, Howard, and Dorothy would have been the only Moonies in San Jose, since the partakers Miss Kim often referred to were not yet members, but only people willing to discuss religion with members.

Chapter 2
The Class Basis of Early Christianity

1. The most distinguished dissenter was the Yale historian Kenneth Scott Latourette (1937:109–110).

2. Albeit some Marxists still insist not only that Christianity was a proletarian movement, but that this remains the dominant scholarly view (cf. Gager 1975).

3. Unfortunately Arrington and Bitton, despite being devout Mormons, readily interpret the characterization of Mormon converts by their nineteenth-century enemies as scum and riffraff to mean that most Mormons were very poor. Presumably the great trek west caused serious financial losses and subsequent hardship for many Mormons, but that is not pertinent to their social origins and essential class position. Moreover, given where and when the Mormons began, the appropriate comparisons are to people in the immediate environment, which was the frontier, not Park Avenue.

4. I have limited the data to cult movements without ethnic ties. Hence Buddhists, Hindus, Muslims, Shintoists, Taoists, Bahaists, and Rastafarians were not included.

CHAPTER 5
THE ROLE OF WOMEN IN
CHRISTIAN GROWTH

1. It should be noted that while secondary converts are often rather lukewarm about joining in the first place, once immersed in the group they often become very ardent.

2. I am indebted to Laurence R. Iannaccone for pointing out this feature of the King James Version.

3. See: Plato, *Republic* 5 (1941 ed.); Aristotle, *Politics* 2, 7 (1986 ed.).

CHAPTER 6
CHRISTIANIZING THE URBAN EMPIRE:
A QUANTITATIVE APPROACH

1. I began from the fact that both cities had been judged by Chandler and Fox as having fewer than 40,000 residents, else they would have been listed with the others. However, since each city often appears in lists of major cities for this period (cf. Grant 1970), it seems reasonable to suppose that they were not much smaller than 40,000. I found the population of Athens estimated to be 28,000 in the second century by J. C. Russell (1958) in his classic work. Because Athens was in a period of slow decline, it seemed reasonable to guess its population as a bit larger in 100. Hence my figure of 30,000. Since Salamis had an economic boom during the first century (Smith 1857), it seemed safe to estimate it as a bit larger than Athens, which is the basis of my figure of 35,000.

CHAPTER 7
URBAN CHAOS AND CRISIS:
THE CASE OF ANTIOCH

1. Max Weber thought it "highly improbable" that Christianity "could have developed as it did outside of an urban" setting (1961:1140).

Chapter 8
The Martyrs: Sacrifice as Rational Choice

1. Albeit the notion of preference schedules is only implicit.

2. For a formal derivation of these propositions, see Iannaccone 1992.

3. Many historians familiar with the book *When Prophesy Fails* (Festinger, Riecken, and Schachter 1956) may wonder why I have not relied on the cognitive dissonance explanation of this phenomenon. Briefly, cognitive dissonance theory predicts that when persons with a strongly held belief are confronted with evidence disconfirming that belief, they typically respond, not by dropping the belief, but by making vigorous efforts to convince others that the belief is true. In the initial application of this proposition to religious prophecies, Festinger and his associates claimed to have observed a small occult group before, during, and after the failure of their prediction that aliens aboard flying saucers would arrive to take the group to other worlds. When this failed to take place, it is claimed that the group redoubled their efforts to spread their message. There have been a number of subsequent tests of the proposition, *none* of which found the predicted outcome. Moreover, recent critics of the initial publication have questioned whether any such increase in missionizing efforts occurred in that instance either (Bainbridge, in press). What seems entirely clear is that this group would never have formed or eagerly anticipated the arrival of the aliens had the woman whose prophecy of this event appeared in the local press not attracted many strangers who showed up, unannounced, at her door expressing their absolute belief in her prophecy and in her prophetic powers. All of these "converts" were social scientists.

Chapter 9
Opportunity and Organization

1. The following indicates the dates by which Isis was established in various cities:

200 B.C.E.—Alexandria, Memphis, Ephesus, Athens, Smyrna
100 B.C.E.—Syracuse, Corinth, Pergamum
1 C.E.—Antioch, Rome

200 C.E.—Carthage, London
300 C.E.—Mediolanum (Milan)
Never—Gadir (Cadiz), Damascus, Edessa, Apamea

Adequate data are lacking for the other cities.

2. Defined as the degree of cultural diversity, the number and variety of distinctive subcultures.

3. The very rapid growth of Soka Gakkai in Japan gives clear evidence of this. Unlike other Japanese religions, it demands exclusive commitment from its followers. The success of the Mormon Church in Asia is also pertinent.

CHAPTER 10
A BRIEF REFLECTION ON VIRTUE

1. So long as the doctrines are not fundamentalist, than which all doctrines are deemed to be better—a view I do not share.

2. Carlin A. Barton (1993) has made an intriguing attempt to do so.

✤ Bibliography ✤

Aharoni, Yohanon, and Michael Avi-Yonah. 1977. *The Macmillan Bible Atlas*. Rev. ed. New York: Macmillan.

Alba, Richard D. 1976. "Social Assimilation among American Catholic National-Origin Groups." *American Sociological Review* 41:1030–1046.

————. 1985. *The Italians*. Englewood Cliffs, NJ: Prentice-Hall.

Argyle, Michael. 1958. *Religious Behaviour*. London: Routledge and Kegan Paul.

Aristotle. 1986. *Politics*. Buffalo, NY: Prometheus Books.

Arrington, Leonard J., and Davis Bitton. 1979. *The Mormon Experience*. New York: Knopf.

Athanasius. [Ca. 357.] 1950. *Life of St. Anthony*. Ancient Christian Writers series. New York: Paulist Press.

Athenagoras. [Ca. 177.] 1989. *The Ante-Nicene Fathers*. Edited by Alexander Roberts and James Donaldson. Vol. 2. Grand Rapids, MI: Eerdmans.

Ayerst, David, and A.S.T. Fisher. 1971. *Records of Christianity*. Vol. 1. Oxford: Basil Blackwell.

Bagnall, Roger S. 1982. "Religious Conversion and Onomastic Change in Early Byzantine Egypt." *Bulletin of the American Society of Papyrologists* 19:105–124.

————. 1987. "Conversion and Onomastics: A Reply." *Zeitschrift für Papyrologie und Epigraphik* 69:243–250.

————. 1988. "Combat ou Vide: Christianisme et Paganisme dans l'Egypte Romaine Tardive." *Ktema* 13:285–296.

————. 1993. *Egypt in Late Antiquity*. Princeton: Princeton University Press.

Bainbridge, William Sims. 1982. "Shaker Demographics 1840–1900: An Example of the Use of the U.S. Census Enumeration Schedules." *Journal for the Scientific Study of Religion* 21:352–365.

————. In press. *The Sociology of Religious Movements*. New York: Routledge.

Bainbridge, William Sims, and Rodney Stark. 1980. "Superstitions: Old and New." *The Skeptical Inquirer* 4:18–31.

Bainbridge, William Sims, and Rodney Stark. 1981. "The Consciousness Reformation Reconsidered." *Journal for the Scientific Study of Religion* 20:1–16.

Baird, William. 1964. *The Corinthian Church—A Biblical Approach to Urban Culture.* New York: Abingdon Press.

Banks, Robert. 1980. *Paul's Idea of Community: The Early House Churches in Their Historical Setting.* Grand Rapids, MI: Eerdmans.

Barker, Eileen. 1981. "Who'd Be a Moonie?" In *The Social Impact of New Religious Movements,* edited by Bryan Wilson, 59–96. New York: Rose of Sharon Press.

————. 1984. *The Making of a Moonie—Brainwashing or Choice?* Oxford: Basil Blackwell.

Barnabas, Saint. [Ca. 100.] 1988. *The Epistle of Barnabas.* In *The Apostolic Fathers,* edited by J. B. Lightfoot and J. R. Harmer. Grand Rapids, MI: Baker Book House.

Barnstone, Willis, ed. 1984. *The Other Bible: Ancient Esoteric Texts.* San Francisco: Harper and Row.

Barton, Carlin A. 1993. *The Sorrows of the Ancient Romans: The Gladiator and the Monster.* Princeton: Princeton University Press.

Barton, Steven. 1982. "Paul and the Cross: A Sociological Approach." *Theology* 85:13–19.

————. 1984. "Paul and the Resurrection: A Sociological Approach." *Religion* 14:67–75.

Bauer, Walter. 1971. *Orthodoxy and Heresy in Earliest Christianity.* Philadelphia: Fortess.

Becker, Gary S. 1976. *The Economic Approach to Human Behavior.* Chicago: University of Chicago Press.

Bellah, Robert N. 1964. "Religious Evolution." *American Sociological Review* 29:358–374.

Benko, Stephen. 1984. *Pagan Rome and the Early Christians.* Bloomington: University of Indiana Press.

Blaiklock, E. M. 1972. *The Zondervan Pictorial Bible Atlas.* Grand Rapids, MI: Zondervan.

Blau, Joseph L. 1964. *Modern Varieties of Judaism.* New York: Columbia University Press.

Boak, Arthur E. R. 1947. *A History of Rome to 565 A.D.* 3d ed. New York: Macmillan.

————. 1955a. *Manpower Shortage and the Fall of the Roman Empire in the West.* Ann Arbor: University of Michigan Press.

————. 1955b. "The Populations of Roman and Byzantine Karanis." *Historia* 4:157–162.

Brown, Peter. 1964. "St. Augustine's Attitude to Religious Coercion." *Journal of Roman Studies* 54:1107–1116.

————. 1978. *The Making of Late Antiquity.* Cambridge: Harvard University Press.

————. 1981. *The Cult of the Saints.* Chicago: University of Chicago Press.

————. 1988. *The Body and Society: Men, Women and Sexual Renunciation in Early Christianity.* New York: Columbia University Press.

Burn, A. R. 1953. "Hic breve vivitur." *Past and Present* 4:2–31.

Cadoux, Cecil J. 1925. *The Early Church and the World.* Edinburgh: T. & T. Clark.

Cahill, Jane, Karl Reinhard, David Tarler, and Peter Warnock. 1991. "Scientists Examine Remains of Ancient Bathroom." *Biblical Archaeology Review* 17 (May–June): 64–69.

Carcopino, Jerome. 1940. *Daily Life in Ancient Rome.* New Haven: Yale University Press.

Case, Shirley Jackson. 1928. "The Acceptance of Christianity by the Roman Emperors." In *Papers of the American Society of Church History,* pp. 45–64. New York: G. P. Putnam's Sons.

Castiglioni, A. 1947. *A History of Medicine.* Translated by E. B. Krumbhaar. London: Routledge and Kegan Paul.

Celsus, Aulus Cornelius. [Ca. 25.] 1935–1938. *De medicina.* Translated by W. G. Spenser. 3 vols. Cambridge: Harvard University Press.

Chadwick, Henry. 1967. *The Early Church.* Harmondsworth, Middlesex: Penguin Books.

Chadwick, Henry, and G. R. Evans. 1987. *Atlas of the Christian Church.* New York: Facts on File.

Champagne, Duane. 1983. "Social Structure, Revitalization Movements and State Building: Social Change in Four Native American Societies." *American Sociological Review* 48:754–763.

Chandler, Tertius, and Gerald Fox. 1974. *Three Thousand Years of Urban Growth.* New York: Academic Press.

Chuvin. Pierre. 1990. *A Chronicle of the Last Pagans.* Cambridge: Harvard University Press.

Clark, Gillian. 1993. *Women in Late Antiquity: Pagan and Christian Lifestyles.* Oxford: Clarendon Press.

Cochrane, Charles Norris. [1940] 1957. *Christianity and Classical Culture*. London: Oxford.

Collingwood, R. G., and J.A.L. Myres. 1937. *Roman Britain and the English Settlements*. 2d ed. London: Macmillan.

Collins, John J. 1983. *Between Athens and Jerusalem: Jewish Identity in the Hellenistic Diaspora*. New York: Crossroad.

Conzelmann, Hans. 1973. *History of Primitive Christianity*. Nashville: Abingdon Press.

Crutchfield, Robert, Michael Geerkin, and Walter Gove. 1983. "Crime Rates and Social Integration." *Criminology* 20:467–478.

Cumont, Franz. [1929] 1956. *Oriental Religions in Roman Paganism*. New York: Dover Publications.

Cyprian [Ca. 250.] 1958. *Treatises*. Translated by Mary Hannan Mahoney. Edited by Roy J. Deferrari. New York: Fathers of the Church.

Danielou, Jean, and Henri Marrou. 1964. *The First Six Hundred Years*. Vol. 1 of *The Christian Centuries*. New York: Paulist Press.

de Camp, L. Sprague. 1966. *The Ancient Engineers*. Norwalk, CT: Burndy Library.

————. 1972. *Great Cities of the Ancient World*. New York: Dorset Press.

Deissman, Adolf. [1908] 1978. *Light from the Ancient East*. Grand Rapids, MI: Baker Book House.

————. 1929. *The New Testament in the Light of Modern Research*. Garden City, NY: Doubleday, Doran & Company.

Demerath, Nicholas J., II. 1965. *Social Class in American Protestantism*. Chicago: Rand-McNally.

Department of Economic and Social Affairs. 1973. *The Determinants and Consequences of Population Trends*. Vol. 1. Population Studies, no. 50. New York: United Nations.

Devine, A. M. 1985. "The Low Birth-Rate in Ancient Rome: A Possible Contributing Factor." *Rheinisches Museum* 128:3–4, 313–317.

deVries, Jan. 1967. *Perspectives in the History of Religions*. Berkeley and Los Angeles: University of California Press.

The Didache. [Ca. 100.] 1984. In *The Apostolic Fathers*, edited by J. B. Lightfoot and J. R. Harmer, pp. 229–235. Grand Rapids, MI: Baker Book House.

Dio Cassius. [Ca. 200.] 1987. *The Roman History: The Reign of Augustus*. London: Penguin Classics.

Dodds, E. R. [1965] 1970. *Pagan and Christian in an Age of Anxiety*. New York: Norton.

Downey, Glanville. 1962. *Antioch in the Age of Theodosius the Great.* Norman: University of Oklahoma Press.

———. 1963. *Ancient Antioch.* Princeton: Princeton University Press.

Droge, Arthur J., and James D. Tabor. 1992. *A Noble Death: Suicide and Martyrdom among Christians and Jews in Antiquity.* San Francisco: HarperSanFrancisco.

Durand, John D. 1960. "Mortality Estimates from Roman Tombstone Inscriptions." *American Journal of Sociology* 75:365–373.

Durkheim, Emile. 1915. *The Elementary Forms of Religious Life.* George Allen & Unwin.

Durry, M. 1955. "Le Mariage des filles impubères dans la Rome antique." *Revue Internationale des Droits de l'Antiquité*, ser. 3, 2:263–273.

Edmonson, George. [1913] 1976. *The Church in Rome in the First Century.* New York: Gordon Press.

Elliott, John H. 1986. "Social-Scientific Criticism of the New Testament: More on Methods and Models." *Semeia* 35:1–33.

Eusebius. [Ca. 325.] [1850] 1991. *The Ecclesiastical History of Eusebius Pamphilus, Bishop of Cesarea, in Palestine.* Translated by Christian Frederick Cruse. Grand Rapids, MI: Baker Book House.

———. 1927. *The Ecclesiastical History and The Martyrs of Palestine.* 2 vols. Translated by Hugh Jackson Lawlor and John Ernest Leonard Oulton. London: Society for Promoting Christian Knowledge.

——— 1949. *Eusebius, The Ecclesiastical History.* 2 vols. Vol. 1 translated by Kirsopp Lake. Vol. 2 translated by John Ernest Leonard Oulton. Loeb Classical Library. Cambridge: Harvard University Press.

———. 1965. *Eusebius, The History of the Church.* Translated by G. A. Williamson. Harmondsworth, Middlesex: Penguin Books.

Farmer, William R. 1986. "Some Critical Reflections on Second Peter." *The Second Century* 5:30–46.

Ferguson, Everette. 1990. "Deaconess." "Mithraism." In *The Encyclopedia of Early Christianity*, edited by Everette Ferguson, 258, 609. New York: Garland.

Festinger, Leon, Henry W. Riecken, and Stanley Schachter. 1956. *When Prophecy Fails.* Minneapolis: University of Minnesota Press.

Finegan, Jack. 1992. *The Archeology of the New Testament.* Rev. ed. Princeton: Princeton University Press.

Finke, Roger, and Rodney Stark. 1992. *The Churching of America, 1776–1990: Winners and Losers in Our Religious Economy.* New Brunswick: Rutgers University Press.

227

Finley, M. I. 1977. *Atlas of Classical Archaeology.* New York: McGraw-Hill.

————. 1982. *Economy and Society in Ancient Greece.* New York: Viking.

Fischer, Claude S. 1975. "Toward a Subcultural Theory of Urbanism." *American Journal of Sociology* 80:1319–1341.

Fox, Robin Lane. 1987. *Pagans and Christians.* New York: Knopf.

Frank, Harry Thomas. 1988. *Discovering the Biblical World.* Rev. ed. Maplewood, NJ: Hammond.

Fremantle, Anne. 1953. *A Treasury of Early Christianity.* New York: Viking Press.

Frend, W.H.C. 1965. *Martyrdom and Persecution in the Early Church.* Oxford: Basil Blackwell.

————. 1984. *The Rise of Christianity.* Philadelphia: Fortress Press.

————. 1990. "Persecution in the Early Church." *Christian History* 9(3):5–11.

Friedlander, Moritz. 1898. *Der vorchristliche judische Gnostismus.* Gottingen: Vandenhoeck and Ruprecht.

Furnish, Victor Paul. 1988. "Corinth in Paul's Time: What Can Archaeology Tell Us?" *Biblical Archaeology Review* 15 (May–June): 14–27.

Fustel de Coulanges, Numa Denis. [1864] 1956. *The Ancient City.* Garden City, NY: Doubleday.

Gager, John G. 1975. *Kingdom and Community: The Social World of Early Christianity.* Englewood Cliffs, NJ: Prentice-Hall.

————. 1983. *The Origins of Anti-Semitism.* New York: Oxford.

Gallup Opinion Index. 1977. *Religion in America.* Princeton: American Institute of Public Opinion.

Gay, John D. 1971. *The Geography of Religion in England.* London: Duckworth.

Gerlach, Luther P., and Virginia H. Hine. 1970. *People, Power, Change: Movements of Social Transformation.* Indianapolis, IN: Bobbs-Merrill.

Gibbon, Edward. [1776–1788] 1960. *The Decline and Fall of the Roman Empire.* An abridgement by D. M. Low. New York: Harcourt, Brace and Company.

————. 1961. *Autobiography.* New York: Median Books.

Gilliam, J. F. 1961. "The Plague under Marcus Aurelius." *American Journal of Philology* 94:243–255.

Glazer, Nathan, and Daniel P. Moynihan. 1963. *Beyond the Melting Pot.* Cambridge: MIT Press.

Glock Charles Y. 1959. "The Religious Revival in America?" In *Religion and the Face of America*, edited by Jane Zahn, pp. 25–42. Berkeley: University Extension.

———. 1964. "The Role of Deprivation in the Origin and Evolution of Religious Groups." In *Religion and Social Conflict*, edited by Robert Lee and Martin E. Marty, 24–36. New York: Oxford University Press.

Glock, Charles Y., and Rodney Stark. 1965. *Religion and Society in Tension*. Chicago: Rand-McNally.

———. 1966. *Christian Beliefs and Anti-Semitism*. New York: Harper and Row.

Goldstein, Jonathan. 1981. "Jewish Acceptance and Rejection of Hellenism." In *Jewish and Christian Self-Definition*, edited by E. P. Sanders, A. I. Baumgarten, and Alan Mendelson, 64–87. Philadelphia: Fortress Press.

Goodenough, Erwin R. 1931. *The Church in the Roman Empire*. The Berkshire Studies in European History. New York: Henry Holt and Company.

Gorman, Michael J. 1982. *Abortion and the Early Church*. Downers Grove, IL: InterVarsity Press.

Gottfredson, Michael R., and Travis Hirschi. 1990. *A General Theory of Crime*. Palo Alto: Stanford University Press.

Grant, Michael. 1978. *The History of Rome*. New York and London: Faber and Faber.

Grant, Robert M. 1966. *Ignatius of Antioch*. Camden, NJ: Nelson.

———. 1970. *Augustus to Constantine: The Rise and Triumph of Christianity in the Roman World*. New York: Harper and Row.

———. 1972. "Jewish Christianity at Antioch in the Second Century." In *Judeo-christianisme*. Paris: Recherches de Science Religieuse.

———. 1977. *Early Christianity and Society: Seven Studies*. San Francisco: Harper and Row.

Greeley, Andrew J. 1970. "Religious Intermarriage in a Denominational Society." *American Sociological Review* 75:949–952.

Green, Henry A. 1985. *The Economic and Social Origins of Gnosticism*. Atlanta: Scholars Press.

———. 1986. "The Socio-Economic Background of Christianity in Egypt." In *The Roots of Egyptian Christianity*, edited by Birger A. Pearson and James E. Goehring, 100–113. Philadelphia: Fortress Press.

Greenspoon, Leonard J. 1989. "Mission to Alexandria: Truth and Legend about the Creation of the Septuagint, the First Bible Translation." *Bible Review* 5 (August): 34–41.

Gryson, Roger. 1976. *The Ministry of Women in the Early Church.* Collegeville, MN: The Liturgical Press.

Guttentag, Marcia, and Paul E. Secord. 1983. *Too Many Women? The Sex Ratio Question.* Beverly Hills, CA: Sage.

Hammond, Mason. 1972. *The City in the Ancient World.* Cambridge: Harvard University Press.

Harkness, A. G. 1896. "Age at Marriage and at Death in the Roman Empire." *Transactions of the American Philological Association* 27:35–72.

Harnack, Adolf. 1894. *History of Dogma.* English ed. London: Williams and Norgate.

———. 1908. *The Mission and Expansion of Christianity in the First Three Centuries.* Translated by James Moffatt. 2 vols. New York: G. P. Putnam's Sons.

Heaton, Tim B. 1990. "Religious Group Characteristics, Endogamy, and Interfaith Marriages." *Sociological Analysis* 51:363–376.

Hechter, Michael. 1987. *Principles of Group Solidarity.* Berkeley and Los Angeles: University of California Press.

Hegedus, Tim. 1994. "Social Scientific Approaches to the Urban Expansion of the Cult of Isis in the Greco-Roman World: An Analysis Based on Forty-four Cities." Unpublished paper. Centre for Religious Studies, University of Toronto.

Hengel, Martin. 1975. *Judaism and Hellenism.* Philidelphia: Fortress Press.

Hexham, Irving, Raymond F. Currie, and Joan B. Townsend. 1985. "New Religious Movements." In *The Canadian Encyclopedia.* Edmonton: Hurtig.

Hine, Robert V. 1983. *California's Utopian Colonies.* Berkeley and Los Angeles: University of California Press.

Hirschi, Travis. 1969. *Causes of Delinquency.* Berkeley and Los Angeles: University of California Press.

Hock, Ronald F. 1980. *The Social Context of Paul's Ministry: Tentmaking and Apostleship.* Philadelphia: Fortress Press.

———. 1986. "Response to Rodney Stark's 'Jewish Conversion and the Rise of Christianity.'" Paper read at the Social History of Early Christianity Group of the Society of Biblical Literature, Atlanta.

Holmberg, Bengt. 1980. *Paul and Power: The Structure of Authority in the Primitive Church as Reflected in the Pauline Epistles*. Philadelphia: Fortress Press.

Homans, George C. 1964. "Bringing Men Back In." *American Sociological Review* 29:809–818.

Hopkins, Donald R. 1983. *Princes and Peasants: Smallpox in History*. Chicago: University of Chicago Press.

Hopkins, Keith (M. K.). 1965a. "The Age of Roman Girls at Marriage." *Population Studies* 18:309–327.

———. 1965b. "Contraception in the Roman Empire." *Comparative Studies in Society and History* 8:124–151.

———. 1966. "On the Probable Age Structure of the Roman Population." *Population Studies* 20:245–264.

Horbury, William. 1982. "The Benediction of the NINIM and Early Jewish-Christian Controversy." *Journal of Theological Studies* 33:19–61.

Iannaccone, Laurence R. 1982. "Let the Women Be Silent." *Sunstone* 7 (May–June): 38–45.

———. 1988. "A Formal Model of Church and Sect." *American Journal of Sociology* 94:S241–S268.

———. 1990. "Religious Practice: A Human Capital Approach." *Journal for the Scientific Study of Religion* 29:297–314.

———. 1992. "Sacrifice and Stigma: Reducing Free-Riding in Cults, Communes, and other Collectives." *Journal of Political Economy* 100:271–292.

———. 1994. "Why Strict Churches Are Strong." *American Journal of Sociology* 99:1180–1211.

———. 1995. "Risk, Rationality, and Religious Portfolios." *Economic Inquiry* 33:285–295.

Ignatius of Antioch. [Ca. 100.] 1946. *The Epistles of Ignatius of Antioch*. Translated by James A. Kleist. Westminster, MD: The Newman Bookshop.

Isaac, Ephraim. 1993. "Is the Ark of the Covenant in Ethiopia?" *Biblical Archaeology Review* 19:60–63.

Jashemski, Wilhelmina F. 1979. *The Gardens of Pompeii*. New Rochelle, NY: Caratzas.

Johnson, Benton. 1963. "On Church and Sect." *American Sociological Review* 28:539–549.

Johnson, Paul. 1976. *A History of Christianity*. New York: Atheneum.

Jongman, Willem. *Economy and Society in Pompeii*. Amsterdam: Gieben, 1988.

Josephus, Flavius. [Ca. 100.] 1960. *The Complete Works*. Grand Rapids, MI: Kregel Publications.

Judge, E. A. 1960. *The Social Pattern of Christian Groups in the First Century*. London: Tyndale.

———. 1986. "The Quest for Mercy in Late Antiquity." In *God Who Is Rich in Mercy: Essays Presented to D. B. Knox*, edited by P. T. O'Brien and D. G. Peterson, 107–121. Sydney: Macquarie University Press.

Justin Martyr. [Ca. 150.] 1948. *Writings of Saint Justin Martyr*. New York: Christian Heritage.

Kanter, Rosabeth Moss. 1972. *Commitment and Community*. Cambridge: Harvard University Press.

Katz, Steven T. 1984. "Issues in the Separation of Judaism and Christianity after 70 C.E.: A Reconsideration." *Journal of Biblical Literature* 103:43–76.

Kautsky, Karl. [1908] 1953. *Foundations of Christianity*. American ed. New York: Russell and Russell.

Kee, Howard Clark. 1983. *Miracle in the Early Christian World*. New Haven: Yale University Press.

———. 1986. *Medicine, Miracle and Magic in New Testament Times*. Cambridge: Cambridge University Press.

———. 1989. *Knowing the Truth: A Sociological Approach to New Testament Interpretation*. Minneapolis: Fortress Press.

Koester, Helmut. 1987. *History, Culture and Religion of the Hellenistic Age*. New York: Walter de Gruyter.

Kosmin, Barry A. 1991. "Research Report of the National Survey of Religious Identification." New York: CUNY Graduate Center.

Kox, Willem, Wim Meeus, and Harm 't Hart. 1991. "Religious Conversion of Adolescents: Testing the Lofland and Stark Model of Religious Conversion." *Sociological Analysis* 52:227–240.

Kraemer, Ross Shepard. 1992. *Her Share of the Blessings*. New York: Oxford University Press.

Kreissig, Heinz. 1967. "Zur socialen Zusammensetzung der frühchristlichen Gemeinden im ersten Jahrhundert u.Z." *Eirene* 6:91–100.

Lactantius. [Ca. 308.] 1964. *The Divine Institutes.* New York: Fathers of the Church.

Larsen, Otto. 1962. "Innovators and Early Adopters of Television." *Sociological Inquiry* 32:16–33.

Latourette, Kenneth Scott. 1937. *A History of the Expansion of Christianity.* Vol. 1, *The First Five Centuries.* New York: Harper & Brothers.

Layton, Bentley. 1987. *The Gnostic Scriptures,* Garden City, NY: Doubleday.

Levick, Barbara. 1967. *Roman Colonies in Southern Asia Minor.* Oxford: Clarendon.

Lewis, Naphtali. 1985. *Life in Egypt under Roman Rule.* Oxford: Clarendon.

Libanius. [Ca. 350.] 1969. *Orations.* Loeb Classical Library. Cambridge: Harvard University Press.

Lightfoot, J. B., and J. R. Harmer, eds. 1988. *The Apostolic Fathers.* Grand Rapids, MI: Baker Book House.

Lindsay, Jack. 1968. *The Ancient World: Manners and Morals.* New York: G. P. Putnam's Sons.

Littman, R. J., and M. L. Littman. 1973. "Galen and the Antonine Plague." *American Journal of Philology* 94:243–255.

Livy. [Titus Livius, ca. 1.] 1959. *The History of Early Rome.* New York: Putnam.

Lofland, John. 1966. *Doomsday Cult.* Englewood Cliffs, NJ: Prentice-Hall.

———. 1977. "'Becoming a World-Saver' Revisted." *American Behavioral Scientist* 20:805–818.

Lofland, John, and Rodney Stark. 1965. "Becoming a World-Saver: A Theory of Conversion to a Deviant Perspective." *American Sociological Review* 30:862–875.

Longenecker, R. N. 1985. "Antioch of Syria." In *Major Cities of the Biblical World,* edited by R. K. Harrison, 8–21. Nashville: Thomas Nelson.

MacLennan, Robert S., and A. Thomas Kraabel. 1986."The God-Fearers—A Literary and Theological Invention." *Biblical Archaeology Review* 12 (September–October): 47–53.

MacMullen, Ramsay. 1974. *Roman Social Relations: 50 B.C. to A.D. 284.* New Haven: Yale University Press.

MacMullen, Ramsay. 1981. *Paganism in the Roman Empire*. New Haven: Yale University Press.

———. 1984. *Christianizing the Roman Empire*. New Haven: Yale University Press.

———. 1988. *Corruption and the Decline of Rome*. New Haven: Yale University Press.

———. 1990. *Changes in the Roman Empire: Essays in the Ordinary*. Princeton: Princeton University Press.

Malherbe, Abraham J. 1977. *Social Aspects of Early Christianity*. Baton Rouge: Louisiana State University Press.

Malina, Bruce J. 1981. *The New Testament World: Insights from Cultural Anthropology*. Atlanta: John Knox.

———. 1986. *Christian Origins and Cultural Anthropology*. Atlanta: John Knox.

Marcus Aurelius. [Ca. 175.] 1916. *The Communings with Himself of Marcus Aurelius Antoninus, Emperor of Rome* [often published under the title *Meditations*]. London: William Heineman.

Marks, Geoffrey, and William K. Beatty. 1976. *Epidemics*. New York: Scribner's.

Martin, David. 1990. *Tongues of Fire: The Explosion of Protestantism in Latin America*. Oxford: Basil Blackwell.

Marx, Karl, and Friedrich Engels. 1967. *Marx and Engels on Religion*. New York: Schocken Books.

May, Gerhard. 1987–1988. "Marcion in Contemporary Views: Results and Open Questions." *The Second Century* 6:129–151.

McNeill, William H. 1976. *Plagues and Peoples*. Garden City, NY: Doubleday.

Meeks, Wayne A. 1983. *The First Urban Christians*. New Haven: Yale University Press.

———. 1993. *The Origins of Christian Morality*. New Haven: Yale University Press.

Meeks, Wayne A., and Robert L. Wilken. 1978. *Jews and Christians in Antioch in the First Four Centuries of the Common Era*. Missoula, MT: Scholars Press.

Meiggs, R. 1974. *Roman Ostia*. 2d ed. Oxford: Oxford University Press.

Menninger, Karl. 1938. *Man against Himself*. New York: Harcourt Brace.

Meyers, Eric M. 1983. "Report on the Excavations at the Venosa Catacombs 1981." *Vetera Christianorum* 20:455–459.

———. 1988. "Early Judaism and Christianity in the Light of Archaeology." *Biblical Archaeologist* 51:69–79.

Miller, Alan S., and John P. Hoffman. 1995. "Risk and Religion: An Explanation of Gender Differences in Religiosity." *Journal for the Scientific Study of Religion* 34:63–75.

Minucius Felix. 1989. "Octavius." *The Ante-Nicene Fathers.* Edited by Alexander Roberts and James Donaldson. Vol. 4. Grand Rapids, MI: Eerdmans.

Mooney, James. 1896. *The Ghost Dance Religion and the Sioux Outbreak of 1890.* Fourth Annual Report of the Bureau of Ethnology to the Secretary of the Smithsonian Institution. Washington, DC: U.S. Government Printing Office.

Morioka, Kiyomi. 1975. *Religion in Changing Japanese Society.* Tokyo: University of Tokyo Press.

Mumford, Lewis. 1974. "Forward." In Chandler and Fox 1974.

Neel, James V., et al. 1970. "Notes on the Effect of Measles and Measles Vaccine in a Virgin Soil Population of South American Indians." *American Journal of Epidemiology* 91:418–429.

Nelson, Geoffrey K. 1969. *Spiritualism and Society.* New York: Schocken Books.

Niebuhr, B. G. 1855. *The History of Rome.* English trans. London: Walton and Maberly.

Niebuhr, H. Richard. 1929. *The Social Sources of Denominationalism.* New York: Holt.

Nock, Arthur Darby. 1933. *Conversion: The Old and the New in Religion from Alexander the Great to Augustine of Hippo.* Oxford: Clarendon.

———. 1964. *Early Gentile Christianity and Its Hellenistic Background.* New York: Harper and Row.

Noonan, John T., Jr. 1965. *Contraception: A History of Its Treatment by the Catholic Theologians and Canonists.* Cambridge: Harvard University Press, Belknap Press.

Nordquist, Ted. 1978. *Ananda Cooperative Village.* Uppsala: Borgstroms.

O'Dea, Thomas F. 1957. *The Mormons.* Chicago: University of Chicago Press.

Origen. [Ca. 230.] 1989. *The Ante-Nicene Fathers.* Edited by Alexander

Roberts and James Donaldson. Vol. 4. Grand Rapids, MI: Eerdmans.

Ostow, Mortimer. 1990. "The Fundamentalist Phenomenon: A Psychological Perspective." In *The Fundamentalist Phenomenon*, edited by Norman J. Cohen, 99–125. Grand Rapids, MI: Eerdmans.

Packer, James E. 1967. "Housing and Population in Imperial Ostia and Rome." *Journal of Roman Studies* 57:80–95.

Parkin, Tim G. 1992. *Demography and Roman Society*. Baltimore: Johns Hopkins University Press.

Patrick, Adam. 1967. "Disease in Antiquity: Ancient Greece and Rome." In *Diseases in Antiquity*, edited by Don Brothwell and A. T. Sandison, 238–246. Springfield, IL: Charles C. Thomas.

Pearson, Birger A. 1973. "Friedlander Revisited: Alexandrian Judaism and Gnostic Origins" *Studia Philonica* 2:23–39.

———. 1986. "Earliest Christianity in Egypt: Some Observations." In *Roots of Egyptian Christianity*, edited by Berger A. Pearson and James E. Goehring, pp. 132–156. Philadelphia: Fortress Press.

Pelikan, Jaroslav. 1962. "Introduction to the Torchbook Edition [of the reissue of Adolf Harnack]." In *The Mission and Expansion of Christianity in the First Three Centuries*, 1:v–vii. New York: Harper and Row.

———. 1987. *The Excellent Empire: The Fall of Rome and the Triumph of the Church*. San Francisco: Harper and Row.

Plato. 1941. *Republic*. New York: Modern Library.

Pliny the Younger. [Ca. 112.] 1943. "Letter to the Emperor Trajan on Christians in Bithynia." In *Documents of the Christian Church*, edited by Henry Bettenson, pp. 5–7. London: Oxford University Press.

Pomeroy, Sarah B. 1975. *Goddesses, Whores, Wives, Slaves: Women in Classical Antiquity*. New York: Schocken Books.

Popper, Karl R. 1959. *The Logic of Scientific Discovery*. New York: Harper and Row.

———. 1962. *Conjectures and Refutations*. New York: Basic Books.

Ramsay, W. M. 1893. *The Church in the Roman Empire before A.D. 170*. New York: G. P. Putnam's Sons.

Rawson, Beryl, ed. 1986. *The Family in Ancient Rome*. Ithaca, NY: Cornell University Press.

Reik, Theodore. 1976. *Masochism in Sex and Society*. New York: Pyramid Books.

Richardson, Cyril C., ed. and trans. 1953. *Early Christian Fathers.* Vol. 1. Philadelphia: The Westminster Press.

Riddle, Donald W. 1931. *The Martyrs: A Study in Social Control.* Chicago: University of Chicago Press.

Riddle, John M., J. Worth Estes, and Josiah C. Russell. 1994. "Birth Control in the Ancient World." *Archaeology* 47(2):29–35.

Rives, J. B. 1995. *Religion and Authority in Roman Carthage from Augustus to Constantine.* New York: Oxford University Press.

Robbins, Thomas. 1988. *Cults, Converts and Charisma: The Sociology of New Religious Movements.* Beverly Hills, CA: Sage.

Roberts, Colin H. 1979. *Manuscript, Society, and Belief in Early Christian Egypt.* London: Oxford.

Robinson, John A. T. 1976. *Redating the New Testament.* Philadelphia: The Westminster Press.

Roetzel, Calvin J. 1985. *The World That Shaped the New Testament.* Atlanta: John Knox.

Russell, J. C. 1958. *Late Ancient and Medieval Population.* Published as vol. 48, pt. 3 of the *Transactions of the American Philosophical Society.* Philadelphia: American Philosophical Society.

Russell, Jeffrey Burton. 1977. *The Devil: Perceptions of Evil from Antiquity to Primitive Christianity.* Ithaca, NY: Cornell University Press.

Sanders, Jack T. 1993. *Schismatics, Sectarians, Dissidents, Deviants.* Valley Forge, PA: Trinity Press International.

Sandison, A. T. 1967. "Sexual Behavior in Ancient Societies." In *Diseases in Antiquity,* edited by Don Brothwell and A. T. Sandison, 734–755. Springfield, IL: Charles C. Thomas.

Schoedel, William R. 1985. *Ignatius of Antioch.* Philadelphia: Fortress Press.

———. 1991. "Ignatius and the Reception of the Gospel of Matthew in Antioch." In *Social History of the Matthean Community: Cross Disciplinary Approaches,* edited by David L. Balch, 129–177. Minneapolis: Fortress Press.

Scroggs, Robin. 1980. "The Sociological Interpretation of the New Testament: The Present State of Research." *New Testament Studies* 26:164–179.

Segal, Alan F. 1991. "Matthew's Jewish Voice." In *Social History of the Matthean Community: Cross Disciplinary Approaches,* edited by David L. Balch, 3–37. Minneapolis: Fortress Press.

Shepard, William R. 1980. *Shepard's Historical Atlas*. Totowa, NJ: Barnes & Noble.

Shinn, Larry D. 1983. "The Many Faces of Krishna." In *Alternatives to American Mainline Churches*, edited by Joseph H. Fichter, pp. 113–135. New York: Rose of Sharon Press.

Simon, Marcel. 1964. *Verus Israel: Etude sur les relations entre chrétiens et juifs dans l'empire romain*. Paris: Boccard.

Smith, Patricia, and Gila Kahila. 1991. "Bones of a Hundred Infants Found in Ashkelon Sewer." *Biblical Archaeology Review* 17 (July–August): 47.

Smith, William, ed. 1857. *Dictionary of Greek and Roman Geography*. London: Walton and Maberly.

Snow, David, and Cynthia Philips. 1980. "The Lofland-Stark Conversion Model: A Critical Reassessment." *Social Problems* 27:430–447.

Snyder, Graydon F. 1985. *Ante Pacem: Archaeological Evidence of Church Life before Constantine*. Macon, GA: Mercer University Press.

Solmsen, Friedrich. 1979. *Sarapis under the Early Ptolemies*. Études préliminaires aux Religions orientales dans l'Émpire romain, 25. Leiden: Brill.

Sordi, Marta. 1986. *The Christians and the Roman Empire*. Norman: University of Oklahoma Press.

Stager, Lawrence E. 1991. "Eroticism and Infanticide at Ashkelon." *Biblical Archaeology Review* 17 (July–August): 34–53.

Stambaugh, John E. 1988. *The Ancient Roman City*. Baltimore: Johns Hopkins University Press.

Stambaugh, John E., and David L. Balch. 1986. *The New Testament in Its Social Environment*. Philadelphia: The Westminster Press.

Stark, Rodney. 1964. "Class, Radicalism, and Religious Involvement." *American Sociological Review* 29:698–706.

———. 1971. "The Economics of Piety." In *Issues in Social Inequality*, edited by Gerald W. Thielbar and Saul D. Feldman, pp. 485–503. Boston: Little Brown.

———. 1984. "The Rise of a New World Faith." *Review of Religious Research* 26:18–27.

———. 1985a. "Europe's Receptivity to Religious Movements." In *New Religious Movements: Genesis, Exodus, and Numbers*, edited by Rodney Stark, pp. 301-343. New York: Paragon.

———. 1985b. "From Church-Sect to Religious Economies." In *The*

Sacred in a Post-Secular Age, edited by Phillip E. Hammond, pp. 139–149. Berkeley and Los Angeles: University of California Press.

———. 1987. "How New Religions Succeed: A Theoretical Model." In *The Future of New Religious Movements,* edited by David G. Bromley and Phillip E. Hammond, pp. 11–29. Macon, GA: Mercer University Press.

———. 1992. *Sociology.* 4th ed. Belmont, CA: Wadsworth Publishing Company.

———. 1994. "Modernization and Mormon Growth." In *A Sociological Analysis of Mormonism,* edited by Marie Cornwall, Tim B. Heaton, and Lawrence Young, pp. 1–23. Champaign: University of Illinois Press.

Stark, Rodney, and William Sims Bainbridge. 1979. "Of Churches, Sects, and Cults: Preliminary Concepts for a Theory of Religious Movements." *Journal for the Scientific Study of Religion* 18:117–131.

———. 1980. "Networks of Faith: Interpersonal Bonds and Recruitment to Cults and Sects." *American Journal of Sociology* 85:1376–1395.

———. 1985. *The Future of Religion: Secularization, Revival, and Cult Formation.* Berkeley and Los Angeles: University of California Press.

———. 1987. *A Theory of Religion.* Bern and New York: Peter Lang.

Stark, Rodney, W. S. Bainbridge, Robert Crutchfield, Daniel P. Doyle, and Roger Finke. 1983. "Crime and Delinquency in the Roaring Twenties." *Journal of Research in Crime and Delinquency* 20:4–23.

Stark, Rodney, William Sims Bainbridge, and Lori Kent. 1981. "Cult Membership in the Roaring Twenties." *Sociological Analysis* 42:137–162.

Stark, Rodney, and Charles Y. Glock. 1968. *American Piety.* Berkeley and Los Angeles: University of California Press.

Stark, Rodney, and Laurence R. Iannaccone. 1991. "Sociology of Religion." In Edgar F. Borgatta, editor-in-chief, *Encyclopedia of Sociology.* New York: Macmillan.

———. 1992. "Rational Choice Propositions about Religious Movements." In *Religion and the Social Order,* vol. 3-A: *Handbook on Cults and Sects in America,* edited by David G. Bromley and Jeffrey K. Haddon, pp. 241–261. Greenwich, CT: JAI Press.

———. 1994. "A Supply-Side Reinterpretation of the 'Secularization' of Europe." *Journal for the Scientific Study of Religion* 33:230–252.

Stark, Rodney, Laurence R. Iannaccone, and Roger Finke. 1995. "Rationality and the 'Religious Mind.'" Paper read at the annual meetings of the Western Economics Association, San Diego.

Stark, Rodney, and Lynne Roberts. 1982. "The Arithmetic of Social Movements: Theoretical Implications." *Sociological Analysis* 43:53–68.

Steinberg, Stephen. 1965. "Reform Judaism: The Origin and Evolution of a 'Church Movement.'" *Journal for the Scientific Study of Religion* 5:117–129.

Stonequist, Everett V. 1937. *The Marginal Man.* New York: Scribner's.

Strecker, Georg. 1971."On the Problem of Jewish Christianity." Appendix 1 in Walter Bauer, *Orthodoxy and Heresy in Earliest Christianity.* Philadelphia: Fortress Press.

Swanson, Guy E. 1960. *The Birth of the Gods.* Ann Arbor: University of Michigan Press.

Tacitus, Cornelius. [Ca. 100.] 1984. *The Histories.* New York: Penguin Classics.

———. 1989. *The Annals of Imperial Rome.* New York: Penguin Classics.

Tcherikover, Victor. 1958. "The Ideology of the Letter of Aristeas." *Harvard Theological Review* 51:59–85.

Tertullian. [Ca. 200.] 1959. *Disciplinary, Moral and Ascetical Works.* New York: Fathers of the Church.

———. 1989. *The Ante-Nicene Fathers.* Edited by Alexander Roberts and James Donaldson. Vols. 3 and 4. Grand Rapids, MI: Eerdmans.

Theissen, Gerd. 1978. *Sociology of Early Palestinian Christianity.* Philadelphia: Fortress Press.

———. 1982. *The Social Setting of Pauline Christianity: Essays on Corinth.* Philadelphia: Fortress Press.

Thompson, Edward H. 1991. "Beneath the Status Characteristic: Gender Variations in Religion." *Journal for the Scientific Study of Religion* 30:381–394.

Thornton, Russell. 1981. "Demographic Antecedents of a Revitalization Movement: Population Change, Population Size, and the 1890 Ghost Dance." *American Sociological Review* 40:88–96.

Thucydides. [Ca. 420 B.C.E.] 1954. *The Peloponnesian War.* London: Penguin.

Thurston, Bonnie Bowman. 1989. *The Widows: A Women's Ministry in the Early Church.* Minneapolis: Fortress Press.

Toby, Jackson. 1957. "Social Disorganization and Stake in Conformity: Complementary Factors in the Predatory Behavior of Hoodlums." *Journal of Criminal Law, Criminology, and Police Science* 48:12–17.

Troeltsch, Ernst. [1911] 1931. *The Social Teachings of the Christian Churches.* American ed. New York: Macmillan.

Volinn, Ernest. 1982. "Lead Us from Darkness." Ph.D. diss., Columbia University.

von Hertling, L. 1934. "Die Zahl der Christen zu Beginn des vierten Jahrhunderts." *Zeitschrift für Katholische Theologie* 58:245–264.

Wallace, Anthony F. C. 1956. "Revitalization Movements." *American Anthropologist* 58:264–281.

———. 1966. *Religion: An Anthropological View.* New York: Random House.

Wallis, Roy, ed. 1975. *Sectarianism.* New York: Wiley.

———. 1982. *Millennialism and Charisma.* Belfast: The Queen's University.

Walsh, Joseph. 1931. "Refutation of the Charges of Cowardice against Galen." *Annals of Medical History* 3:195–208.

Walsh, Michael. 1986. *The Triumph of the Meek: Why Early Christianity Succeeded.* San Francisco: Harper and Row.

Warner, R. Stephen. 1993. "Work in Progress toward a New Paradigm for the Sociological Study of Religion in the United States." *American Journal of Sociology* 98:1044–1093.

Watt, W. Montgomery. 1961. *Muhammad: Prophet and Statesman.* London: Oxford University Press.

Weber, Max. 1946. "The Sociology of Charismatic Authority." In *From Max Weber: Essays in Sociology*, edited by H. H. Gerth and C. Wright Mills, 245–252. New York: Oxford University Press.

———. 1961. "Religion and Social Status." In *Theories of Society*, edited by Talcott Parsons, Edward Shills, Kaspar D. Naegele, and Jesse R. Pitts, 1138–1161. New York: The Free Press.

Weiner, Eugene, and Anita Weiner. 1990. *The Martyr's Conviction: A Sociological Analysis.* Atlanta: Scholars Press.

Weiss, Johannes. [1937] 1959. *Earliest Christianity: A History of the Period A.D. 30–150.* 2 vols. New York: Harper Torchbooks.

White, K. D. 1984. *Greek and Roman Technology.* London: Thames and Hudson.

White, L. Michael. 1985. "Building God's House: Social Aspects of

Architectural Adaptation among Pagans, Jews, and Christians." Paper presented at the annual meeting of the Society of Biblical Literature.

White, L. Michael. 1986. "Adolf Harnack and Early Christian 'Expansion': A Reappraisal of Social History." *Second Century* 5:97–127.

———. 1987. "Scaling the Strongman's 'Court' (Luke 11:21)." *Foundations and Facets Forum* 3:3–28.

———. 1990. *Building God's House in the Roman World: Architectural Adaptions among Pagans, Jews, and Christians.* Baltimore: Johns Hopkins University Press.

———, ed. 1992. *Social Networks in the Early Christian Environment: Issues and Methods for Social History. Semeia* 56. Atlanta: Scholars Press.

Wilken, Robert L. 1971. *Judaism and the Early Christian Mind.* New Haven: Yale University Press.

———. 1983. *John Chrysostom and the Jews.* Berkeley and Los Angeles: University of California Press.

———. 1984. *The Christians as the Romans Saw Them.* New Haven: Yale University Press.

Williams, Michael. 1985. *The Immovable Race: A Gnostic Designation and the Theme of Stability in Late Antiquity.* Nag Hammadi Studies, vol. 29. Leiden: E. J. Brill.

Wilson, Bryan. 1961. *Sects and Society.* Berkeley and Los Angeles: University of California Press.

———. 1970. *Religious Sects.* New York: McGraw-Hill.

———. 1975. *Magic and the Millennium.* Frogmore, England: Paladin.

Wire, Antoinette Clark. 1991. "Gender Roles in a Scribal Community." In *Social History of the Matthean Community,* edited by David L. Balch, 87–121. Minneapolis: Fortress Press.

Wrigley, E. A. 1969. *Population and History.* New York: McGraw-Hill.

Wuthnow, Robert. 1976. *The Consciousness Reformation.* Berkeley and Los Angeles: University of California Press.

Zinsser, Hans. [1934] 1960. *Rats, Lice and History.* New York: Bantam.

✦ Index ✦

Only authors named in the text are listed in the index. Those merely cited are included in the bibliography.

About the Author

RODNEY STARK is Professor of Sociology and Comparative Religion at the University of Washington. He is the author of many books, including *The Churching of America, 1776–1990*, with Roger Finke, and *A Theory of Religion*, with William Sims Bainbridge.